WEAVING A FUTURE

ELAYNE ZORN Weaving

a Future

TOURISM, CLOTH, & CULTURE ON AN ANDEAN ISLAND

University of Iowa Press

IOWA CITY

University of Iowa Press, Iowa City 52242
Copyright © 2004 by the University of Iowa Press
All rights reserved
Printed in the United States of America
http://www.uiowa.edu/uiowapress

All photographs by the author unless otherwise indicated.

The University of Iowa Press is a member of Green Press
Initiative and is committed to preserving natural resources.

Printed on acid-free paper

Library of Congress Cataloging-in-Publication Data
Zorn, Elayne.
    Weaving a future: tourism, cloth, and culture on an
    Andean island / by Elayne Zorn.
       p.   cm.
    Includes bibliographical references and index.
    ISBN 0-87745-915-0 (cloth), ISBN 0-87745-916-9 (pbk.)
       1. Quechua textile fabrics—Peru—Taquili.
    2. Quechua business enterprises—Peru—Taquili.
    3. Quechua Indians—Peru—Taquili—Clothing.
    4. Hand weaving—Peru—Taquili.   5. Textile design—
    Peru—Taquili.   6. Taquili (Peru)—Social life and
    customs.   7. Taquili (Peru)—Economic conditions.
    I. Title.
    F3429.1.T36Z67   2004
    985'.3600498323—dc22   2004051651

04 05 06 07 08 C 5 4 3 2 1
04 05 06 07 08 P 5 4 3 2 1

I dedicate this book

to my son, Gavriel,

and to the people of

Taquile Island

CONTENTS

Preface ix

Acknowledgments xvii

1. Introduction: Tourism, Cloth, and Culture 1

2. Taquile Island in Lake Titicaca 26

3. The Cloth of Contemporary Incas 51

4. Transforming Value by Commoditizing Cloth 82

5. Visit Taquile — Isle of Peace and Enchantment 111

6. Conclusion: Weaving a Future? 147

Afterword: Traveling to Taquile 165

Notes 167

Glossary 177

References 183

Index 215

PREFACE

Like many recent researchers who have been fortunate enough to do fieldwork in a region over many years, my original research agenda has been sidelined to some degree by the tumult of rapid transformations affecting rural indigenous peoples in the past half century. June Nash, who has carried out long-term research in Mexico, Bolivia, and the United States, argues that "the most radical changes are those that have occurred in the settings that were in the past the most marginal to the centers of power" (J. Nash 2001: xi). Her observation aptly applies to the farmers and artisans in highland Peru who are the focus of this study.

My long-term involvement is with people from Taquile Island (fig. 1), on the Peruvian side of Lake Titicaca, the highest navigable lake in the Americas (see map, p. 7). In the 1970s Taquileans were small-plot cultivators and artisans working in artistic traditions that go back thousands of years and whose lives centered almost overwhelmingly on their community — religiously, economically, and culturally. A central theme of this book is how this community focus has transformed through Taquileans' interactions with regional, national, and global phenomena.

Anthropologists who work long term often feel that their research site is a very special place, as indeed I do. In part, this feeling has been interpreted, I think correctly, by postcolonial (or cynical) visitors as anthropological nostalgia, or understood as the pleasure of fieldwork removed from the mundane routines of daily life. I know that there always is "trouble in paradise" and that the kinds of problems that occur in small, poor, peasant communities occur in Taquile too. Taquileans experience family feuds, battles over land and other scarce resources, ill will and enmity, and so on.

Nevertheless, the beauty of this terraced island located in the shining waters of Lake Titicaca (fig. 2) and set against the brilliant blue of

1. Alejandrina Huatta and Alejandro Huatta with their children, Julia, María (hands on belt loom), and Orlando. Terraced fields and a small house are behind them. July 2002.

the Andean sky, the gorgeous textiles that virtually all Taquileans create, the quiet of a community "without dogs or police" — and, most importantly for me, the people of Taquile — continue to draw me. I am not alone in being impressed: time and time again my friends, colleagues, and the hundreds of visitors who have posted diaries and photos on the Internet have become enchanted with Taquile and with Taquileans.

I live near Orlando, Florida, capital of a certain kind of world fantasy, one not particularly appreciated by the region's many local low-wage workers, so I am well aware that the paradise that tourists experience does not necessarily correspond to the ways a place is experienced locally (see for example Jamaica Kincaid's novel *A Small Place*, which skewers outsiders' myths about the small Caribbean island of Antigua). However, many or most Taquileans feel that their island is a special and desirable place to live. This is so, I argue, because despite tourism Taquile still primarily belongs to Taquileans, not outsiders.

2. *Lake Titicaca, seen from Taquile. Boats (upper left) sail west to Puno. Taquile's stone jetties of Port Alisuno lie below. July 2002.*

The tale I tell here begins with my interest in Andean cloth, which dates to a weaving class given by the U.S. fiber artist Debra Rappaport at the University of California at Berkeley in 1970. The very first day of class, I fell in love with the brilliantly colored scraps of Peruvian cloth she showed us. Interested in the textile arts since childhood, I realized that I had never seen anything as beautiful.

I first traveled to the Andes as a backpacker in 1972 while an undergraduate art student at the California College of Arts and Crafts. Following graduation in 1975, I was awarded a fellowship by the Institute of International Education to research the rather arcane, but to me exciting, topic of Andean textile structure and technology. Ramiro Matos Mendieta, my supervisor at Peru's venerable Universidad Nacional Mayor de San Marcos, supported my intention to do this by learning how to weave using local techniques. Lima textile scholar and exporter Gertrudis de Solari suggested Taquile Island, in the southern highland department of Puno, as a good place to meet many weavers.

When I started my research, studies of textiles were limited to the work of a very few people who had done fieldwork on contemporary Andean textile technology (J. Cohen 1957; Goodell 1968a, 1968b; A. Rowe 1975), scholars investigating ancient Andean textiles (Bird 1968; Bird and Bellinger 1954; Conklin 1971; d'Harcourt 1974; Murra 1962; O'Neale and Kroeber 1930; Rowe, Benson, and Schaffer, eds., 1979), and handweavers interested in contemporary Andean textiles (Cason and Cahlander 1976). Textile studies were marginalized, and thus research on cloth was not encouraged. Archaeology graduate students interested in material culture examined ceramics, not cloth, for their dissertation research, in a trend that continued until the 1990s (Clark 1993).

Nevertheless, perhaps due to the social movements of the 1960s, and an increased interest in crafts, a shift occurred in the mid-1970s and more research began on contemporary Andean textiles and their creators, leading to long-term studies. Researchers include Lynn Meisch (1980, 1986, 1987a, 1987b, 1991, 1997, 2002), Christine Franquemont (1986), Edward Franquemont (1986a, 1986b; Franquemont and Franquemont 1986), Blenda Femenías (1987, 1991, 1994, 1997, 2004), and Verónica Cereceda (1978, 1986, 1987, 1990, and 1992 with Gabriel Martínez, among others).

Though not trained in anthropology, I did speak passable Spanish and rudimentary Quechua, was an experienced photographer, knew how to weave, and understood textile structures. My hope was to apprentice myself to one or more local weavers, to learn a full range of textile technologies (spinning, plying or doubling, dyeing, warping a loom, weaving, and finishing). I took an apprenticeship-and-practice approach in trying to learn the kinds of bodily habits and mental conceptions related to daily performance, which Pierre Bourdieu calls habitus and schema (Franquemont, Franquemont, and Isbell 1992).

Thus late one December 1975 afternoon, I went to the nearly deserted dock in Puno, southern Peru, to meet people from Taquile, who Gertrudis de Solari had told me landed there on their infrequent visits to town. I met Francisco "Pancho" Huatta Huatta, who had time to chat, in Spanish, while keeping an eye on his extended family's sailboat because his relatives were in town doing errands. He invited me to visit Taquile in early February when he and his wife

Natividad Machaca Quispe would sponsor the Festival of the Virgin of Candlemas (Candelaria, February 2), which starts Taquile's annual festival cycle.

Francisco "Pancho" Huatta and Natividad Machaca (fig. 3), their children, and the members of their extended families became the people I was closest to on Taquile, a friendship that has lasted a quarter century. For cultural anthropologists, the people who end up becoming our closest advisors (formerly called "informants") shape our view of the society we study. Thus, despite the hundreds of hours spent with other Taquileans, my relationship with the Machaca-Huatta extended family is central to this book. I spent countless hours with them, sleeping in their home, cooking and eating in their kitchen, spinning and weaving, learning to help in their fields, traveling with various members to run errands and on excursions, and, much of that time, talking. As I hope this study will make clear, I am indebted to them profoundly for their years of kindness and help.

During the first half of 1976, I spent many, many days spinning, doubling thread (plying), and weaving. Despite the physical strain and pain that these processes cause (lower backache from bending over, shoulder pain from beating down the weft, blisters, calluses, hand strain), I enjoyed those hours spent weaving next to my teachers.

I became increasingly concerned with the lives and circumstances of Taquileans, however, more than with their textiles. In hindsight, I was on my way to "becoming" an anthropologist, even though it was not until 1985 that I began graduate study in anthropology. Tourism to Taquile began mid-year 1976, and though I continued to research textile technology, I spent the second half of that year documenting how Taquileans were responding to the opportunities tourism presented.

My multi-sited fieldwork on Taquile between 1975 and 2002 has consisted of long-term residence, brief visits ranging from a few days to a few weeks, and work with groups of Taquileans in the United States. During 1983 and 1984, I worked with the community to make a textile collection for the Textile Museum in Washington, D.C. From 1987 to 1989, I carried out fieldwork for my dissertation research in highland Bolivia among the large Quechua-speaking Sakaka ethnic

3. *Natividad Machaca and Francisco "Pancho" Huatta, my* compadres, *pose for a goodbye photograph. Pancho Huatta wears the medal he was awarded as the 1996 Grand Master of Peruvian Crafts. July 2002.*

group in the north of northern Potosí (Zorn 1997a, 1997b, 1999, 2002). I continued to visit Taquile but conducted research in Bolivia in part because I wanted to study a large ethnic group with distinctive cloth traditions and history. I also was concerned that my presence in another Peruvian community might become dangerous to local people and to me because of the undeclared civil war between the Maoist guerrilla group Sendero Luminoso (Shining Path) and Peruvian military and paramilitary groups. I made the switch to Bolivia fully cognizant that during those years (1980–1995) most Peruvians did not have the luxury of going elsewhere (Mayer 1992; Palmer 1992; Poole and Rénique 1991, 1992; Rénique 1998; Stern 1998). Taquile was fortunate: neither the guerrillas nor the army entered the island. Taquileans saw a big drop in tourism, but otherwise were spared.

In 1991 and 1994, I served as translator and "presenter" for Taquileans participating in the Smithsonian Institution Festivals of American Folklife. After thirteen years away, I traveled to Taquile again during July 2002, as part of a team that collected textiles and documented cloth traditions for the reinstallation of the Brooklyn Museum's Hall of the Americas in New York (see chapter 1).

My early research on Taquile focused on textile technology; subsequently, influenced by the times in anthropology and the spell of John Murra's article on the "functions" of cloth in the Andes (1962) as well as his interest in "*lo Andino*" (Andeanness), I shifted to examination of the "special" nature of cloth. During the 1980s my research expanded again to incorporate economic anthropology, as reflected in my M.A. thesis (Zorn 1983), titled "Traditions Versus Tourism in Taquile, Peru: Changes in the Economics of Andean Textile Production and Exchange Due to Market Sale." The thesis examines Taquileans and their textile arts before and after the initial arrival of tourists in 1976, emphasizing Taquileans' agency, that is, their active efforts to shape the people and institutions that attempted to shape them.

Writing now from the perspective of twenty-five years later, I still believe that our mutual interest in cloth and weaving bridged many gaps despite our huge differences. Unlike many anthropologists who have witnessed a steady erosion of quality of life for the indigenous people they work with, I have been privileged to see most Taquileans being able to make the world a better place for themselves. In contrast to erroneous accounts by mainland tour agencies and some guides who claim credit for promoting tourism to Taquile, this development occurred because of years of Taquileans' individual and community initiatives and efforts. It is Taquileans' agency in this process that I would like to show in this book.

ACKNOWLEDGMENTS

Acknowledging help with research that has lasted half a lifetime and involved many, many people would fill its own slim volume, so here I will thank the people of Taquile, where I did research; the institutions that generously supported my work; and the colleagues and friends who helped me put this book in its final form. I recorded my thanks to many individuals in Peru and the United States in my M.A. thesis and Ph.D. dissertation. My debt to so many others is clearly visible throughout this book, and I hope I will be forgiven for not acknowledging everyone by name.

I take this opportunity to publicly thank the many people in Peru and Bolivia who warmly received me and talked with me or helped in other ways with my research, especially my weaving teachers and *compadres* in Taquile, Sakaka, and other communities, and the many community authorities who have helped me over the past two decades. It is a pleasure to again thank my *compadres* Natividad Machaca Quispe and Francisco "Pancho" Huatta Huayta, members of their extended families and their children and families, and I especially extend my gratitude to my weaving teachers, Lucia Huatta, Alejandrina Huatta, and Natividad Machaca. For their hospitality in 2002, I thank my *compadres*; Alejandrina Huatta, Alejandro Huatta, and their children; Juan Quispe Huatta, his parents, and his family (especially for recent logistical support and answers to questions); and the authorities and community of Taquile for their exceptional hospitality and trust over twenty-five years.

Nancy Rosoff at the Brooklyn Museum invited me to work as a consultant on two exhibitions that are part of the reinstallation of the Hall of the Americas, which made a return trip to Taquile possible. I warmly thank her for that invitation and her camaraderie. My early fieldwork in Taquile was funded by the Institute of International Education, and then by the Inter-American Foundation (M.A. fellowship). Olivia Cadaval at the Smithsonian Institution twice invited me to serve as "presenter"/translator for people from Taquile at the Smithsonian's Festival of American Folklife; Ismael Calderón, then at the American Museum of Natural History, invited me to do the same there, and I thank them, other staff members, and their institutions for those opportunities. The Wenner-Gren Foundation for Anthropological Research granted me a fellowship that, to my great regret, I was unable to use at that time. At Cornell University, my Ph.D. dissertation committee of Billie Jean Isbell, Thomas Holloway, Davydd Greenwood, and Kathryn March, with assistance from Berndt Lambert, provided a stimulating and supportive environment for writing my dissertation. The National Endowment for the Humanities awarded me a Fellowship for College Teachers and Independent Scholars for research on Taquile's calendars, which provided a wonderful year for writing. I thank the Department of Sociology and Anthropology and the College of Arts and Sciences at the University of Central Florida for making it possible for me to take up that fellowship, and for all their subsequent support. I also thank my colleagues at UCF for other assistance, including UCF's wonderful librarians (especially Winnie Taylor at Inter-Library Loan), Tami Pullin, and my college's computer staff Sae Schatz, Walter Peters, Scott Thompson, and especially the late Tony Travaglini. I also thank my students who asked me questions about Taquile when I presented portions of this book in several classes, and Austin Kamm, who visited Taquile in 2003 and kindly obtained names and permissions from people in several photographs.

I would like to express my appreciation to the following colleagues and friends who provided conversations, comments, and suggestions on portions of earlier drafts of this book: Catherine Allen, Chris Bolton, Nan Brown, Andrew Canessa, Diane Chase, Kristin Congdon, Blenda Femenías, Kathleen Fine-Dare, Mary Frame, Amy Fried, Leslie Sue Lieberman, Lisa Markowitz, Enrique Mayer, Susan Niles, Kenna Noone, Ben Orlove, Nancy Rosoff, Marcia Stephenson, and Cassandra Torrico. Kevin "Benito" Healy shares my lifelong interest in Taquile, and I thank him yet again for decades of conversations, coauthorship, and sources on Taquile Island.

I thank the Inter-American Foundation for permission to use photographs by Ron Weber.

I would like to thank friends and colleagues for carefully commenting on sections of the manuscript, including Nan Brown, Andrew Canessa, Amy Fried, Ben Kohl, Lisa Markowitz, Ben Orlove, and Nancy Rosoff. I especially thank Linda Farthing and Blenda Femenías, wizards with the editing pen, who came to my aid at a moment when health matters impeded further progress on the text. Linda read two complete drafts, and Blenda tore apart (and rewove) two chapters: the book is far, far better for their help. I also thank Shayna Michaels for carefully checking the bibliography; Chris Bolton, who brought an artist's eye to my photographs as well as providing logistical support, and Kenna Noone and Leslie Sue Lieberman for other assistance.

It has been a pleasure to work with Holly Carver, director, and Charlotte Wright, managing editor at the University of Iowa Press. All authors should have the opportunity to work with such enthusiastic and expert editors. I also wish to thank the anonymous reader and Jeffrey H. Cohen for their careful and thoughtful reviews, advice, and comments that helped make this a much more readable book.

I gratefully acknowledge my Florida friends who provided childcare and enthusiastic support, especially Deborah and Dru Boulware, Joy and Keith Lay, and Elaine and Larry Broome. I warmly thank my mother, Sandra Gordon, and appreciate her ongoing pride in my work.

I thank my greatest supporter, my son, Gavriel, who cheerfully persists in inviting me to play catch and reminds me to go for a walk around tiny Lake Charm, my miniature representation of the larger lake I still miss. Gavriel, along with Paul Fisk, helped with the index.

I have not followed all the good advice I have received, and all errors are my responsibility.

When I started this book, I knew that I would want to share any money it earned with the community of Taquile, in partial *ayni* for their kindness and hospitality. A portion of my royalties from this book will go into a fund for the education of Taquilean youth on and off the island, administered by local authorities.

WEAVING A FUTURE

1 INTRODUCTION
TOURISM, CLOTH, AND CULTURE

TAQUILE'S CHOICE

"We can only buy a few textiles," we told the Taquileans[1] who had agreed to advise us which weavings to choose for the Brooklyn Museum's soon to be reinstalled Hall of the Americas. On that dazzlingly sunny Andean winter day in late July 2002, the brilliantly hued handwoven belts, shawls, and coca leaf purses were arrayed on the women's black shawls spread on the dirt and green stubble of a field (fig. 4). The colorful wool textiles contrasted with hundreds of shriveled corklike freeze-dried potatoes, or *ch'uñu*, sunning on dark cloths nearby. The *ch'uñu* reminded me that the primary occupation on the island of Taquile in southern Peru remains subsistence farming, even though people from Taquile create some of the finest textiles in the Andes.[2]

The terraced field we gathered in lay directly below the hand-built home of Taquile's enthusiastic young Cultural Promoter, Juan Quispe Huatta. Juan had coordinated my trip to Taquile with Nancy Rosoff, Andrew W. Mellon Curator of the Arts of the Americas, Brooklyn Museum, via e-mail and cell phone. This task was quite a challenge because Taquile still has no electricity, except for a few solar-powered installations, and using e-mail requires a three-and-a-half hour motorboat trip to a mainland Internet café in Puno.

Our quest for textiles began after an enormous lunch of white rice and crispy Lake Titicaca fried trout followed by pungent herbal *muña* tea in the Quispes' chilly formal dining room. We paused to thank Francisca Huatta (Juan's mother) and María Huatta (his wife), who had cooked the meal but, I knew, would eat separately in the kitchen. I had hoped to spend some time with Juan's female relatives to catch up in Quechua on news as well as to ask about a recent big meeting

4. *A group of Taquilean women and men decide which textiles anthropologists should purchase for the Brooklyn Museum. July 2002.*

concerning tourism, but they gently hurried us outside to look at the textiles they hoped to sell.

In the photograph are twelve Taquileans. They are from three intermarried, extended families, and they range in age from an older teenager to individuals in their late fifties. Also in the photograph is a representative from the Brooklyn Museum (Georgia de Havenon, to the far right, partly hidden). Just before this photograph was taken, Nancy and I were talking about the Brooklyn Museum project with my *compadre* "Pancho" Huatta (standing to the right, in profile). Pancho is my host and a friend of several decades. When we spoke with him, we also addressed Juan and Julio Quispe (Juan's father) and the younger men who in the photograph are behind the tall bunch grass, sitting quietly.

Meanwhile Wilton Callañaupa, a serious young Cusco college student who spoke Quechua and was working with us on the project, started filming several women who had set up their looms in an adjoining field, the preferred Andean weaving site. The front edge of such a loom is barely visible as small upright bars in the center of

5. Alejandrina Huatta (left), helped by her sister Petrona Huatta, warps an Andean-type staked-out ground loom on which to weave a belt. 1981.

figure 4. I noticed that the weavers' traditional Andean-type ground loom (fig. 5) was like one modified for indoor use by members of the "Natives of Taquile" Folklore Association in 1994, working with staff from the American Museum of Natural History in New York.[3]

Various men and women walked up and placed textiles on the shawls on the ground. My perpetually busy friend Alejandrina Huatta, daughter of my *compadre* Pancho and one of my first weaving teachers, had arrived carrying additional textiles with her husband Alejandro Huatta, one of Taquile's master boat builders. In figure 4, they are to the left, laying out one of Alejandrina's excellently woven wedding shawls. I still hadn't met everyone, and had many questions, but I was busy translating between Spanish and Quechua and taking photographs and notes.

Initially the Taquilean men gathered around the textiles, while the women sat weaving farther away at their Andean looms. Typical of almost any group interaction when tourists are not present, the Taquileans good-naturedly joked in Quechua almost nonstop. A few men gently jostled for position, before the younger men went to sit on the side, near the tall bunch grass. All the people were of course interested in what Nancy, as curator, would select. I suggested asking the Taquileans to choose which textiles we should buy, because they are, after all, the expert weavers, but also because I was interested to learn what they would recommend.

The situation was a little awkward because they would be judging textiles that included their own or their relative's. Also, such judging was both artificial and routine. I was well aware that people judged textiles all the time in private, and in small groups, since seemingly everything everyone wears is noted and critically evaluated. Taquileans also judge textiles when pricing them for sale in their community cooperative store. Furthermore, tourists evaluate textiles daily when considering what to buy. I knew that in South America's tiny handful of successful textile cooperatives public judging was integral to the development and maintenance of high standards. I also realized that there were potential conflicts of interest because money is very scarce in the impoverished Andean *altiplano* and everyone present certainly would be happy to have a guaranteed sale at the presumably good price that the Brooklyn Museum could offer. Within Peru, our request for their advice was still rather unusual because while indigenous people may be invited to give folklore presentations, or sometimes demonstrate crafts, they rarely are consulted as experts.

When the women continued to sit at their looms rather than join the group of men beside the textiles, I quietly and jokingly encouraged them in Spanish and Quechua to come over to voice their opinions and vote too. I wanted to hear their opinions because women created the beautiful and technically complex textiles we were examining. Yet, although Taquilean women are astonishingly articulate visually, they rarely speak in public. But slowly, by ones and twos, the women stood up and came to stand as a group, to better see the textiles, and figure 4 records that moment.[4]

Though all eight belts offered for purchase to the Brooklyn Museum clearly were examples of a single, distinctive regional substyle, numerous differences illustrated the ways that Taquilean weavers have been transforming "traditional" textiles since they began marketing them in the 1970s. Transformations included using purple instead of the usual red as the belts' main color, factory-spun instead of handspun yarns, double cloth instead of the more traditional complementary warp "pebble" weave, and densely packed representational and naturalistic images instead of more widely spaced abstract and geometric ones.

The astonishing quiet of the island without cars or electricity and set in vast Lake Titicaca, where sound travels immense distances, was interrupted by Juan's cell phone. Somewhat abashed, he broke away to answer. As people got ready to vote, we stopped again when someone pointed out that the afternoon boats were leaving the island for the mainland city of Puno. We walked to the edge of the field to quietly watch the vessels quickly become glittering specks in the shining water.

By that time there were thirteen Taquileans, so a decisive vote would be possible. There was no conversation but plenty of careful looking. After two minutes, each person voted aloud. Several of the younger men I didn't know commented that they liked one of the purple belts, but it was eliminated because of its nontraditional background color. I was intrigued by two belts with wide color stripes next to the central pattern stripe. The stripes made them look very different from other Taquilean belts, but they were well woven. I was somewhat surprised they too were quickly eliminated. Were the Taquileans concerned that these were not "representative" of Taquile, and therefore not "authentic"? Several people in the group had traveled to museums in Lima, Mexico, and the United States and thus had a sense of collections there. Taquileans have performed in folklore events in Peru, the United States, France, and Poland; they also have coped daily with mass tourism, and thus are well aware that the issue of authenticity is very important.

In the end, they chose an extremely well-woven example of a traditional-style belt to represent Taquile in New York. How much this determination was based on their preferences and how much on perceptions that Westerners ascribed a higher economic and aesthetic value to "traditional" weaving is unclear.

The selection process, including the decision to opt for a "traditional" weaving, reflects recent transformations in the production and uses of handmade cloth. The textile arts have been of singular importance in the Andes for thousands of years. Even now, handmade clothing remains central to racial and ethnic identity and cultural expression, while also serving as an important source of income for artisans. The production of textiles with symbolically meaningful geometric and representational images is the major form of expressive culture for indigenous women. Taquilean women are actively transforming textiles both in response to the tourist market, which has grown since the late 1970s, and to represent new ideas and experiences in their society.

The beautifully made clothing created and worn by Alejandrina, Juan, María, Francisca, Pancho, and Julio is part of what draws tens of thousands of visitors a year to their tiny island. Income from selling textiles has propelled Taquileans to develop a unique, world-renowned model for community control of tourism. However, this success also means that Taquileans increasingly purchase factory-spun yarns rather than bartering for fleece and handspinning the yarn themselves. During my 2002 trip, I also observed that many Taquileans have become so busy obtaining an education and attending to tourist-related businesses that they have far less time to weave than when I first visited in the mid-1970s.

How, I wondered, would they be able to maintain their traditional arts and customs while also working so hard to obtain the material comforts of modern society? How would women's increasing literacy and public assertiveness affect their creation of cloth, and the island society itself? Would Taquileans exert increasing power in their region due to Taquile's tourism clout, or would regional elites find ways to co-opt, ignore, or sidestep them? Would the positive Indian identity they were creating, through cloth and tourism, function as an antiracist strategy?

Faced with the same dilemmas that so many other rural indigenous people confront worldwide, could Taquileans manage to find an alternate path between what has long been posed as the seemingly irreconcilable choice between tradition and modernity? Would their community unravel due to the conflicts between these two extremes, or could they weave a new future that combined both? Many Taquileans were asking themselves the same questions.

TAQUILE

Approximately 1,700 Quechua-speaking people live on Taquile, located in the Andean *altiplano* (high plain) at 3,808 meters, or almost 13,000 feet, above sea level. Taquile is one of three permanently

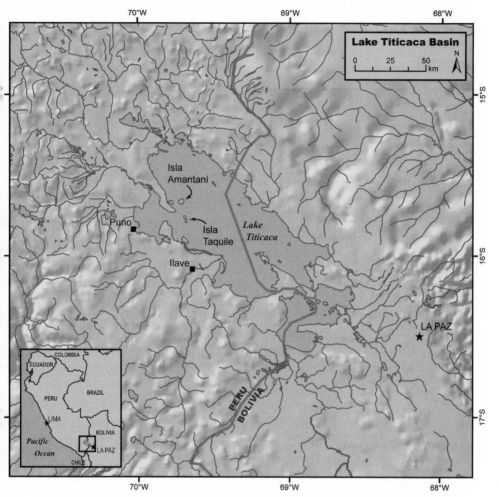

Map of the Lake Titicaca Basin. Map by Steve Wernke.

inhabited islands on the Peruvian side of Lake Titicaca. Before Taquileans began using motorboats in the 1970s, it took about eight hours to sail the 45 kilometers between Taquile and the nearest city, Puno on the mainland, and before sailboats, days to travel by reed boat. Taquileans identify themselves as *runa*, or Indians. All the people are related, and almost all share one of nine Quechua, Aymara, or Spanish surnames, including Quispe and Huatta. They are subsistence farmers using unirrigated agriculture in an arid region to grow potatoes, other Andean tubers, barley, broad beans, and some corn; they also fish in the lake. Their small, rocky island supports some sheep and cows. The community (Taquile *ayllu*) has two moiety *ayllus* ("upper" and "lower");[5] it still does not have electricity, running water, or a sewage system. It has an elementary school and a recently completed high school.

The Puno Region (formerly Department) is one of the poorest areas in the nation. Puno suffered, though not as much as other regions, during Peru's undeclared civil war of the 1980s and early 1990s that left some sixty thousand Peruvians (primarily peasants) dead or disappeared (Mayer 1992; Poole and Rénique 1992; Rénique 1994; Stern 1998). From the perspective of the creole elites of Peru's capital city of Lima and other metropolitan centers, as well as Puno's *mestizo*[6] residents, the town and surrounding region are considered "wild" and violent, according to a nineteenth-century discourse that links geography, race, and character together (Orlove 1993). At the same time, Peruvians call Puno the "heart" of Peruvian folklore.

For many in Peru and Puno, Taquile represents the backwardness and isolation of native Andeans, considered distant heirs of the great Incas whose glory was forever lost with the Spanish Conquest. Taquileans thus are at the bottom of the social ladder in a region already marginalized within the nation, which in turn is marginalized in the wider world (Jacobsen 1993; Painter 1991; Smith 1991).

The period that I examine here (1976–2002) saw profound changes within Taquile, as well as within Peru. That country, destination of desire and mystery to many Europeans and North Americans for centuries, underwent a military dictatorship, democratic elections, a debt crisis, astoundingly high inflation, a violent undeclared civil war, cycles of floods and drought, a dictatorship in all but name, neoliberalism, and once again democratic elections. Peru transformed from a predominantly rural country of some 15.5 million people in 1976 to an urban nation of 27 million by 2000, in a process occurring throughout Latin America.

During this period, the population of Taquile increased from around 900 to 1,700, primarily the result of return migration, improved nutrition, and decreased mortality. (My impression is that most returning migrants came from Peru's Pacific coast, having left Taquile to earn cash and learn Spanish.) Many Taquileans now speak some Spanish in addition to Quechua, and quite a few are fluent in Spanish. The trip from the mainland city of Puno to the island now can be made in three or four hours by motorboat. Few girls studied at Taquile's primary school in 1976; now Taquile has a secondary school, and Taquileans, both males and females, are studying in high schools in Puno as well, while some are preparing to enter the university.

Some of the technological changes of the late twentieth century have helped Taquileans, along with other people in geographically isolated regions, to improve communication. Although there is no mail service and Taquileans are off the electrical grid, unable to get Internet service that some so desperately want, some families now have cell phones, and travel on the lake is less dangerous when help is, at least in theory, a phone call away.

Taquileans are conservative in some ways (they were late to build wooden sailboats, for example) but innovative in others (certain Taquilean families purchased title to their lands beginning in the 1940s, ahead of any other peasant community on that side of the lake).

CLOTH

Cloth was of paramount importance for pre-Conquest civilizations for more than three thousand years (Murra 1962; Rowe, Benson, and Schaffer 1979). Weaving remained important during the colonial period for the economies of both church and crown, and even though Andean textile production was transformed substantially, in virtually every way imaginable in terms of technology and iconography, rural Andeans continued to produce massive amounts of fine cloth. However, the combination of a series of factors in the twentieth century makes it surprising that today any Andeans weave at all. By factors I mean the almost complete collapse of the regional wool economies (Zorn 1997a, 1997b) that supplied raw materials to weavers, the discrimination that wearers of ethnic dress face throughout Peru and Bolivia, the difficulty of weaving while working in urban areas, and the relative low cost and ubiquity of factory-made clothing (especially used Western dress). Nonetheless, many Andeans still weave. In many areas, despite increased commoditization, cloth continues to hold local meanings, as commoditized arts do in Mexico (J. H. Cohen 1999, Stephen 1991b) and elsewhere. However, by the twenty-first century, as was clear to me during my trip to Peru and Bolivia in 2002, much highland weaving had ceased.

People who still weave do so for a series of reasons: because producers can obtain basic materials without spending money, because handwoven cloth still fulfills many of its economic, communicative, and symbolic roles, and because cloth can provide a significant source of income in the impoverished Andes.

Where cloth remains important, it codifies the changing experiences of young Andeans and their ongoing process of defining their identity (Cassandra Torrico, personal communication 1994). Although recently made Andean textiles look vastly different from their predecessors, cloth continues to be a site for investing enormous resources and creativity, requiring major investments of time and money. Creating handwoven textiles is still in many places second only to subsistence activities (though other forms of craft production in Latin America are a primary source of income: Chibnik 2003). Increasing participation in the cash economy due to the severe decline of the Andean agro-pastoral system however, has substantially eroded the ability of *runa* to obtain the raw materials they need to make cloth. Thus Andeans now need money to purchase most or all of the materials they require to make handmade textiles.

Taquile is one of a few places in Peru where people continue, on a community-wide level, to produce cloth that they wear every day. In this book, I focus on how Taquileans have changed their textiles as part of their efforts to carve out a space where one would think there is no space at all (Davydd Greenwood, personal communication 1996) — at the bottom of the social hierarchy in the Andean nation of Peru.

Both men and women are involved in these recent changes in the production, use, and meaning of cloth in Taquile, and *Weaving a Fu-*

ture shows how gender is central to the creation of cultural expressions as well as to responses to globalization. Because tourism has led Taquileans to become increasingly self-conscious about their lives and society, and to interpret their "culture" for outsiders, I pay special attention to gendered cultural expressions that Taquileans created in the "contact situations" (cf. Pratt 1995) that arise from tourism and commercialization of art.

I want to emphasize, however, that my celebration of Taquilean creativity must be understood within the context of the terrible poverty and discrimination that indigenous Andean people face each day. Many of the choices Andeans make, such as the decisions to stop weaving, adopt Western-style clothing, and migrate to urban areas, are based on their desire to escape daily hardships. Many indigenous Andeans feel forced to choose between their rich cultural traditions and the perceived economic improvements offered by modernization. In these circumstances, it is not surprising that many seek modernization and urbanization, with nary a backwards glance. Others wonder, Are both possible? As I will show, Taquileans, although with uneven results, have placed themselves at the forefront of those indigenous people who seek both worlds.[7]

COMMODITIZATION

Before 1968, few Taquileans sold their exquisitely beautiful weavings, which represented tens of thousands of hours of work and enormous resources. The increase in commoditization[8] (sale) of textiles that previously were made almost exclusively for personal or family use caused profound changes in Taquilean society.

The initial suggestion that Taquileans consider selling textiles in a Cusco-based cooperative came from Peace Corps volunteer Kevin Healy, who lived nearby on Capachica. Experience selling textiles, first through the cooperative and then through Taquilean intermediaries in Peruvian cities, gave them knowledge of the tourist market and income that made it possible to benefit from tourism when the opportunity presented itself. During all that time, both female and male Taquileans experimented with many aspects of their textile traditions, altering some textiles and inventing others, in their efforts to diversify products and increase sales. Their experiences and the money earned from selling textiles gave rise to a new class of male entrepreneurs who would prove important for the evolution of tourism. This new generation of male agents of change is the latest version of the young entrepreneurial men described by Peruvian anthropologists Rosalía Avalos de Matos and José Matos Mar in the 1950s. Matos Mar wrote of their rise to power by a nontraditional route, which included learning Spanish, in addition to Quechua, and interacting more extensively with outsiders.

Taquile shows that the commercialization of culture — more particularly the commoditization of handmade cloth — does not inevitably lead to the destruction of local traditions and cultures, though it appears to increase the pace of changes.[9] Andean peoples continue to produce new styles of art, such as the new art object recently created by some Taquileans: a calendar belt, which has both a woven form (made by women) and a written form (made by men).[10]

Handicraft production, however, is often reorganized to meet market demands (García Canclini 1982, 1990, 1993), and indigenous control varies greatly (Graburn 1976, 1993, 1999; Zorn 1983, 1987a). Many people in the industrialized world crave handmade objects, and earning some income from sales of crafts allows people in many areas of the world to survive on their land. Tourist purchase of objects made by people such as Taquileans can reinforce local identity and express resistance to capitalist hegemony, as well as nurture utopian dreams of alternatives to the regularization of consumption that engulfs (post)modern life.

Increasing population pressure and parcelization of land in Taquile and the aggravated economic crises in Peru have encouraged Taquileans to produce textiles for differentiated markets. At the same time, Taquileans' distinctive dress has served to reinforce local identity and pride, and to advertise their island, while reconfirming its "Indianness," to tourists.

TOURISM

Travel to Taquile by outsiders was long limited to a priest who visited yearly to perform marriages, teachers who appeared sporadically, occasional government officials, anthropologists (Avalos de Matos 1951a, 1951b; Matos Mar 1951a, 1951b, 1957a, 1960, 1964, 1986), and a few travelers.

In 1976, following publication of a brief report praising Taquile in a popular traveler's guide, tourism arrived on the tiny island, soon reaching one thousand visitors monthly and now totaling forty thousand a year. Taquileans responded quickly, creating tourism-related infrastructure that formed a model of indigenous control of tourism.

Taquileans came up with an impressive array of individual, group, and communal enterprises and institutions to service tourists and to market their textiles to them. These consist of a cooperative store for selling handicrafts, a system for lodging overnight guests in individual Taquilean homes, a community museum, and associations of boat owners/operators for transporting tourists and Taquileans between the island and the mainland. They also created a festival-fair to showcase dances and market textiles.

Income from tourism derives primarily from transportation (carried out primarily by men) and selling textiles (produced primarily by women). These gendered differences are an important element in analyzing the Taquileans' creation and operation of tourist-oriented enterprises for those seeking a glimpse of the "real Peru."

Textile sales and tourism have brought a series of economic benefits to Taquile, especially a reduction in off-migration and a return of former migrants (see Chibnik 2003 on short-term success in Mexico). Taquileans also have created new businesses and industries. More generally, they are seeing their standard of living rise, overall health improve, and lifespan lengthen somewhat. Taquileans are creating new products for sale, learning to speak Spanish while retaining Quechua, and increasing their ability to read and write in Spanish. Women are playing a more prominent role in public life, and the consumption of manufactured goods clearly is up. Nevertheless, benefits are not shared equally.

Taquileans interpret their island, cultural traditions, and weaving for the outsiders who visit them. On the island itself, Taquileans have, for example, built new "Inca" roads and ruins (*musuq ruinas*), with stone benches at scenic views, and colonial-style arches.

Ironically, Taquile's isolation has turned out to be one of its greatest strengths, since the islanders maintain many traditions, such as weaving, that people in other communities no longer practice. This cultural preservation has enhanced the island's desirability. Taquile's isolation facilitated control of transportation, protected the island during Peru's recent civil war, and helped Taquileans reject attempts by outsiders to build hotels on the island, giving Taquile, at least for a few decades, a competitive advantage.

Taquileans, like some other indigenous groups, have been relatively successful, at least in the short term, in "leveraging" their international experiences from tourism into regional and sometimes small national victories (Matos Mar 1997a, 1997b, 1998; Zorn 2000, n.d.d), as when they gained national notice because presidential candidate Alberto Fujimori helicoptered onto Taquile for a campaign stop (fig. 6). They achieved their measure of success through individual and family initiative in some cases, and in others through collective work in groups and associations. Some of these organizations predate tourism, such as the various wooden-sailboat "cooperative" groups that became motorboat groups; other organizations were new, such as the expanding number of folklore associations.

Taquileans have drawn on two sociocultural forms ideologically conceptualized as having great historical, pre-Conquest depth: first, cultural products, including cloth, music, and dance, and, second, the *ayllu*, as community, though in both cases I want to underline the importance of the intellectual knowledge and practices (habitus and schema, per Pierre Bourdieu), and not just the products. The definition of community as one that could incorporate strangers (Urton 1991) was flexibly manipulated as Taquileans drew on relationships with outsiders in contexts both political (CISA 1998a, 1998b, 1998c; Matos Mar 1951a, 1951b, 1964) and personal, the latter frequently cemented through the Spanish/Andean institution of *compadrazgo* (ritual or spiritual kinship).

By the 1990s, thanks to tourism, Taquileans' racial and ethnic identity had become a positive sign, both because they looked beyond Peru for their identity and because Indian identity had become a commodity in attracting tourism to the Puno region and the nation. Previously Taquilean men literally covered up their Indian identity by wearing Western-style clothing over native dress when traveling off the island, in an attempt to mitigate white and *mestizo* racism that left them, and other indigenous people, subject to ill treatment, taunts, or worse.

That Taquileans now look to transnational sites (New York, Washington, D.C., London) to construct their identity can be understood as an antiracist strategy in the context of prevailing racism in their

6. *Former Peruvian president Alberto Fujimori (center, wearing glasses) helicoptered onto Taquile when seeking reelection in 2001. He wears numerous items of Taquilean men's clothing (cap, vest, scarf, coca leaf purse, belt) and a tourist item (gloves). Note community authority (back turned, left); Pancho Huatta (center); and presidential bodyguard (right). Photograph in possession of Pancho Huatta. Used by permission.*

own region and nation. One way that Taquileans cope with globalization and mass tourism is by creating novel objects and institutions that are both "traditional" and "modern." Globalization and transnationalism in the form of community-controlled tourism have not only allowed many Taquileans to alleviate some of the terrible poverty on their island, but also to look beyond their nation to create positive Indian identities.

COMMODITIZATION AND TOURISM

Both tourism and the commoditization of cloth developed in the context of broad regional, national, and global processes that shaped their impacts on this and other communities. Tourism expanded steadily after the 1960s with the improvements in air travel and greater accessibility to areas once considered remote by Europeans and North Americans. The importance of tourism to communities in low-income countries is magnified because of poverty in these regions and nations, in no small part the legacy of centuries-old processes of colonialism and postcolonialism. Before the 1970s, many of these areas, Taquile included, had minimal relationship with a cash economy, the populations surviving as subsistence farmers who relied largely on barter.

My research shows clearly that tourism and commoditization of cloth, and of culture, are interrelated processes. First, the same people in this island community are involved in both. This was crystallized for me when I spent the day with my friend and former weaving teacher Alejandrina Huatta and saw her "typical" day (as she said). She spent the morning cooking for her family and helping her children get ready for school, then managed a few hours weaving a section of a calendar belt before heading off at mid-day to the island's "control" to pick up a tourist who lodged with her family that night. After serving lunch to the tourist (and snacking on something herself), Alejandrina worked on another section of the textile, before breaking off to help her older daughter cook dinner. Following dinner, though tired, she and her husband, Alejandro, walked to the community plaza to rehearse a dance for both their community festival and the tourist fair, knowing that their folklore association would fine them if they failed to appear. Nevertheless, in the interrelationship of tourism and commoditization we see gendered distinctions: women make certain kinds of textiles and men make others, and women and men participate in managing tourism in different ways.

Second, the processes of tourism and commoditization are intertwined in many ways, as seen in the opening anecdote. Selling textiles that previously were made only for personal and family use provided a rare opportunity for Taquileans to earn money. They invested this money to create a tourism infrastructure, and without this source of income, they might not have been able to develop their model of community tourism. At the same time, tourists to Taquile were attracted in large part by the community members' beautiful handmade clothing, making it possible for Taquileans to sell far more textiles and at better prices than would have been possible through other channels. Decades later, community members have become so busy managing tourism on top of subsistence agriculture that textile production has diminished in importance.

Finally, both tourism and the commoditization of local cultural products and performances are being experienced hand in hand by thousands of communities worldwide. Together the two can affect nearly every aspect of peoples' lives and society — their time, their land, their ideas about themselves and others. Tourism and commoditization have been blamed, sometimes correctly, for significantly contributing to the destruction or loss of natural resources, long-standing cultural traditions, and the integrity of local life. To take advantage of rare economic opportunities, the people on Taquile, sometimes individually, sometimes in groups or united as a community, have found creative ways to encourage the positive aspects of tourism and commoditization, while challenging or resisting the negative.

INTERDISCIPLINARY APPROACHES FOR MULTI-SITED ETHNOGRAPHY

By the later twentieth century, scholars began to analyze the apparently new forms of identity that arose as many people, often from formerly remote rural areas, migrated in great numbers all over the world yet retained multiple and transnational allegiances. Globalization, defined as the flow of capital and information around the world, affected people in areas remote from centers of power in ways that intensified their roles in the world capitalist economy.

The transnational lives of anthropology's "subjects" required new forms of ethnography that moved beyond the "closed corporate peasant community" (Wolf 1957, 1986). Though my initial project on Taquile was to study textile technology, my research expanded as I traveled and interacted with Taquileans outside the island in various Peruvian cities. Travel by Taquilean "folklore" groups to the United States during the 1990s gave me opportunities to work with them in Washington, D.C., and finally on my home island of Manhattan in New York City. My interdisciplinary theoretical approaches and multi-sited ethnography thus came about in part by following the trajectory of the Taquileans, which mirrored movements of people across borders worldwide.

This book arose from my interest in the roles of cloth in the contemporary Andes, or to phrase the issue more simply, what specific groups of Andean people "do" with, and think about, cloth today. Since an ever-increasing articulation to the market, frequently at disadvantageous or disastrous terms, has been one of the most important features of late twentieth-century Andean life,[11] I have been concerned with phenomena that have had special impact on handwoven "traditional" cloth production, which in the case of Taquile has been the production of textiles for tourists.

There is a surprising lack of anthropological case studies on tourism in Peru, despite the hundreds of thousands of tourists who have traveled there and the importance of tourism to the region's economy. This book is part of filling that gap, and by focusing on a single island, the case study offers an unusually long-term, multi-sited study of tourism in one region.

I use theory from diverse fields (political economy, race, gender, semiotics, performance, identity, tourism, commoditization, material culture, and aesthetics). I strongly believe that change has long been at the center of "traditional" textiles, and culture, and that while earlier scholarship on the Andes has understandably concentrated on continuity in culture and society, I am looking on the other side of the two-faced textile to examine the side of change. Continuity and change, like other dichotomies, have meaning through a continuous, mutually self-defining interlacing. In this process, issues of race, gender, and class intersect.

In seeking to combine both semiotic and political economic approaches to the production, use, and exchange of contemporary Andean cloth, I have found García Canclini's (1982, 1990, 1993) approach to popular culture and (post)modernity in Mexico particularly valuable. His statement on modernity and anthropology neatly sums up my (ironic) recognition of my nostalgia for traditions whose passing I lament: "It seems that we anthropologists have more difficulties entering modernity than do the social groups that we study" (1990: 230).

Hobsbawm and Ranger's pioneering edited volume on the "invention of tradition" (1983) was important to me (as it has been to many other scholars) when I returned from fieldwork on Taquile and other Peruvian communities to grapple with conceptualizing the varied textiles that Taquileans sold. Hobsbawm and Ranger caution that, while so-called traditions are "invented" all the time, ongoing traditions also can be quite adaptable.

Hobsbawm and Ranger's work intertwined with the growing, transdisciplinary field of material culture studies (Hodder 1982a; Myers 2001, Myers, ed. 2001). This juncture was marked by Appadurai's groundbreaking volume on the "social life of things" (1986), as anthropology rediscovered the importance of objects, though I focus on processes of change in Andean cloth, rather than on individual textiles.

Anthropology has long looked at processes such as commoditization in noncapitalist societies (Parry and Bloch 1989) and at social change in what formerly were called primitive or tribal societies. Theorizing change, however, has been problematic for the discipline, and for me. My discussion of the creation of new art objects/styles such as the calendar belt continues an examination of ways that peasants participate in markets and attempt to exert some control over them (Painter 1991).

Change at the center of "traditions" (cf. Baizerman 1987, 1990; Hobsbawm and Ranger 1983) inform my analysis of Andean cloth production, because I believe that the concept of fashion is applicable to indigenous cloth production and use. I do not, however, discuss whether the textiles Andeans weave and wear are crafts or art (Phillips and Steiner 1999; Phillips and Steiner, eds., 1999), though aesthetics is central to many aspects of Taquilean social and cultural life, and certainly the story with which I started this chapter raises questions about the boundary between crafts and art. I believe it useful to think about textile production/art not as an autonomous aesthetic sphere but as a site of social identity (Turino 1991, 1993), and therefore of power (Gramsci 1971), whether between men and women (Arnold 1988), peasants and the state (O'Brien and Roseberry 1991), or local and global agents.

Gender is a primary lens through which to create and understand society. I emphasize women and issues of gender here since women in southern parts of the Andes, as in many other parts of the world (Weiner and Schneider 1986, 1989), have a "special" relationship with cloth, producing the textiles that are most symbolically meaningful, as well as those that have been most heavily commercialized. Transformations in the production, use, and marketing of Taquilean textiles affect the relations of power between men and women. Taquilean women, like Andean market women, derive power precisely because of their control of their own earnings.

Here, the use of interdisciplinary perspectives from anthropology, economics, and art to analyze tourism and culture shows how, under certain conditions, communities can control and benefit from tourism. How gender is central to development and modernization is revealed by examining the different processes through which women and men create and manage institutions and forms of cultural representation in novel contexts.

METHODOLOGY

This multi-sited ethnography is based on long-term research which started December 1975 and continued through 2002.[12] During those decades, many older Taquileans I knew have died, and the children I met when I began are now grown and have their own families and children.

Many methodological and ethical problems arise in the course of researching and interpreting investigations with living subjects, especially when the researcher is from a class, race, sex, language group, and/or nationality ranked higher than the people she or he studies. Anthropology's long-standing and much-critiqued interest in the so-called "exotic Other" has meant that, until recently, researchers almost without exception came from urban societies and studied people in poorer, rural undeveloped regions. Issues of subjectivity, power, and general ethics are inevitable.[13] Is knowledge only subjective, not external or objective? Can subjects of research refuse to participate when the researcher comes from a more powerful group? To whom does a researcher owe loyalty if the interests of the community of study conflict with interests of the host region or nation? How can the subjects of research be compensated for their time and trouble? Who owns the data collected? Whose interpretations are valid, and how should they be presented? Such methodological and ethical issues are foregrounded when using the method I did—the now-classic participant observation, where the researcher tries to observe what is going on in a society while participating in the full range of activities of peoples' lives. These were all questions that I wrestled with during my research and which have neither easy nor definitive answers.

Taquileans are generally remarkably hospitable, and I benefited especially from being one of the first outsiders to stay on the island.[14] Like many anthropologists, I had a special relationship with the family who invited me to stay in their home, and since I spent a great deal of time with them, what I learned from them was important in shaping my understanding of the community. Many members of the Huatta-Machaca family welcomed me, and overall, I was treated or tolerated with great politeness, and often with kindness, warmth, and concern. It is common for researchers such as anthropologists to form relationships with elite male members of a society, in part because community leaders' responsibilities include interacting with powerful outsiders, while gender or linguistic boundaries limit interaction with others. This of course influences the vision one has of a society and places limits on the people with whom one should, or should not, interact.

In my case, Francisco "Pancho" Huatta, who first invited me to Taquile, spoke Spanish and was part of the initial generation of Taquileans who traveled off the island to market weavings—both of which meant that he was a high-ranking male. During that first year my primary means of addressing this issue was to improve my Quechua (particularly so I could communicate with women), regularly spend time away from his family compound so I could interact with non-family members, rent a room in the city of Puno so that Taquileans could visit me away from the island, and apprentice myself to weavers, who are female.

Like other researchers, I tried to make myself useful, though it is hard to repay years of friendship and hospitality. I provided news, income (for rent and purchases of textiles), food, and gifts, though I struggled to set limits on who should receive them and what I should give. Over the years, I served as recording secretary at various community assemblies (at a time when Taquileans were not as literate as they are now), helped draft and present petitions to regional au-

thorities (to try to gain a high school), and helped write a successful grant application for Taquile's first outside donation, by the Inter-
American Foundation (IAF), a U.S. governmental agency.[15] In the
United States, I have given as gifts and sold what seems like endless
quantities of Taquilean textiles, a chore that is part of the reciprocity
that structures Andean life, and one that outsiders such as anthropologists fail to participate in at their peril. In the course of research
and writing, all anthropologists have to make judgments about the
boundaries between research and advocacy. I chose a middle path.

My initial research provided both qualitative and quantitative
data and focused on learning and documenting textile technology
(spinning, plying, warping, weaving, finishing), but I also researched
costs and labor-time invested in making Taquile's many types of textiles. There is no doubt that since I was the first outsider who lived
there to study weaving, people were not sure how to handle my request to learn the skill because they could not ascertain if I was serious. Their perception, as they later told me, was that it could be a
waste of their time trying to teach a *gringa* (foreigner), who generally
was perceived as capable of working impressive modern equipment
but incapable of doing anything with her hands. They wondered how
they should teach weaving to an adult lacking the basic skills that
should have been learned in childhood, especially one who was a
high-prestige foreigner. They questioned why I would even want to
learn, since *mestizos* thought what Taquileans did of no value. Would
I take that knowledge and somehow make money from it, like other
outsiders who over centuries have stolen objects and knowledge from
them and other *runa*?

Since I was the first outsider Taquileans taught textile skills,[16] the
women I asked to teach me to weave insisted that I would need to first
learn to spin (make thread) and then ply (double the thread to make
it stronger) before I started warping (setting up a loom) and, only
then, could I move on to weaving. In retrospect, these women — my
host's wife and my *comadre*, Natividad Machaca, their daughter Alejandrina Huatta, and Pancho's sister Lucía Huatta, forced a pedagogical model on me, that of learning in stages what I initially, in a typically Western impatient way, wanted to skip. The children were less
inhibited about spying on me, so I spent a fair amount of time with
the preteens and teenagers living in my house compound. Since some

of them had only recently mastered the skills I was struggling to learn, I found that my most tolerant teachers were children, and I still remember how Calixto Huatta, then the young son of my *compadre*, taught me how to ply. I eventually learned enough to weave a narrow patterned belt on the Andean loom, but my progress stopped due to the rise of tourism, which drew my attention away from cloth.

My apprenticeship to Taquilean women weavers was unusual at the time in terms of general anthropological methodology, except for researchers interested in studying apprenticeship (Coy 1989a, 1989b; Coy, ed. 1989), but one that was frequently adopted by other textile researchers. I had learned to weave before studying weaving in Taquile, which was both an advantage and a disadvantage. Prior study was advantageous because I understood the basic operation of the loom and had a degree of manual dexterity. On the other hand, this knowledge was a disadvantage because I went to the Andes socialized to learn weaving according to a Western pedagogical model, based on writing and ongoing encouragement, neither of which is part of traditional Andean pedagogy.

During five years of fieldwork in three regions (Taquile Island; Macusani in Puno, Peru; and Sacaca in northern Potosí, Bolivia) I had the opportunity to work with eight principal teachers: two women per region plus two men who taught me to braid slings. In every locale, I also met several other "part-time" teachers who offered short-term advice, criticism, and occasionally help. Thus much of what I learned about Andean cloth and weaving came from this apprenticeship to the true textile experts — women weavers who taught me to weave small textiles, such as narrow ties, belts, and a coca leaf purse. Taquilean, Macusani, and Sakaka men also told and showed me much about both men's and women's cloth.[17]

In retrospect, it was a huge advantage to interact with Taquilean society through a highly valued aspect of the culture such as weaving, rather than as an intellectual solely gathering verbal or visual data. More importantly, as my teachers and I wove, we spoke about the art of weaving (though we often worked in silence), and those conversations ranged over the community, my project, and our lives.

When tourism developed, I shifted research and spent an increasing amount of time studying Taquileans' active responses to the opportunities that tourism presented. I obtained data from community records on tourists, as well as cooperative records of textile sales, plus general community economic data used to write grant requests to external agencies, again combining qualitative and quantitative approaches.

As I still have not completed any large textiles, my teachers jokingly and seriously pointed out my need to return to do so, which I certainly hope to do some day. As part of the *ayni* (reciprocal exchange) of fieldwork, including the gifts of food and textiles and time that I was given, many Taquileans also reminded me that I owed them a book about their community, which documents their remarkably successful efforts to manage tourism, as well as their current struggles to regain that control.

ORGANIZATION OF THE BOOK

Chapters 2 and 3 provide background on Taquile and Taquileans' beautiful textiles. Chapter 2 introduces the island community, paying special attention to its unusual history, including the various ways that Taquile was an "exception" in its region, and to the communal forms of social organization and reciprocal labor exchange that Taquileans drew upon when they responded to new opportunities created by tourism. Chapter 3 looks at the unique importance of cloth in the southern Andes in general and in Taquile in particular, focusing on the ways that cloth is gendered and on women's "special" relationship with cloth.

Chapters 4 and 5 examine changes on Taquile related to commoditization of its cloth, which started in 1968, and tourism to the island, which started in 1976. Chapter 4 analyzes the process of commoditization and commercialization of Taquilean cloth. The chapter shows how sales of textiles provided the best alternative for Taquileans to earn money, and how the money earned from marketing cloth provided the capital Taquileans used to develop tourism infrastructure. It examines the recent creation of Taquile's unique woven and written calendar belts, which "explain" Taquile to outsiders at the same time that they record information important to islanders.

Chapter 5 looks at Taquile's remarkable and sudden success responding to tourism by analyzing Taquile's unique model of community-controlled tourism, as well as ongoing challenges to Taquilean control of tourism to the island. The chapter examines the argument about Taquilean "exceptionalism," showing how strong community organizations, ownership of all its land, and refusal to let outsiders build on the island made it possible for Taquileans to take advantage of tourism. Both chapters pay special attention to gendered aspects of these processes.

Chapter 6 presents the conclusions, showing how both commoditization of traditional arts and tourism are complex processes whose multifaceted effects on communities and individuals cannot be predicted in advance. I believe that peasants such as Taquileans can benefit from globalization through sale of their handicrafts and tourism to their community in certain circumstances, though gendered aspects of these processes constrain those benefits. I also show that money, recognition, and prestige from selling handicrafts, participating in crafts fairs and folkloric events, and traveling abroad can constitute an antiracist strategy that helps Indians bypass or more effectively challenge racism and discrimination at home.

The conclusions pose the question of whether the Taquileans' effort to find an alternative development path, which would allow them to interweave modernity together with their extraordinary crafts and other cultural traditions, is possible.

2 TAQUILE ISLAND IN LAKE TITICACA

They called these islands by the name of the Guacas *[sacred shrines]
that the Devil revealed to them; one [is] Amantani. . . . Taquilli is the
other island, where they worshiped another Guaca of the same name.*[1]
— Father Martín de Murúa (1946 [1605]: 215)

FIRST IMPRESSIONS

Anthropologists often compare stories of awful first journeys to a
field site as one of them leaves home to experience the rite of passage
known as fieldwork, sine qua non of our profession. These stories
provide common ground but also are a way to "prove" that one has
really "been there."[2]

Abercrombie (1998b), among others, examines these stories of
problems, incomprehension, confusions, and conflicts, many of
which are part of the "shop talk" at anthropology gatherings. As anthropologists increasingly have realized, these anecdotes and inci-
dents are also part of the research record. They record the creation
and maintenance (or dissolution) of the intersubjective social relationships at the core of qualitative research, part of the very conflicts
between Andeans and others since at least the Spanish invasion that
continue in the postcolonial frontier. While confusions, misunderstandings, and conflicts certainly occur among people from the same
society, the gulf between colonizer and colonized, or even foreign anthropologist and local resident, lead to misunderstandings that become part of the historical record. The quotation by the colonial
chronicler Father Martín de Murúa that starts this chapter, the earliest reference to Taquile I know of, is ambiguous. Either there were
two islands, one named Amantani and the other Taquilli (Taquile), or
there were two islands and both had the same name: Amantani.
Since Taquile likely was named after the colonial landowner Pedro
González de Taquila, it is likely that Taquile once had another name,
which may never be known.

My first trip to Taquile really was awful — the worst trip to or from the island I have experienced in twenty-five years. Unusually severe storms turned what should have been an overnight sail in a hand-made boat, holding about fifteen people and their tightly packed belongings into a voyage lasting two nights and three days. It is amusing in retrospect as a classic "rite of passage." It was very unpleasant at the time, and the story stays in my mind because it reminds me of the ever-present dangers and hardships of traveling on powerful Lake Titicaca, something that Taquileans never forget. Like farmers and fisherfolk worldwide, Taquileans always read the signs of nature, and the texts of the natural world along with those of the social world, which are not separate in the Andean thought, as they are in Western thought.

We set off on an evening in February, which is midsummer and the end of the rainy season, from the dock at Puno, since the winds of the lake blow east at night, towards Taquile. The wooden sailboat was crowded and included four nonislanders, all of us invited to participate in a local festival. No one had planned for a multiday boat trip, with overnight stops and almost constant rowing by the male passengers and crew and constant bailing by the women. The boat was piled with staples obtained in Puno, such as onions and flour for cooking, but we quickly ran out of food to eat. People laughed and joked, though I felt lost — I didn't speak Quechua very well and I didn't know what to expect. Mostly I wondered when we would get to Taquile and when our next meal would come. I experienced patterns of behavior different from those of my own culture: a communal ideal that mandated sharing whatever food (or hunger) one had with everyone and a great sense of humor, especially manifest in practical jokes, which I had to learn to appreciate rather quickly.

Eventually the sight I would become accustomed to, and never fail to appreciate, came into view: the rocky, terraced island of Taquile. The island was green with summer growth, dotted with stone and thatch houses and a few eucalyptus trees. People wearing Taquilean dress waited on the dock and along the island's stone paths. I was somewhat ill from the trip but was rushed up more than five hundred Inca-type stone steps and across stone and dirt paths to my host's home, where I was given something to eat and dressed in twenty pounds of wool skirts (a dozen *polleras*) and other Taquilean women's garments. The many *polleras* made me well dressed, as would be expected of a guest of Pancho Huatta and Natividad Machaca, my hosts and sponsors of the Festival of the Virgin of Candlemas. The three other nonislanders were similarly given Taquilean dress.

Next I was urged to trot up and down yet more paths and stone steps to Taquile's beautiful central plaza. There, amusingly in retrospect, I faced a second "test" of fieldwork. Struggling to keep my head shawl on and to not trip over my skirts when climbing up stone walls (which I invariably knocked over), I soon was pulled out of the crowd by a Taquilean authority. He invited me to dance in the central plaza, where (it seemed to me) the entire island could watch. I was a rather shy person and rarely attended parties, preferring quiet dinners and small groups. To my horror, exacerbated by little food and exhaustion, I realized that one of my worst nightmares — dancing while everyone watched — was about to unfold in real life.

At the time, I thought that if I refused the invitation I would never be allowed to carry out research in the community. Facing my personal moment of truth, however silly it seems now, I had to toss away my shyness and get out and dance. Would "everyone" laugh at me? Possibly. I lived through that festival, though a faded photograph shows me clutching my heavy black-wool head shawl that threatened to fall at every whirling turn, looking faint while struggling to dance through the twenty-minute-long *waynos* (Andean songs) at 13,000 feet. I later came to enjoy the festival breaks in the monotony of yearlong arduous agricultural work, though perhaps with less enthusiasm than Taquileans.

TAQUILE AND ITS HISTORY

Taquile lies between Peru and Bolivia in a high flat plateau called the *altiplano* (map, p. 7; see also Matos Mar 1986: 18). Taquile and Amantani (the larger island to its north) are in the Bay of Puno just past the Capachica and Chucuito peninsulas.

Only 5.7 kilometers in length by 2.2 kilometers in width, or 3.5 × 1.4 miles (ibid.: 22), Taquile consists of numerous heavily terraced rolling hills (fig. 7). The island's population appears to have been stable, at 215 people until about 1940, and then increased rapidly in the next sixty years. Of its 754 hectares (1,862 acres), only 490 (1,210 acres) are cultivable (ibid.).

7. Taquile Island, with stone and adobe houses, stone paths, and terraced fields. 1981.

Although many Taquileans marry young (age fifteen or sixteen for women, eighteen or nineteen for men), family size in the 1970s and early 1980s typically was small, averaging two to three children.[3] Better nutrition and general health, plus return migration to Taquile, is likely to lead to further population growth. This will exacerbate the strain on already small landholdings and the double ecological challenge of sustainability on an island, in a mountainous region.

The community of Taquile is nearly 100 percent endogamous, that is, people marry among themselves, although there are isolated instances of Taquileans marrying *runa* from Capachica Peninsula to the north or Aymara speakers on the southern shore of Lake Titicaca. I know of one marriage of an island-dwelling Taquilean with a Puno *mestizo* but none with tourists, despite the numerous joking stories that would lead one to expect the latter nearly any day (see Meisch 1995) on intermarriage between Otavalo *runa* in Ecuador and foreigners.

In addition to speaking the southern dialect of Quechua, many Taquilean men now also speak some Spanish, and some speak it fluently; an increasing number can read and write it. Literacy is increasing, and Taquile finally has its own high school. It is still the case that few women speak Spanish, and even fewer are literate; this is a common pattern in rural areas of low-income countries. A small number of Taquileans speak or understand Aymara, the other principal highland Andean language, which they use for business or learned as a child.

Before the Spanish invasion in the sixteenth century, Taquile was part of the great Inca empire, but before that it formed part of a pre-Inca Aymara polity ("nation" or federation[4]), and a language that predates Aymara, called Puquina, may have been spoken there. Taquile was part of either the Lupaca (Lupaqa) or the Colla (Qulla) Aymara "kingdoms" (*señorios*) in what is now Peru, and probably belonged to the Urcosuyo[5] (Urqusuyu) division of the *altiplano* (Bouysse-Cassagne 1987: 211, map 13; cf. Julien 1993).

Sometime around 1450, more than seventy-five years before the sixteenth-century Spanish invasion, the Cusco-based Inca took over the island and incorporated it into the southern Collasuyo (Qullasuyu) province of Inca Tawantinsuyu (Bouysse-Cassagne 1987). The province was named after the powerful and prestigious "kingdom" of the Qullas (Qullaw; Choque Canqui 1993: 16 ff.). It is likely that the Incas settled Quechua-speaking *mitmaq*[6] on the island and this led to Quechua becoming the dominant language.

Lake Titicaca and its larger islands, now part of Bolivian territory, were sacred to the Incas. It is possible that the smaller islands, such as Taquile, also fulfilled special functions, based on their location in the lake, which was considered a giant shrine, and on their favorable microclimates.

Taquile today is famed locally for the high quality of its potatoes and *ch'uñu* (freeze-dried potatoes), and it is locally thought, by some Taquileans and people in nearby Puno, that Taquile may have been an agricultural station where seed potatoes were grown for the Inca state. It also is possible that Taquileans performed services for the Incas that would have exempted them from military service, such as farming and attending a shrine and, possibly, weaving.

Taquile once may have had another name, as I note above, which would explain its absence from any early Spanish document. The following history of Taquile is from Matos Mar (1951a). In the late sixteenth century, Taquile, with Amantani, was auctioned off by Carlos V, king of Spain, to the Spaniard Pedro González de Taquila. After his death, Taquile most likely reverted to the possession of its indigenous inhabitants.

The island of Amantani, Taquile's neighbor, was depopulated in 1604 by order of a Dr. Recalde, Judge of Charcas, apparently because of the continued practice of idolatry (pre-Christian religion). It is likely that Taquile also was depopulated at that time and both islands were again declared royal property of the Spanish crown. José Huatta, an elderly and highly respected community leader I met in the 1970s, told me that Taquile was repopulated by families from various regions. The Machacas came from the Aymara area of Juli, and the Flores family from the floating Urus islands.

According to Matos Mar, Amantani was auctioned off again in 1644, to Don Pedro Pacheco de Chávez, and Taquile (written as Taquila) was sold as an annex of Amantani. Haciendas, or landed estates, were set up and ownership changed hands several times until the end of the eighteenth century, when the Cuentas family bought most of Taquile. Later other hacienda owners purchased parts of the island and also forced the Taquileans to work for them. Taquileans residing in Lima told Matos Mar (1986), in repeated and eloquent testimony, of the abuses they suffered in servitude as peons.

Undoubtedly due to its isolation, Taquile served as a site to house Peruvian political prisoners from the end of the nineteenth century to the early twentieth century, including the future president Luis Sánchez Cerro, who was befriended by Taquileans. Their island's most famous prisoner helped them stop some of the most onerous personal servitude to landlords, and assisted them in regaining title to their lands by lawsuit and purchase years ahead of their indigenous neighbors—an early example of Taquilean ability to use friendship and contacts with nonislanders to achieve their goals. The process of purchasing title to their lands, which began in the 1930s, was almost complete by 1960, when outsiders owned only 6 percent of the island's cultivated lands (ibid.). The islanders' ability to mobilize to take advantage of opportunities was repeated in the 1940s, when they were among the first communities to construct wooden sailboats, and again in the late 1970s in responding to Peru's tourist "boom" (Healy and Zorn 1982–1983; Zorn 1983).

By the 1950s, as Matos Mar shows, the majority of the island's cultivated land was held by two or three Taquilean families. This land concentration occurred because one person, Prudencio Huatta, initiated and largely carried through the lengthy and dangerous land-titling process. Matos Mar's (1986) extended interviews of Taquilean families living in Lima contains many accounts of the abuses and jailings suffered by Huatta and others. He writes that in addition to Prudencio Huatta, five other Taquileans obtained title to Taquilean land bought from the Zuñiga family — Juan de Dios Cruz, Bernabé Flores, José Marca, Justo Machaca, and Vicente Huilli (ibid.: 128) — but Pancho Huatta told me that other families also contributed funds initially. Poorer Taquileans called those families *gamonales* (exploitative landowners), and community pressure eventually forced them to sell land to poorer relatives. Since 1960, land transfers have been made of ever-tinier parcels as titles change hands among islanders through inheritance or sale. Taquile's *minifundización*, or the parcelization of land into ever-smaller plots that diminish with each generation, so common throughout Latin America, is particularly acute because the community is an island. Some land disputes between islanders have dragged on for decades.

The island still lacks irrigation, running water, and sewerage, though a growing number of islanders obtain electricity through solar power (see Horn n.d.). With a few exceptions, Taquileans remain poor peasants, who still suffer high infant mortality rates and low life expectancies. These conditions have been exacerbated by Peru's ongoing political and economic crises, but at the same time Taquileans overall are faring better than their rural neighbors.

SOCIAL ORGANIZATION

All Taquileans are related to one another, and almost without exception all share from nine surnames: Cruz, Flores, Huatta, Huilli (Willi), Machaca, Mamani, Marca, Quispe, and Yucra. The island is divided into two "halves" or moieties, called *ladus* (from the Spanish *lado*, or "side"), which are called *Janaq* (upper) and *Uray* (lower). The Inca moieties, based on Cusco, also were designated "upper" (*hanan*) and "lower" (*hurin*). These halves are described in geographic and spatial terms; they organize members of Taquile into two groups. The two moieties have parallel authorities, and "compete" when sponsoring festivals, as occurs in many other Andean communities. Dual moiety divisions exist worldwide; in this region, they predated the Inca Empire. There are no large ayllus in Peru today comparable to those still in existence in highland Bolivia (Zorn 1997a). *Runa* generally identify themselves locally by community, no matter what its size.

Only *runa* own land on Taquile. Taquileans have steadfastly resisted all efforts by outsiders to gain title. Land is owned privately by individuals, with the exception of the island's central village square and its three ports — Alisuno, Collino (Kollino), and Chilcano — which are public. Taquileans who have considered selling land to outsiders were pressured by the community to not do so. They were told that if they were to sell land to an outsider, the community would revoke their membership in the community, thus invalidating the sale.

Taquile is divided for purposes of crop rotation and administration into six *suyus* (or divisions), named (from north to south) Chilcano (or Lakayano) Suyo, Estancia (Pampa) Suyo, Chuño Pampa Suyo, Collino (Kollino) Suyo or Tahuichuño Suyo (Matos Mar 1986: 22), Huaillano (Huayllano) Suyo, and Cullata (Kollata) Suyo. Juan Quispe Huatta points to the *suyus* on a map in Taquile's travel agency located in Puno (fig. 8). Some Taquileans call their *suyus "barrios"* (from the Spanish for neighborhoods).

Ideally, families own land in each of the six *suyus*. Three *suyus* are cultivated each year, while three lie fallow and are used as communal pasture. Each household also plants crops in the tiny fields surrounding the family's house compound (*canchón*). Taquileans use those fields to plant primary crops (potatoes) or crops that need ongoing care, or to experiment with raising supplemental plants, such as salad vegetables. The six-triangle image that repeatedly appears in all Taquilean weavings represents a "map" of this community division of land, and thus of Taquile itself (fig. 9).

POLITICAL DIVISIONS

Together, the islands of Taquile and Amantani make up the political district of Amantani, in the province of Puno, region of Puno. (Peru's former departments are now called regions.) Taquileans depend on Amantani authorities for state functions, including the registration of births, deaths, and marriages. Taquileans, like many peasant communities, continue to lobby for separate district status.

Similar to other highland Peruvian peasant communities, gover-

8. *Juan Quispe Huatta points out a map of Taquile in the community's Puno travel agency. The map shows the island's six-sector division and ports. The lower left map shows Taquile and Amantani islands in the Puno bay. July 2002.*

nance on Taquile is a mix of both traditional and Peruvian national authorities. "Traditional" authorities (*mandones* — those who give orders) were becoming less important in the 1970s, but even in 2002 they continued to fulfill key functions and therefore their offices continue. Service in these offices is part of a potentially lifelong career ladder (South America's *fiesta-cargo* system), in which people advance by serving in office and sponsoring community festivals. In Taquile, all authorities have been male, though islanders are well aware that the "real" authorities are a married couple, since it is virtually impossible to fulfill the obligations of office without the agreement, support, and assistance of the official's wife.[7] To date, no Taquilean authorities have been affiliated with any political party.

Community members who have spent decades in service, fulfilling all public offices and sponsoring all festivals (including the most elaborate and costly), are called *pasadu runa* (passed, or completed people); men who hold the highest offices are called *hombres cesantes*.[8] Taquileans who have completed all of the community festival/

9. *Section of a Taquilean calendar belt, woven by Teodosia Marca Willi, ca. 1983.*
The image of a hexagon divided into six sections is six suyus *(six divisions)/rosas*
(roses), representing Taquile. Handspun alpaca fleece and sheep wool. Collection of
the Brooklyn Museum (2002.62.15). July 2002.

religious *cargos* (obligations) are expected to offer advice to authorities and the community as a whole at the island's weekly assemblies, and they often hold office on Taquile's numerous committees that organize and manage tourism-related enterprises.

SOCIAL DIVISIONS IN TAQUILE

Traditionally, Andean wealth meant access to land and to labor and the accumulation of personal property, particularly textiles. During the second half of the twentieth century, wealth increasingly came to mean knowledge of Hispanic society, including such skills as the ability to speak Spanish and deal with *mestizos*. In the early 1950s, the Peruvian anthropologists Avalos de Matos (1951a, 1951b) and Matos Mar (1951a, 1951b) defined three strata of Taquilean society — wealthy, "just-enough," and poor — based on access to land.

Similarly, Matos documented the rise of a "new" elite, consisting of young men who spoke some Spanish and were thus able to serve as brokers with nonislanders, increasing their prestige. In the late 1970s and early 1980s (Zorn 1983), I observed increased growth of this male Taquilean elite, again based on their knowledge of Spanish and contacts with *mestizos* and, increasingly, foreigners, including anthropologists.[9]

In Taquile the *qapaq* (powerful and wealthy) *runa* is someone who has numerous plots of land in many parts of the island, can host expensive festivals (including hiring musicians and feeding hundreds of people over several days), takes on the full gamut of expensive community responsibilities (*cargos*), and dresses well, wearing new, fashionable, and expensive clothing. The *qapaq runa* stand counterpoised to the *pobres* (poor), or *waqcha* (literally, orphans), who can do none of this and barely have enough clothing and food for subsistence.

TRADITIONS OF COMMUNAL WORK

While people all over the world exchange labor, most contemporary Andean practices took shape during pre-Conquest times (Candler 1993). Various types of exchanges exist throughout the Andes, and the terminology for identifying them differs somewhat. What is universal in the Andes is that reciprocal labor exchanges are fundamental to the organization of society and serve to link together individuals and households, as well as the two *ladus* (moieties) at festivals. The *ayllu* itself can, in a sense, be seen as functioning through reciprocal exchanges of labor. Reciprocal labor exchanges are fundamental to Taquilean society, although it appears that as individuals become wealthier, the importance of nonreciprocal labor exchanges will increase.

On Taquile, the most fundamental form of exchange is *ayni*, which probably is the most well-known form of exchange throughout the Andes. Ideally, it is an equivalent trade of labor (like for like: setting up a loom for setting up a loom, roofing a house for roofing a house, and so forth). *Mink'a* usually is an exchange of labor for a product, either food or cash. *Mink'a* is especially common during harvest, when the person or family needing assistance will offer a cooked meal, beverage, and coca leaf; a share of what has been harvested; and sometimes some cash in return for labor. Wealthier peasants prefer *mink'a*, since they do not have to return the labor. *Mañarikuy* is a system of borrowing that should be reciprocated in kind (Prochaska 1983: 49–50); this could extend to unspun fleece or seed, but also money. Modes of labor that are not directly reciprocal include *ayuda*, which is the giving of a small gift, and *yanaparikuy*. The latter is a request for labor between nuclear families that cannot (ideally) be refused, and usually does not have to be strictly accounted for (unlike *ayni* and *mink'a*).

Partners in boat groups (called *socios*) share construction and maintenance costs and rotate boat operation duties (though periodically the three-person crew receives a small stipend). This pre-Conquest labor rotation system is called *mit'a*, which means "labor rotation" or "forced labor turn" (see n. 6). Spaniards during the colonial period exploited that system as the basis of forced labor services by Indians, the most onerous of which was in the mines, but which also included textile sweatshops. Taquileans also handle ongoing community needs through public work parties (*faenas*). At these "parties," each family is expected to send at least one adult member. Both men and women participate, though their tasks differ (fig. 10). Men quarry and build with stone, and make adobe bricks; women haul water and, if required, braid ropes. Community authorities supervise the labor, and provide coca leaf and beverages.

WOMEN, MEN, AND GENDER IN TAQUILE

Taquilean images of the ideal woman (held by both women and men) show her as abundantly productive, fertile, and fecund (fig. 11). She is elegantly dressed in full skirts, carrying a purse or carrying cloth that holds food, coca leaf, or money, with a baby wrapped snugly in her heavy mantle on her back; she endlessly spins, or serves food from abundant storehouses that never run out.[10]

Women's productive and managerial abilities (especially in regard to each family's herds and storehouse) are highly respected and recognized by both sexes as essential to Taquilean society. Marriage is a goal of virtually all men and women, since an unmarried person is considered a minor, can assume no public office, and receives virtually no respect in the community. Both men and women usually want many children; although this seems to be changing, fertility (of humans, of herds, of crops) remains highly prized.[11] Households without children are considered sad, empty, and silent: *llaki, ch'usaq, ch'in,*

10. *Antonio Quispe (left) and Victorio Marca make adobe bricks as part of a community-wide* faena *(work party) in Taquile's central plaza. Women (background) have brought water for brick-making. 1981.*

silencio. Blame for a childless family goes to the woman: men are not considered the culprits.

Despite the high value put on women's abilities, domestic violence in the Andes appears common, with women far more likely to be beaten then men. (Despite physical damage, Andean women are far less likely to be cowed by domestic violence, and being beaten is not cause for shame, as it is in Western societies.) In Taquile, a young man who comes from a family where the father is known to severely and regularly beat his wife generally is considered an undesirable potential son-in-law. On the other hand, Andean love-play can be rough, on the part of both sexes, as expressed in the proverb, *maqanakuy, munanakuy* (hit one another, love one another) (Isbell 1976; Platt 1986).

Taquilean women exercise no formal, public power, with a few exceptions (offices in "female" organizations such as the Club de Madres, or Mother's Club). Instead, women assert their power through the home, or work through men, as Allen well illustrates (2002); few men make decisions in assemblies without at least discussing the issues first with their wives. At the same time, in the An-

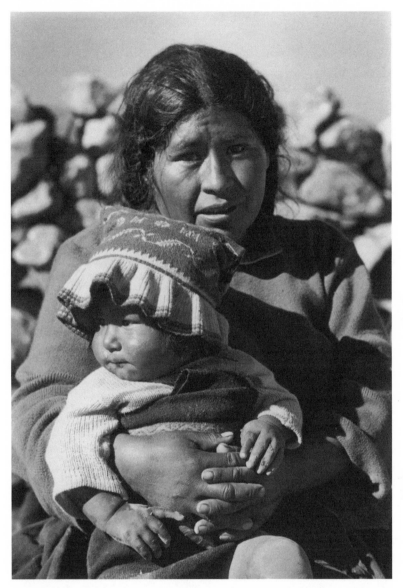

*11. Natividad Machaca holds her youngest son, Elias Huatta, before the Rutuchiy
ceremony when I cut his hair for the first time, becoming his godmother and her
comadre. 1976.*

dean social hierarchy of food, women are served after men, and generally receive smaller portions (elder males are served first). Although Peruvian law mandates that women inherit equally with men, some Taquilean women told me that they inherit less land than do male siblings, though by the late 1980s this had begun changing in women's favor.

A sexual division of labor prevails for agricultural tasks, as for others; with extremely rare exceptions, men plow the earth and women store, select, prepare, and plant seed.[12] Both men and women harvest crops. The general pattern in Taquile is for the entire household to store together the harvest from its fields. Produce is stored in the household's dispensary (*dispensa*), which is one of several buildings around the household's courtyard, next to the kitchen/sleeping house. The *dispensa* is a key space in the home, one that, like the oven/hearth in the kitchen/sleeping room, is considered a female domain.

Herding of camelids and sheep is the second-most important subsistence activity after agriculture (and primary for Andeans who live in the high *puna*), and it is in this sphere that women may have an equal or greater share of inherited wealth than men, although in Taquile herds are less important than in other areas. Generally, herds are considered to "belong" to women, who (with small children) care for the animals daily; this especially is true for camelid herding in *puna* communities. Men, far more often than women, make the long trading trips (from a few days to many weeks) between highlands (*puna*) and valleys.

Economic differences that exist within Taquile divide women, since there are both wealthy and poor peasants. While *runa* in Taquile are no exception to the general rule that access to land, and family (or other) networks to work it, form the basis of wealth, in both respects knowledge of modern society outside the community is increasingly important. This is especially significant for women's changing status, as they are far less likely than men to interact with and therefore learn about modern, national society.

The issue of women's status in the Andes is a contested one. Anthropological studies of Andean women (and men) in the 1970s and 1980s emphasized a conceptual and real "complementarity" of gender roles between human males and females, as well as between gendered supernatural beings (Isbell 1976; Harris 1978).

Women perceive themselves as a group opposed to the group of men, but also as forming half of the married *qhariwarmi* (man-woman) pair. The division into male/female is aligned with other divisions, including right/left, upper/lower, and so on. This model of Andean gender complementarity, which produce a "natural," married whole is linked, as Isbell points out (n.d.), to a conceptual model of dual organization. In Andean sociopolitical organization, dual organization clearly had a hierarchical sense, such that the two "halves" of an *ayllu* or a polity were regarded as representing units ranked as superior and inferior.

Scholars, feminists, and activists have sought to understand when the relationship between women and men is egalitarian, though they each hold power in different spheres, and when the ideology of complementarity masks hierarchy and male dominance, including male violence (Arnold 1997).

In popular and academic discourses, as well as in much development literature, Latin American women are portrayed as passive, backward, socially conservative, and victims — "'beasts of burden,' mothers and wives, staunch traditionalists, or heroic guerrilla fighters" (Escobar 1995: 177). This applies especially to indigenous women, who usually are nonliterate, don't vote, don't speak Spanish, and wear "traditional dress." Indian women face the heaviest burden of discrimination in their societies. The challenge, as Escobar points out (ibid.), is how to maintain awareness of and, indeed, expose the suffering of impoverished women, while also recognizing or foregrounding their creative work and social contributions.

SUBSISTENCE AGRICULTURE

Taquileans cultivate potatoes, other Andean tubers (principally *oca*), barley, broad beans, and some corn in unirrigated fields where frost can occur three hundred days a year. In the southern Andes, the year is divided into a rainy season and a dry season. Ideally, rains begin in September, lasting through January or February; planting begins in November; and harvest is done in May and June. During the end of June and most of July, Taquileans process their crops for long-term storage, including processing potatoes into *ch'uñu*. These freeze-dried potatoes, which were essential to the success of Inca Tawantinsuyu, remain the primary food of last resort in the Andes and, in certain circumstances, an essential sign distinguishing *runa* from *mestizos*.[13] Some families fish, but more obtain this protein source through barter or purchase it from peasants in neighboring communities. Barter of foodstuffs was, and remains, an important way to obtain products from off the island.

Many Taquilean families raise a few scrawny sheep and a few have some cattle; animal manure is the field's principal fertilizer. Taquileans are enormous consumers of wool, and their sheep provide some of the fiber needed for basic garments, but they must barter or buy alpaca fleece, as pasturage is extremely limited on their tiny island. They have periodically tried to herd camelids on Taquile, to no avail (Zorn 1983).

Taquileans also barter local production for coca leaf, and wood for house posts and large loom parts (ibid.: 31). They trade at the regional market at Socca, the Sunday weekly market at Ilave (fig. 12), and in the city of Puno (on the dock, at markets, and in individual homes).

In the 1960s, Peru's camelid wool production began to decline, and it had almost completely collapsed by the early 1980s (Zorn 1997a, 1997b, 1999) due to erosion, urbanization, droughts and floods, continued low prices for camelid fiber, and the civil war. Herders either stopped maintaining flocks completely or increasingly preferred to sell their animals' wool for money rather than bartering. Herders also are increasingly breeding white animals for the export market, reducing the amount of wool in other natural colors available to local weavers. This development forced people like Taquileans into the cash economy in order to get wool.

THE CASH ECONOMY

Access to cash was extremely limited until quite recently: older Taquileans recall not even "knowing twenty cents" (Matos Mar 1986). Prior to the commercialization of Taquile textiles, Taquilean men occasionally earned money working in the city of Puno as *picapiedras* (stone masons), cutting and shaping stones for house foundations and patios, work that their neighbors to the north in Amantani

12. *Market in Ilave, Peru, on the southern shore of Lake Titicaca, where local people speak Aymara (not Quechua). The man receiving payment (center, foreground) sells sheep, llama, and alpaca hides with attached fleece. 1978.*

are famous for. In Taquile, the specialization of *pica-piedras* is associated only with the poor, a point my *compadre* Pancho made about his father. Taquileans, up until the 1940s or 1950s, cut and sold their island's wood (primarily as firewood), leading to deforestation. However, permanent migration off island has been minimal. By 1982, only nine Taquilean families lived in Lima (ibid.: 13–14).

Population pressure led to erosion and degradation of land quality, which until the 1970s increased the numbers of Taquileans seeking work off-island as seasonal laborers. They worked in commercialized coastal agricultural plantations, commercial chicken farming, and, to a much lesser degree, in the mines that ring Puno. Young men sometimes still migrate as seasonal agricultural laborers to the warm valleys of Arequipa and Tacna. In the 1980s, several Taquilean families moved to the jungle "colonization zones." By the mid-1990s, all except one had returned to Taquile.

The only mode of transportation on Taquile, for people or burdens, is by foot over often-narrow and steep paths. According to Taquileans Alejandro Flores and Paula Quispe, "Outsiders do not come into the community to live, because we have no donkeys, trucks, or

13. *The Taquile motorboat* San Miguel, *captained by Casimiro Marca Flores, departs Puno in the early morning, carrying islanders and tourists east to Taquile.* *1989.*

horses. It is hard to move around Taquile's terrain and altitudes. We do everything ourselves—we carry our own burdens up the hills. That is difficult for others, but we are used to it and for us it is very easy" (Flores and Quispe 1994: 167–68).

Travel between Taquile and the mainland before the 1940s was by reed boat (*walsa*, from the Spanish *balsa*). According to elderly Taquileans, they used to spend up to two days traveling to Puno and up to a week each way voyaging across the lake to the Bolivian side to obtain coca leaf. Even after Taquileans built wooden sailboats starting in 1946, until the late 1980s many continued to fish close to the island using reed boats. Sailboats also were used for fishing, not just travel, as Orlove (2002) shows in his study of fisherfolk around the lake. Taquileans still fish using the cheaper sailboats. In 1978, following the rise of tourism, they bought motors and, using only hand tools, built larger and sturdier boats (fig. 13).

HEALTH

The harshness of *altiplano* life extends to Taquilean health and life expectancy, which as in all highland Peru is lower than the national average. While a few Taquileans remain vigorous to a very old age, most live only into their fifties. Death during childbirth remains a constant menace for women. The great majority of Taquileans rely on Andean native medicine, with its specializations that include herbal medicine, bone setting and massage, and spiritual/psychological treatments, and distinctive medical traditions have great meaning for Andean ethnic groups. Since the 1980s, Taquile has had a sanitary post, staffed by a Peruvian nurse or health aide paid by the government, though service is intermittent and most Taquileans still prefer native medicine. A few foreign nurses and doctors, enchanted with the island, have lived there for relatively long periods (up to a year), offering medical services as part of reciprocal hospitality. Taquileans' recent income from selling textiles and from tourism appears to be helping improve their health compared to their neighbors, however, and certainly increased height and weight of Taquileans, observable since the 1990s, suggests improved diet, or at least increased calorie consumption.

EDUCATION

As in many parts of the world where people continue to live apparently "traditional" lives, often in remote, rural locations, little of the knowledge needed to become an adult and make a living on Taquile is learned through formal education. The skills — conceptual, technical, and religious — needed to successfully farm in the immensely challenging environment of the Andean *altiplano*, and to create textile masterpieces, constitute key areas of knowledge transmitted through the domestic sphere, in the Quechua language, based on thousands of years of cultural development and social memory.

Despite this, the Taquilean community has fought long and hard throughout the twentieth century to obtain schools in their community, despite understandable ambivalence about the value of formal schooling and a history of often-bitter encounters with the school as an institution of the state that, among other values, reinforces racist discrimination against *runa*. Until the 1990s, Taquile's few literate people had difficulty reading complex texts. In the late 1980s, only a few young women had attended the island's elementary school, but this number has steadily increased.

A few Taquileans tried attending high school in the city of Puno in the late 1970s but didn't last more than a year or two, primarily due to racism and homesickness. Finally, in 1988, probably because of national and international interest in their island, Taquileans were able to obtain regional support they needed to construct a high school. Now a director and several teachers live there from mid-day Monday to mid-day Friday. However, some families are sending their children to high school in Puno, where they believe the education is superior to that on Taquile. By 2002, a few Taquilean families had sent their children to live with relatives in Lima to attend school there.

HOUSING

Housing, like that of most Andean peasants, is homemade; Taquileans' rectangular homes have traditionally been built of stone and adobe bricks with thatch roofs that have to be replaced approximately every five years. Doors are made of wood, as are locks. Houses generally do not have windows. Inside walls contained interior niches, which is a feature common to pre-Conquest Andean residential structures. These were the type of homes that one could expect to find in any peasant community throughout the Andean highlands, with few exceptions.

For good and bad, few Taquilean houses are now adobe brick and stone with tightly packed, quiet, thatch roofs; many or most houses have *material noble* (literally, "noble" material, or cement) facades, are two or three stories, and have corrugated iron roofs (*calamina*), smooth painted wooden doors, and windows. Though scattered among the fields, Taquilean houses look like what one would find in a prosperous neighborhood in any *altiplano* city, but not in a "quaint" peasant village. This change has not been well received by tourism professionals who fear that Taquile is "losing its look."

The island has had a reservoir for water since the early 1980s, which brings water from a faucet to the central plaza (*pueblo*) of the island. There are still no water taps either within or near individual homes.

RELATIONS WITH NON-TAQUILEANS

During the second part of the twentieth century, Taquileans' closest relations off the island were with *runa* from nearby Capachica Peninsula, who sometimes visit them for festivals (fig. 14). Taquileans allow people from Capachica to come to Taquile to fish for, and then

14. Taquileans, author (center, dressed as a Taquilean), and Capachica runa *(seated right) during a festival. 1976. Photographer unknown.*

dry, *ispi*, a variety of small carp. Many are linked by relations of *compadrazgo* (ritual or fictive kinship).

Relations with neighboring Amantani Island generally have been frosty since Taquile's tourist "boom," which meant the island was no longer secondary (in size, political status, general status) to Amantani, which has been generally unsuccessful in competing with Taquileans for tourists. Tourism has increased commercial relations between the islands as some Amantani textiles are now sold in the Taquile cooperative store. Relations with Aymara-speaking *runa* on the southern shore of Lake Titicaca have always been primarily commercial, and most recently some Taquileans work there as boat builders.

Relations with people from the floating Urus islands are longstanding, because the shortest route between Puno and Taquile is through the Urus and because many Taquileans buy or trade for fish there. At the turn of the twenty-first century, despite some disputes over tourists, Taquileans were working to build alliances with their island neighbors based on common concerns, including environmental threats to the lake and the perceived lack of *runa* input into the policies governing it.

Taquileans often categorize their relationships with outsiders in terms of perceived ethnicity (*runa* or *mestizo*). Their closest collaborative relationships are with other *runa*, but Taquileans have ongoing economic relationships with *conocidos* (people known to them) of varying ethnic/racial statuses. Taquileans now build boats for people in other lake communities and the city of Puno. Itinerant vendors still come to the island to barter wool and manufactured goods. Taquileans, like other Andeans, have long had to deal with people in positions of power, typically defined as *blancos* (whites) or *mestizos*.

Since Taquileans have recently had problems with tour agencies based in Puno, over the years I repeatedly heard that they were competing with the "*mestizos*" in Puno, which is a statement that expresses frustration in racialized terms, from the Taquileans' subaltern position.[14] Past relations were hierarchical and, at the best, unpleasant. Taquileans, who once slunk into Puno disguised in ill-fitting cosmopolitan dress in the hope of getting in and out of town relatively unnoticed, since the advent of tourism go to Puno to consult with ministry officials, Catholic priests and nuns, lawyers, teachers, and the like.

Due to this legacy of racism and discrimination, many Taquileans told me that relations with foreigners were sometimes perplexing but generally a pleasant relief from problems with many or most mainland *mestizos* and *blancos*. The early *gringo* visitors went to Taquile because of an interest in cultural practices and typically developed friendly, long-lasting relationship with islanders. Stereotypes abounded on both sides, but generally Taquileans enjoyed the positive contacts. Among these early foreign visitors were John Cohen (1957), who documented Taquilean textiles in the 1950s, and Kevin Healy, who as a Peace Corps volunteer in the 1960s first suggested that Taquileans sell their beautiful textiles. But generally, Taquileans had limited relationships with non-*runa*.

Even into the 1980s, Taquileans' primary, ongoing relation with outsiders was with Padre Pepe Loits, the Catholic priest based in Capachica Peninsula, to the north of Taquile, who traveled to Taquile once or twice a year, primarily to celebrate marriages. In the 1980s, an Evangelical church began on Taquile, mirroring the process occurring in many others areas of Latin America (cf. Stoll 1990). Conflict between Catholic and Protestant Taquileans has never been great, though at moments there has been tension. At one point Protestant Taquileans formed their own motorboat group, and they have built a private school on the island, whose subscription costs U.S.$5/month: a significant sum for a Peruvian peasant. Catholic children also attend the school. The goal, according to the families involved, was not so much religious instruction per se, but rather the creation of a private school whose teachers would be accountable to Taquileans, who paid their salaries and thus could expect a longer instructional week.

Since the development of tourism, Taquileans have worked with many national and international government and nongovernmental organizations. Taquile was the pilot project for solar energy in the lake region, through agreements with Peru's National Engineering University (CER-UNI) and Ministry of Energy and Mines (PAE-MEN). The Taquileans received development assistance from the U.S. governmental agency the Inter-American Foundation (IAF) and other organizations, and partnered with private youth organizations on exchange programs, which have allowed Taquilean youth to travel to Denmark and Bolivia. Students from various foreign universities visit Taquile as part of study groups, such as the La Paz–based "Duke in the Andes." Taquileans also have made hundreds of transnational relationships, which led to opportunities to travel abroad.

Taquileans have stayed out of politics and have not allied in any numbers with Peru's few indianist organizations, such as CISA (Consejo Indio de Sud América), although they did allow CISA to hold a Statutory Convention on the island (CISA 1998a, 1998b, 1998c). The percentage of Taquileans voting in elections tends to be extremely low, even compared to nearby indigenous communities, though this may change with the current generation. Young Taquilean men who voted in the 1980s (I don't know of any young women who did) told me that they voted for the Peruvian leftist coalition, Izquierda Unida (United Left), though others voted for the social democratic party APRA, which made more promises to provide infrastructure to the island. In the 1990s elections, the number of Taquileans who voted continued to increase, with votes, I was told, being split between Fujimori's Cambio 90 party and several center and left-of-center parties. By 2000, some Taquileans had become more sophisticated about politics, trying to hold out for more than the usual "soccer balls and T-shirts" that rural communities were promised, though again, very few women voted, and turnout was still low.

By 2002, after former president Fujimori's helicopter visit to the island (fig. 6), Taquileans told me that they enjoyed the publicity and bargaining for "gifts" (sewing machines, building materials for Taquile's still-unfinished community inn), but that didn't make them feel obligated to vote for Fujimori.

CONCLUSION

While Taquile's isolation made it a special "unspoiled" place to study Andean culture, this combined with its spectacular physical location in Lake Titicaca has meant that it has been transformed by tourism. Before tourism, Taquile was largely self-sufficient, if poor, living off what its land produced and what islanders could trade with their neighbors. A key component of this self-sufficiency was Taquileans' ability to create superb textiles. These textiles became central to the development of tourism on the island and, as the next chapter shows, play an important role in all aspects of Taquilean society.

3 THE CLOTH OF CONTEMPORARY INCAS

*This is what hurts Indians most. . . . They think our costumes
are beautiful because it brings in money, but it's as if the person
wearing it doesn't exist.*

—Rigoberta Menchú Tum (1991: 209)

THE CLOTH OF TAQUILE: FIVE INTERWOVEN SCENES

Browsers in Puno markets on a brisk winter day find a few Taquilean belts and caps fluttering from the top of kiosks or hidden among
mounds of dolls, sweaters, gloves, and scarves handmade elsewhere.
The Taquilean textiles, typically woven and knit by teenagers, are
generally higher in quality than the others on display, but still inferior
to those Taquileans themselves wear.

Visitors on the Puno dock awaiting Taquile-bound boats encounter Taquilean cloth on the bodies of Taquilean people. The fine
clothing—in dramatic red, black, and white—crosses boundaries of
ethnicity and authenticity. Once an icon of despised indianness, it
now serves as a source of pride that advertises the island, and its
people, to tourists. The islanders find themselves (or their dress) the
object of desire.

Audiences at major Puno folklore events distinguish Taquileans by
their clothing, which tells *runa* and *mestizos* the performers' community of origin. Such folkloric competitions are staged on November 4,
the anniversary of the colonial founding of Puno, and February 2,
Festival of the Virgin of Candlemas (Candelaria), patron of that city.

Customers shopping on Taquile at its community cooperative
store admire dazzling, patterned vests. Elsewhere in Peru and Bolivia, old cut-up textiles often appear on garments or handbags; on
Taquile, however, this is extremely rare. Instead, Taquileans have designed new knitted vests expressly for sale. Customers favor the "musician's vest," with its brightly colored, densely figured front panels,
over the plain navy blue vests Taquilean usually wear.

Taquileans in New York City to perform at the American Museum of Natural History endured a long, unforgiving hot June day, arriving late at night at our hotel. Their elegant wool clothing, designed for a cooler climate, attracts attention. A man rushes out from the hotel restaurant, enthusiastically greeting them in Spanish, telling them that he, too, is Peruvian, that he identified them as compatriots by their clothing but, he confides, in Peru he never wore handmade ethnic dress.

As these vignettes show, Taquileans display and produce cloth in diverse contexts. From their island homes to New York City, it shapes their approach to life and pervades many levels of being. Because cloth is so central to Taquilean society, this chapter provides information that I believe is necessary for understanding Taquile.

Cloth is a paramount sign in the representation and construction of identity in manifold forms: individual and social, racial, ethnic, class, and gendered. In this communicative system, the meanings and values of textiles evoke, express, and constitute a coherent whole for their wearers. Not only is cloth an art, but also this most important expressive visual medium is linked to poetry and song. It constitutes wealth, whether displayed in public, stored in their homes, or inherited. Religion, as well, permeates the process of creation of cloth. In multiple spheres of Andean belief and experience, its political significance is connected to community authorities, who are invested with special textiles and who signal their position through special dress.

In Taquile, cloth plays multiple roles today in terms of functions, production, gender, and identity. Taquile is one of a few areas in Peru where people still make and wear Andean textiles on a daily basis. What they make and how they do so is in flux, continuing a process of change that began with the arrival of the Spaniards. I argue that producing and wearing cloth remains a major creative focus for Taquileans and many other Andeans, as they invest substantial resources of time, materials, money, and labor and simultaneously make statements about themselves. I further argue that style, fashion, and distinctions in dress remain important in marking and symbolizing identity on multiple levels: international, national, regional, ethnic, community, racial, class, gender, individual, and, finally, human/nonhuman.

This chapter explores cloth in the context of twentieth-century social and economic changes in Andean societies and explains why Taquilean cloth persists, although at the turn of the twenty-first century
few *runa* elsewhere still make it. The changes encompass both weaving and dress. In the 1970s, most *runa* in Ecuador, Peru, and Bolivia
wove and spun or knitted, or both, and many wore handmade dress.
By the 1980s, far fewer *runa* did so, and today the daily practices continue in very few Andean communities. In this chapter and the one
that follows, I explain not only what traditional Taquilean textiles are
and how they relate to other Andean textiles, but what has happened
to the practice of cloth-making in the past three decades, and why.

INTERPRETING ANDEAN CLOTH

The importance of cloth in Taquile derives in part from the now
well-documented importance of Andean textiles. In the Andes, one
of the world's greatest textile traditions has continued for five thousand years. Andean fiber arts "represent a philosophy built of visual
and tactile ideas rather than verbal ones, a philosophy that finds no
parallel in contemporary western society but powers the engine of
Andean creativity" (Franquemont 1986b: 86).

John Murra (1962, 1995) concluded that in the Inca Empire no important event took place without cloth playing a prominent role,
which in other societies was filled by objects made in other media.
His assessment of the multiple functions of cloth in the Inca Empire,
notably its political function, emphasizes its great value in Andean
society, surpassing even the colonial Spaniards' interest in cloth.

While much of what contemporary Andeans do and think about
cloth echoes the Incas, by no means are contemporary Andeans
"frozen" in time. They do not live just like their ancestors. Differentiation relating to cloth in the Andes stems from the differences between rural social groups (*ayllus*), each having its own historical experiences of the Inca state, Spanish colonial empire, subsequent
republican administrations, and contemporary nation-states.

Although native Andeans were prohibited from wearing indigenous dress under Spanish colonial rule, this prohibition was not
entirely successful, as my examination of contemporary Andean
dress demonstrates. Variations of clothing from Spain — pants, vests,
jackets, shirts, and skirts — became part of "native" ethnic dress.

Through bloodshed and sometimes less violent means, including the manipulation of dress codes, native Andeans under colonialism became "Indians," and people of mixed-blood and social status became *mestizos*.

In today's Andes, making and thinking about cloth on a daily basis still provides an underlying structure for conceptualizing far more than clothes, including political organization and time. Andean clothing can consist of simply or complexly patterned garments, including the man's poncho, belt, and coca leaf purse and the woman's mantle or large carrying cloth, coca-carrying cloth or purse, and belt (fig. 38). Utility cloth (or household textiles) comprises storage bags of varying sizes, food carrying-cloths, ropes, and blankets. Some textiles have exclusively ritual uses, such as those in a herding family's ritual bundle (Zorn 1987b), or military uses, such as those used as armor or weapons when fighting ritual battles (Zorn 2002). In addition to clothing, Andean textiles are used as tools, altars, sacrifices, and symbols of authority.

For ancient Andeans, textiles were the single most important medium, encoding meaning and wealth in multiple ways that are difficult for non-Andeans to appreciate fully. Under the Incas, fine cloth, possibly tapestry (*qumpi*), was produced by and for the elite; local weaving (*awasqa*) was for the less privileged.[1] Following the Spanish invasion, *qumpi* declined but *awasqa* continued, becoming the direct precursor to contemporary Andean cloth production.

Cloth is, however, a supremely time-consuming medium in which to encode meaning, wealth, and cosmology. After agriculture, creating cloth takes up the major part of Andeans' time and labor (Zorn 1983). Both "traditional" handmade and urban Indian dress cost far more in time and resources (whether fibers or cash) than cosmopolitan, Western-style dress. A handwoven patterned belt, such as those worn by my *compadres* Natividad Machaca and Pancho Huatta in figure 3, takes a week to weave, and a patterned shawl requires two to four weeks of labor, ten hours a day, six days a week. An elaborately patterned poncho may require three to six months of concentrated daily work. The labor time for yarn preparation is easily double that for weaving.

Virtually all the Andean cloth makers I have known seem perpetually busy juggling multiple projects: one textile has just been finished, but others are in progress, and mental bookkeeping is ongoing; some are in the planning stages, and others must be rushed because of a deadline (typically, a festival). Fleece or yarn always is needed; money or items to trade must be found. Yarn must be spun, dyed, and plied, and looms must be set up. Textiles must be made for family members, and some time found to weave something for oneself. The organization of labor and resources that enable all these activities has changed significantly since the mid-twentieth century, as I demonstrate here and in chapter 4.

Though textile production is tiring and time-consuming and a task that some approach with little interest (Goodell 1968b), weaving is, on many levels, a holy act. Weavers may request supernatural as well as human assistance. The idea that a textile on the Andean loom is a living being, with zoomorphic features (hands, mouth, butt, teeth), is supported by linguistic evidence from many Andean areas (Cereceda 1978, 1986; Desrosiers 1982; Meisch 1987b; Zorn 1993). In Bolivia, weavers have expressed that "to cut a [four-selvedge] textile is to kill it" (Desrosiers 1982: 21). Thus, besides representing society, a textile is one of many beings in the Andean cosmogony, along with humans, animals, the earth mother, and the mountain spirits (Zorn 1987b).

William Conklin, among others, points out that multiple meanings are also "conveyed by the structure of the cloth and the process of weaving itself" (Conklin [1983] quoted in E. Franquemont 1986b: 83). My approach to meaning combines structuralist and post-structuralist perspectives, linking a theory of structure to a theory of agency and praxis. I believe, following Antonio Gramsci, that material-culture production can be a site of social power and identity. I am convinced that objects do more than merely "reflect" the society where they were produced. The design styles in objects can "comment on, transform or disrupt the styles in other aspects of life. Design styles do not 'reflect' behaviourally, but they are made to 'transform' structurally" (Hodder 1982a: 207).

My approach to Andean cloth supplants and to some extent rejects earlier studies of limited historical depth that frequently, and incorrectly, assumed timelessness. Code is used in semiotics (particularly by Umberto Eco) to analyze clothing styles and fashions, but Davis (1992: 5, 11) argues that the "clothing-fashion code [has] . . . low semanticity" and is much closer to an aesthetic code than a conventional sign code (e.g., writing, semaphore, or traffic signs). What clothing chiefly communicates, he maintains, has to do with the self and social identity. Western fashion is particularly concerned with ambivalences of social status, sexuality, and gender.[2] Studies in Guatemala make it clear that dress forms a semiotic system, which can be decoded to reveal information about the social status of the wearer, the social status of the individual within the community, coded according to origin, age, sex, economic level, and *cargo* (office) in the civil-religious hierarchy, and the event in which they are used (Mayén de Castellanos 1986: 101). By studying Scottish tartan, Martin argues, however, that "Barthes' metaphor of a sign system in textiles is inaccurate and insufficient" because textiles have a shifting interpretive potential; their uncertain or contradictory meanings, not easily "translated into words and made into equivalents," are ever-changing and evolving (1988: 51–52, 60). Trevor-Roper (1983) illustrates this by contextualizing tartans within the "invention of tradition" (see Hobsbawm 1983; Hobsbawm and Ranger 1983), that is, of objects such as textiles that are valued as "ancient" and "traditional," though recently created.

Taquilean women with whom I wove rarely talked explicitly about what the textile codes mean, though male textile sellers did. I found that experienced weavers often think about cloth in aesthetic, not verbal, ways, having internalized the codes such that language is not necessary to explain what is going on. In response to my questions, novice and experienced weavers provided terms for spaces in a textile, such as *ñan* (path) for the narrow stripes that flank the central design row in coca leaf purses and in belts, but experienced weavers didn't use these terms when talking to me or among themselves about weaving. My experiences paralleled those of Cereceda (1992) who worked with Tarabuco weavers in Chuquisaca, Bolivia. In contrast, however, members of the Macha ethnic group in Chayanta, Bolivia, were quite explicit about their textile codes (Cassandra Torrico, personal communication, 1989).

Ironically, while increased research over the past twenty-five years has greatly expanded outsiders' knowledge of twentieth-century Andean textiles, many Andean peoples no longer weave, and a massive traffic in antique textiles has removed an inestimable number of woven objects from the homes and communities of origin. In one famous case, ancestral textile bundles (*q'ipis*) were illegally removed from the community of Coroma, Bolivia. The people of Coroma prepared a rare written document supporting their claim to recover the bundle (Bubba et al. 1990). Losing the textiles, they wrote, would destroy the entire history of their community (not only of the textiles themselves) and cause the *ayllus* to disperse, rupture religious beliefs, and displease the ancestors, as well as destroy social organization. Such is the power of old textiles, the work — and the embodiment — of the ancestors.[3]

One central question remains: are Andean textiles a visual language? If so, do they have rules that can be decoded, a grammar and syntax? Verónica Cereceda's pioneering analysis of the structure of "ideal" cloth began with a deceptively simple textile: striped bags (*wayaqas*). Her analytic model (1978, 1986) builds on the work of the French semiotician Algirdas Julien Greimas (1987). Similarly, Cassandra Torrico demonstrates how the striped sacks of Macha herders are a spatial map of social relations of exchange throughout their territory (personal communication, 1994). Cereceda's subsequent work (1992; Cereceda, Dávalos, and Mejía 1993) employs historical perspectives on ethnicity and change, which she relates to divisions between fabrics used by both men and women, but woven by women in ethno-development projects (Dávalos, Cereceda, and Martínez 1992).

The question of whether cloth is more like language, or like writing (see Arnold 2000 for Bolivia) is important and awaits further study. Like Cereceda, I consider Andean textiles a form of visual language. My research has shown that experienced Andean weavers do not need written diagrams or instructions, though weavers sometimes use words to talk about textiles, particularly in the initial stages of teaching novices to weave. That is, this Andean textile language, at least in the *ayllus* where I have done research, does not depend on writing. In this sense, weaving is "like" writing because it is one step removed from oral language.

I think that comparisons between weaving and writing, as interesting as they might be, are accurate only in this sense, of being one step removed from speech, even though some scholars have been interested in proposing Andean cloth as a replacement graphic system for Andeans who "lack" writing. I think, however, it is more accurate to think of Andean cloth as a language, parallel to speech, probably functioning cognitively at a higher level than writing.

THE TECHNOLOGY OF CLOTH PRODUCTION

Agustín Machaca Huatta, a Taquilean man living in Lima, described how "each person in Taquile makes his or her clothing, according to personal taste": "We all use sheep wool, very little llama or alpaca, some buy that in Puno or get fleece as payment when they go to work on the Aymara side [of Lake Titicaca]. We buy aniline dyes in Puno. Clothing is made well and thick, so that it lasts and keeps us warm when it's very cold" (Matos Mar 1986: 59).

The great majority of Andean textiles are woven.[4] Knitting and crochet (techniques introduced by the Spanish) and braiding (a traditional Andean technique) are secondary to weaving in importance. Other traditional Andean techniques (twining and, for decoration, embroidery) are employed to make products such as hat frames, stiff belts, baskets, and reed boats. Production must often fit into time not spent on agriculture, though herding is compatible with some phases of textile production. People spin and ply on the drop spindle while walking to and from fields or watching animals.

Contemporary Andean weavers have long preferred camelid fiber from two domesticated species (llama and alpaca), from hybrid mixes, and from the wild vicuña, a threatened species whose fleece is currently unavailable to local weavers.[5] Sheep wool, though widely used, is less desirable. Other animal hair is used for special textiles or ritual purposes. For example, several Taquilean men told me that ponchos worn by newly inaugurated Taquilean male authorities used to be woven with a few rows of fox hair, said to "scare" people so they would obey authorities. Taquilean men sometimes use women's hair as the warp for their underbelt.

Acquiring alpaca fleece became difficult for many *runa* after the mid-1950s (Orlove 1977; Thorp and Bertram 1978). Fluctuations in world interest in alpaca fiber periodically led to higher prices paid to Peruvian-based multinational wool industries, but little of this trickled down to *runa* herding families in Puno Department, members of whom told me in the 1980s that they were still paid the same for a pound of fleece as two decades earlier. Several grassroots development projects in Peru and Bolivia worked, sometimes successfully, with herding communities to improve prices for fleece (Healy 2001: 216–24). However, as I learned repeatedly from *runa* in Peruvian herding communities, in comments echoed by frustrated weavers in communities including Taquile, most herders now raise white alpacas because white fleece brings a higher price. Other beautiful natural colors — tans, grays, browns, and blacks — have become scarce.

Another problem is that environmental factors and overpopulation have reduced supplies of natural dyestuffs. The synthetic dyes available in Peru are notoriously poor, and better suited to dyeing sheep wool than alpaca fiber. All these factors have pushed Taquilean weavers into using more sheep wool, as Agustín Machaca Huatta noted, more factory-spun wool, and more factory-made synthetic yarns.

To acquire fiber or yarn by barter or purchase, a family must expend a significant part of its wealth. Tremendous family labor and wealth is invested to help young weavers prepare textiles before marriage. Many Taquileans of several generations consider a potential mate's skills in spinning, plying, weaving, and knitting, which they believe reflect other productive skills.

Contemporary Andean textiles typically feature complex warp patterning to achieve decorative effects, far outpacing weft patterning (A. Rowe 1977). They are also characteristically four-selvedged, having no cut ends. A loom with a continuous warp and applied (and therefore removable) shedding devices, such as the Andean-type loom, is needed to produce four-selvedge cloth (ibid.). In contrast, fabrics woven on the European-type treadle loom have only two side selvedges; the warps must be cut to warp the loom and to free the finished textile from the loom. Four-selvedge textiles are woven in rectangles or squares. Large garments (ponchos or mantles) are made by seaming two or more sections. In warp-patterning virtually the entire textile must be previsualized and thus enormous mathematical effort is required. Not only the length and width of the finished textile, but the colors, patterns, and, to a certain extent, structures and weaving motions are determined when warping.

In the Andes, both men and women weave, but in the gendered division of labor in most of Peru and Bolivia, women weave on the Andean-type loom and such weaving is generally considered female,

15. *Francisco Huatta (standing) knits a man's cap, his brother Casimiro Mamani (hidden, center) weaves yardage on a European-type treadle loom, and Casimiro's wife, Marta Huatta (right), weaves half a blanket on the Andean-type staked-out ground loom. 1976.*

whereas men weave on the more mechanized European-type treadle loom, shown in figure 15 (cf. Meisch 1997).[6] Women make patterned belts, mantles, ponchos, coca leaf purses, carrying cloths, and blankets. Taquileans start learning to make cloth when they are children, by observing their parents (Prochaska 1983, 1988, 1990; Zorn 1983, 1997a). Taquileans, like other Andean weavers, slowly progress through many stages to learn the technology, and aesthetic and semiotic codes, necessary to create cloth, and as they learn to weave (see figure 16) they learn about their culture and society (see also C. Franquemont 1986; Franquemont and Franquemont 1986; Franquemont, Franquemont, and Isbell 1992; Medlin 1986).

The Andean loom (*awana*, literally, a thing for weaving) is simple — a collection of sticks, poles, strings, and ropes that are put together each time the weaver prepares to make a four-selvedge cloth (A. Rowe 1978; Zorn 1983). The weaver is the most important part of the technology, as I quickly learned when I struggled to transform balls of string and a pile of poles into a loom. Wood for most loom parts must be brought from lower altitudes, and so may be difficult

16. Pancho Huatta (center) knots on a new warp on a man's European-type treadle loom, helping his now-deceased godson. Huatta's son Calixto (right) learns by watching. 1981.

to get. Taquilean women generally weave on a staked-out horizontal ground loom, like the one Alejandrina Huatta uses in figure 17, and a body-tension loom for narrow bands. Weaving on the Andean loom is physically demanding, causing back strain and, sometimes, repetitive-motion injuries; the tiring position can be seen as Petrona Huatta bends close to the ground to select threads to weave an image (fig. 18). For this type of weaving, the single most important weaving tool is a polished and pointed camelid-bone weaving pick (*wich'uña*).[7]

Yardage is almost always woven by men on the European-type treadle loom (fig. 16), a legacy of *obrajes*, colonial Spanish sweatshops (Golte 1980; Money 1983; Salas de Coloma 1979; Seligmann and Zorn 1981; Silva Santisteban 1978). The yardage (*wayta*, from Spanish *bayeta*) is cut and sewn into European-type garments, including head shawls, dresses, skirts, shirts, tailored pants, vests, and jackets.

Men on Taquile make some small textiles on other, small looms. They make the black and white thick-wrapped underbelt that Taquileans wear under woven belts, such as the belt that Taquileans chose for the Brooklyn Museum (see fig. 1, left; see also Femenías 1987:

17. Alejandrina Huatta concentrates as she carefully inserts the first weft of a new belt, warped on the Andean-type staked-out ground loom. 1981.

18. Petrona Huatta selects threads (pallay) to weave an image in a belt. Weavers lean over during work, which results in back strain. 1981.

plate 8), on a rigid frame loom. Men weave poncho fringe on a hole-and-slot heddle loom (Zorn 1983). Elsewhere, they also braid ropes and slings (Zorn 1986, 1987b).

The basis of fine weaving is good spinning, which is why my Ta-quilean teachers automatically assumed, and insisted, that I needed to learn to spin and ply thread before I started to weave. Both male and female *runa* spin, although men commonly do more plying (fig. 19). Male herders spin the thick thread used for making ropes and slings.[8] Today, however, fewer *runa* spin, and men generally give up spinning sooner than *runa* women do. The reasons include de-creased availability of fleece, increased availability and use of factory-spun yarn (which saves time), and the association of spinning with "Indianness" and, perhaps, femaleness.

The Andean work ethic is so strong, however, that even ill or nearly blind people try to spin thread. This was resoundingly dem-onstrated to me when my *compadres'* relatives, Lino Huatta and his wife, Regoria, shyly invited me during a visit to see what they had been working on. I knew they both had suffered illness during the past year, so I wasn't sure what they meant. From their storeroom, they dragged two enormous woven sacks overflowing with huge balls of spun and plied yarn, which they had produced during that time — "inheritance for our children," they both proudly told me.

Most items made on the Andean loom are woven with two-plied yarns, separately spun. Such yarns are finer, stronger, and more elas-tic than single yarns, so they support the great tension required to weave on the Andean loom and do not fray from the repeated hard blows of the pointed *wich'uña*. Only single yarns are needed to weave cloth for yardage on the European-type treadle loom. There-fore, yarn preparation for the Andean loom is significantly more time-consuming than for the treadle loom.

CLOTH AND IDENTITY

Taquilean Cayetano Flores Quispe, who wore Western clothing while being interviewed in Lima, expressed pride in the clothing he no longer wore: "Our clothing is unique, ours, and that is the only kind of clothing Taquileans want to wear. . . . When traveling, any-where, people looked at us and knew us, because our clothing was

19. Pancho Huatta experiments with a homemade spinning wheel to ply (re-spin) factory-spun yarn. He wears Western-style clothing while working at home. Taquileans traditionally spin using the slower but portable Andean drop spindle; the wheel never became very popular. 1981.

characteristic of our region" (Matos Mar 1986: 59). To wear *runa* dress, however, means risking discrimination, and the fact that many Taquileans do so testifies to its importance. The visual presentation of self through clothes, along with language, establishes the weaver's identity, according to the parameters of gender, race, ethnicity, class, and age. Yet, the wearer may attempt to reinforce, subvert, or escape from these social categories. "Taquile" dress to outside observers is emblematic of the wearer's separate — and to many, inferior — identity as Indians. To the wearers, however, such dress marks a fundamental division between clothed, indigenous humans (*runa*) who wear *runa p'acha*, human (Indian) dress, and "shorn" (*q'ara*), foreign outsiders who are less than human precisely because they do not. While hegemonic non-Indian evaluations of Indian separateness denigrate Indianness, the Taquilean view inverts the hierarchy.

Taquilean involvement with cloth begins at birth. The newborn baby is received on cloth and then tightly swaddled. The newborn is not considered entirely human, and cloth is key to turning the "prehuman" into a *runa*, or human being.[9] Both male and female Taquilean babies are dressed almost alike, in a small skirt, belt, shirt, and knitted cap. Only the color of the cap differentiates boys from girls (girls' caps are white, boys' are vicuña-brown). Until first haircutting, the hair is left to grow uncombed. When the child is two or three, she or he can "walk, talk, and think." Then, in the first haircutting (*Rutuchiy*) ceremony, the godparents cut the child's long hair and give the toddler a set of new handmade clothes. When Guillermo Pulido and I became godparents to Elias Huatta, we gave clothing we bought in Puno, which was appreciated partly for its novelty.

At the other end of the life cycle, Andeans use cloth to harness the power of the dead. Both the recently deceased and the ancestors intervene in agricultural fertility (see Harris 1982 on Bolivia). Among the Sakaka of northern Potosí, Bolivia, each community receives an annual visit of its "ancestors," who are authorities dressed in ancient clothing that walk the entire hamlet's boundaries and thereby recreate the community (Zorn 1997a). On Taquile, as in many other societies, the dead are dressed in special clothing — a shroud — for burial.

Identity through the life cycle is complexly expressed through style. I observed a continuum, with "handmade" dress at one pole and "factory-made Western" dress at the other. "Handwoven" or "handspun" refers to garments made completely by the user and/or a family member (or sweetheart), including the processes of spinning the yarn, weaving the fabric, and sewing the finished garment. Such garments usually are made within the ethnic group. An intermediate category is "cottage-industry-made" dress, consisting of garments or fabric handmade outside the ethnic group, in indigenous communities, small towns, or provincial cities in rural regions. "Factory-made" (factory-woven, factory-spun, or industrially manufactured) refers to yarns, fabrics, or garments made in factories of varying size, using industrial looms. Large cottage industries and small factories overlap in scale, and sometimes in technology.

Taquilean dress is visually distinctive. Taquileans still wear many traditional garments, some clearly of pre-Columbian origins, but have adopted others. Their dress has changed only slightly in the past few decades and far less than for many Andean groups. Certain garments have disappeared, and there has been an overall shift toward synthetic fiber for many handmade garments.

Women's good daily or festival dress consists of a black head-shawl, a shirt, a belt, a black mantle, and many pleated skirts (*polleras*) such as those worn by Natividad Machaca in figure 3. Women formerly wore a somberly elegant, voluminous, black over-skirt (*aqsu*) over the *polleras*. Since the 1980s, few women continue to weave and wear this expensive, labor-intensive, finely woven alpaca garment. The *aqsu* was a shorter version of the single-piece black tubelike dress called a *t'ipana* (Quechua, "something for pinning") that Taquilean women wore into the early part of the twentieth century, which went over the shoulders and was attached with Inca-type shawl pins (see Prochaska 1990: 48 and figure on facing page). Since the 1970s, married women usually wear a red sweater instead of the red woven blouse (*aymilla*) they formerly wore. Married women wore red, and unmarried females wore white, though more recently, girls and some women wear other colors, such as pink. Other relatively recent changes include the use of sandals and wearing their hair in two rather than multiple braids. A few women studying and working in Puno wear pants, such as the young woman seen in figure 38.

Male dress has changed little in appearance over thirty years, al-

20. *Taquileans performing Sikuris (panpipe players) de Santa Cruz during the fiesta on May 3. They wear wigs of long braided hair, the pre-1940s style for Taquilean men and now the style worn only by older women. 1989.*

though most Taquilean men now weave tailored garments with syn-thetic-fiber yarns, and fewer men wear the traditional wide white scarf on a daily basis. Men's good daily or festival dress consists of a knitted cap, white shirt, short black-and-white vest, black pants, white long under-pants, coca leaf purse (carried by married men), wide belt, poncho, and rubber-tire sandals. Traditionally, unmarried men wear white caps, whereas married men, especially authorities, wear a red cap, as numerous tourist accounts posted on the Internet frequently remark. Some men wear a factory-made shirt under the woolen one, and many use the white scarf. Several people told me that at the turn of the twentieth century, Taquilean men formerly wore a long tunic, rather than a shirt and vest. Taquilean men wear their hair short; they formerly wore long braided hair, but now only as a wig for certain festivals (fig. 20), a style still common in Otavalo, Ecuador.

Rules governing choice of dress vary in day-to-day practice, even as dress styles and their names crosscut regional and socioeconomic boundaries. The full-pleated skirt (*pollera*) worn by women indexes urban Indian status, but it may polysemously signal higher status vis-à-vis a rural Indian, or lower status vis-à-vis a *mestiza* city dweller. A factory-made *pollera*, however, generally costs less than handmade ethnic dress, though some luxurious *polleras* cost more than factory-made working-class Western-style dress (Barragán 1992; Femenías 2005; de Sahonero 1987; Stephenson 1999).

Ethnic and gender cross-dressing also occurs. Members of the elite wear a national variant or imported Western-style dress, but men and women may use ponchos (worn by male *runa*) to symbolize their identity as Peruvians. Gender distinctions in Andean dress are very important, but *mestizas* and white women, especially students, increasingly wear pants. The young Taquilean Juana Marca, in front of Taquile's travel agency at Puno in figure 38, put on a man's colorful muscian's vest to advertise the island's famed textiles, though she probably would not wear the vest on the island.

Mestizos wear a less expensive version of elite dress, but poor rural townswomen (called *vecinas* in highland Bolivia), who consider themselves non-Indians, may wear a type of wool or synthetic-fiber *pollera*, along with a hat, which to some indexes their "true" identities as *cholas*, or urban Indians (see fig. 12). *Mestizas* who wear pants sometimes wear them under skirts, citing reasons of practicality (certainly apt in the frigid highlands), while also asserting a female gender identity. *Chola* market women who wear pants under skirts may also assert an ambiguous identity, claiming certain masculine prerogatives in the male-dominated Andean societies (Weismantel 2001). Transvestism is practiced ritually; men dress as women for dances across much of the Andes (Femenías 2005), as in Taquile's May 15 Festival of Saint Isidore (San Isidro).

Such instances of cross-dressing both reinforce and subvert boundaries and distinctions. Andeans use dress to assert a change in social status, and therefore in class, ethnic, and racial identity.[10] In addition, a person considered middle class or even wealthy in a small Andean community is often seen as poor by the urban elite.

Many *runa* routinely change their clothing when they leave their community, often because of the deep, anti-Indian racism in Peru. Taquilean men sometimes wear items of Western dress on the island, typically at home, as did my *compadre* Pancho, seen in figure 19. For public presentation in the plaza, work party, or assembly, they still adhere to Taquilean dress. In the 1970s, only a few, young male entrepreneurs wore Western garments, thereby signaling access to and knowledge of the off-island world. However, I saw many Taquilean men "button up" their Taquilean identity when traveling to the mainland. They donned a Western shirt, pants, jacket, and fedora hat — over their Taquilean garments — as the boat approached the Puno dock, seeking to appear and be treated as a generic Puno peasant, rather than a Taquilean "hick." On the return voyage, unbuttoning their Western clothing, they revealed the community-based aspect of their Taquilean selves as their island home came into view. Such changes clearly show how and why racialized identity in Peru is cultural, not biological.

Taquilean men's literal cover-ups changed in the 1980s, as tourism expanded (Healy 1991; Healy and Zorn 1983; Zorn 1994). Being recognized as Taquilean began to convey an advantage in regional politics, and the islanders began to develop pride in their distinctive costume, countering the censure and superiority of *mestizo* mainlanders. More Taquileans soon were wearing ethnic dress on the streets of Puno or Lima and, later, even New York City.

At home, some islanders amuse themselves by "dressing up" visitors in Taquile clothing, as my *comadre* Natividad dressed me to attend a festival the first day I was in the field (see fig. 14). We all enjoyed this experience, but I also recall sweating in the hot Andean daytime sun with my heavy wool clothing and freezing in the frigid Andean night without pants. My hips hurt from wearing fifty pounds of skirts, and my tightly cinched wide belt constricted my waist. Accustomed to Western-style clothing, I usually wore pants to keep warm at night, but Taquilean men and women, some of whom I barely knew, routinely commented favorably when I wore a skirt, even if Western-style.

Taquileans who return to the community after living off the island for a short time usually resume wearing Taquilean dress. During the 1980s I knew a few Taquilean women who worked off the island as domestic servants in Lima, where they changed to urban Indian (*cholita*), working-class, and sometimes middle-class dress. They arrived back in Taquile with pierced ears, short hair, and narrow skirts, but within a few years they resumed wearing Taquilean dress and become indistinguishable from other Taquilean women (except, perhaps, for tiny earrings). My sense is that they did this to symbolize being Taquilean. Both returning and interacting with tourists encourage the use of Taquilean dress and finery. Tourists expect Taquileans to look a certain way, which is "freezing" the local style but also stimulating Taquileans to wear some of the textiles they created for sale, notably the musician's vest for festivals.

Not all *runa* have access to Western clothes, even if they want to wear them, though Western clothing is far more available than it was when I first traveled to Taquile in 1975. *Runa* who live in very remote villages may have only limited contact with people who provide used Western clothing (such as Mother's Clubs or political candidates). Others may wear used Western clothing that does not fit well. But no matter the dress, the bent posture of someone who has carried burdens all her or his life marks that person as a member of the peasant or laboring class. Yet though poor, sometimes wrenchingly so, most *runa* do manage to acquire enough items of non-*runa* dress so that it is possible to "cross-dress" and change ethnicity. Some do so rarely if at all, while for others it is a regular part of one's work week. Lynn Meisch pointed out in the late 1980s that for Ecuadorian *runa*, "by young adulthood, dress is a choice. A person can choose to dress as an *indígena* [indigenous person] or as a white, or as one or the other depending on the occasion. Ethnic identity is malleable" (1991: 146, brackets mine). This has increasingly become an option for Taquileans, too.

Yet some clothing is more comfortable than others, and since dress remains one of the major markers of ethnicity in the Andes, returning to *runa* dress can provide the comfort of returning to one's preferred ethnic identity as well. Yet because language also marks ethnic identity, even though one may "dress the part," the moment comes when one has to speak. Can one pass as white? Should one have to? The semiotic code of dress is not fixed, and the clear demarcations of identity made possible by dress also can be blurred, and manipulated.

Changes within dress and cloth clearly correlate with sociohistorical phenomena. Among the Tecpán Maya, Hendrickson (1995) shows that indigenous Guatemalans mobilize the wearing of *traje* ("traditional" dress) in identity politics (also see Schevill 1985). Because contemporary "traditional" Maya dress combines Mayan and Spanish elements, it expresses change in Maya society. Similarly, in

New Mexico, Hispanic weavers manipulate tradition and modernity (Baizerman 1987, 1990). They pass on not simply a product but a "constellation of materials, techniques, aesthetics, support systems, [and] ways of learning . . . that determine the final product" (1990: 234). Textiles made for tourism are not the only ethnic textiles that change. In addition, some objects that are sold were previously used by their makers, providing both use and exchange value (Femenías 2004; Lambert 1990; Phillips 1990; Zorn 1991).

In studying changes in Andean dress, several important investigations of meanings are particularly concerned with practice and technology, especially weaving (Desrosiers 1992; Frame 1986; Franquemont, Franquemont, and Isbell 1992; A. Rowe 1981). A few studies address changes both in the object and its meanings. Among those that have strongly influenced my perspectives is Medlin's (1991) examination of dress in Calcha, Bolivia, where festival use superseded daily use in the 1960s. This happened because wearing handmade dress identified Calcha people as Indians, and therefore subject to discrimination. Women also had less time to weave and spent more time feeding their families. In Peru's Colca Valley, however, Femenías (1996, 2004) argues that embroidered dress has become more elaborate and "a more important component of local culture, in tandem with increased commercialization of the valley's economy" (1996: 180). Still and all, given the tremendous continuity in the importance of Andean cloth, it is notable that handwoven garments are sometimes no longer mandatory. Factory-made items now often fulfill social and ritual roles formerly held by their handwoven counterparts (Ackerman 1991: 231). Yet Meisch observes that new elements of dress are continually defined as part of "'traje típico' [traditional costume] so that there is always a distinct costume that identifies the group" (1991: 147).

Nevertheless, many indigenous people have recently abandoned ethnic dress, sometimes for extreme reasons such as death threats. In twentieth-century Peru, Guatemala, and El Salvador, guerrilla, military, and paramilitary violence forced such abandonment, as traditional clothing was used to identify reputed subversives.

The close relationship between ethnic cloth and hand weaving, then, is changing. Weaving textiles, not only wearing Taquilean dress, has maintained ethnic, gender, racial, and class boundaries.

Runa weave, whites and *mestizos* do not. However, weaving no longer is ubiquitous. Today, *runa* who stop spinning and weaving, wearing traditional dress, and chewing coca have found ways to remain *runa*, if they choose to so regard themselves.

Some Taquilean *runa* who migrate seasonally to the coast (and one group that tried life in the lowlands) have returned to their communities to farm, herd, and weave. In southern Peru more generally, few urban *runa* who have received a formal education continue to make cloth for themselves or for their families. The more formal education young *runa* acquire, the less likely they will continue to weave. The long apprenticeship required to weave Andean cloth appears to be incompatible with urbanization and schooling. Furthermore, wearing ethnic dress is not useful while attending school. *Runa* often are not admitted to classrooms if they do not wear the national school uniform, though during the 1990s people on Taquile and nearby Amantani and Urus islands successfully lobbied the Peruvian government to allow children to wear local dress to school. For those who leave school to seek employment — as domestic servants, for example — changing from handmade dress to Western, cosmopolitan dress is necessary; again, uniforms may be required. Given the wide-ranging social and economic changes, and the reality of discrimination, perhaps most surprising is that some *runa* continue to weave at all.

CLOTH AND GENDER

Women often produce the most symbolically important Andean cloth, which is patterned.[11] Cloth itself is also gendered: several primary aspects of cloth production and the resulting textiles are considered female. Creating cloth constitutes a significant source of prestige for women in the southern Andes, which changes according to women's (re)productive roles and stage in the life cycle. Cloth has a "silent language" spoken through the visual art of weaving (Arnold 1988, 1994; Arnold and Yapita, 1996; Harris 1980). Both men and women can read these codes, but in many regions and on many occasions, they nevertheless interpret codes differently, and consistently by gender.

Taquilean women weave the most "traditional" textiles, which are highly patterned or finely striped. While some appear virtually identical in form and iconography to cloth woven before the Spanish Conquest, the images have been given different meanings through the radically different context for their interpretation.

Taquilean women's mastery of the semiotic codes of cloth helps construct and define kinship and ethnicity in their *ayllus* and between *runa* and non-*runa*.[12] In this arena of active participation, *runa* women reflect on and partly structure the encounters between their indigenous communities and the world outside. Through the practice of cloth, Taquilean women order and reproduce tradition, glossed as the ways of the ancestors and the Incas, as well as negotiate modernity through the medium of ethnic, generational, and individual changes in fashion.

As in so many parts of the world, a significant source of Andean women's power comes from economic exchange (Babb 1989; Femenías 2004; also Larson, Harris, and Tandeter 1995), such as Taquilean women's income from selling textiles (chapter 4). Taquilean female weavers have modified textiles for sale since the 1970s, experimenting with various features (background colors, materials, dimensions, and so on) to increase marketability.

At the same time, purely for the aesthetic and technical challenge, Taquilean female weavers also have introduced changes in textiles made for personal and family use, some of which are not sold. Innovations include learning to weave new textile structures, as when Feliciana Huatta Huatta, late wife of Gerardo Huatta and daughter-in-law of my *compadres*, became the first Taquilean weaver to figure out how to weave the complex textile structure of double cloth (Zorn 1987a) by studying a textile from another region purchased by her father-in-law, Pancho Huatta. The results of this visibly different technical innovation (fig. 21), which slowly spread throughout the island, could be spotted "across the plaza," as the textile scholar Mary Frame commented to me (personal communication, 1987). The new weave structure allows weavers greater freedom to create curvilinear designs, including naturalistic images copied from school textbooks and "x-ray" images that show both the exterior and interior of animals and buildings. This weave structure subsequently became important in the development of Taquile's calendar belt, since some weavers chose to use it to create this belt's new images.

The Taquilean case encourages a reevaluation of changes in gen-

21. Older- and newer-style belts. Older belts (top), woven in 3/1 complementary warp ("pebble") weave, have widely spaced images. Newer belts (bottom), such as this one woven in double cloth, have densely packed images. 1998.

dered activity. Women's apparent conservatism, in language and dress particularly, greatly supports the community in resisting outside attacks (de la Cadena 1995; Silverblatt 1987). In Sonqo, Peru, for example, men feel that community well-being is associated with Sonqo women's continued use of *runa* dress (Allen 2002). Negotiating modernity and mediating relationships with outsiders, on the other hand, usually have been considered reserved for men, especially political authorities (Abercrombie 1998b; Rasnake 1988). Taquilean women, however, define and code the new as well as the old. Perhaps both tasks have been part of "women's work" for a very long time.

Gender also shapes access to weaving-related resources: materials, tools, knowledge, and labor allocation. Indeed, my long-term research demonstrates that until the latter part of the twentieth century, much of Andean society was structured to supply resources and free up time for women to produce cloth; Cassandra Torrico finds the same for Bolivia (personal communication, 2001). Obtaining fiber, especially alpaca, is the greatest challenge in textile production and is facilitated for women who own herds or whose families do, as they have rights to the wool sheared from their animals and, to some extent, from their children's animals. Women also barter or sell small amounts of produce within what Harris (1987) calls the "ethnic economy" of exchange within and across *ayllus*, or to *mestizo* vendors to obtain wool. Interzonal exchange, a key component of Andean economies since early pre-Conquest times (Murra 1972, 1975, 1978), is particularly essential on Taquile, which lacks space and appropriate pasturage for alpacas and whose scrawny sheep produce tiny amounts of wool.

As an example of the ongoing concern, or near obsession, of Taquilean weavers with obtaining fiber, I recall a conversation I had with my *comadre* Natividad on a winter afternoon in the early 1980s, following the June 24 Festival of San Juan, which left us with postfestival hangovers that impeded my efforts to pack to catch a boat back to Puno. Neither Natividad, her husband Pancho (my *compadre*), nor I were feeling very talkative.

When I mentioned, however, that the following week I might accompany my then mother-in-law to the little town of Ichu, Natividad practically jumped up, as she bombarded me with questions:

Would I go? Was my mother-in-law going to trade alpaca fleece? Could I bring back fleece? "Black fleece," she emphasized. "Good black alpaca fleece," she added, spreading apart her thumb and index fingers to remind me of the desired fiber length. "I need," she said, "two, no, three hides." Natividad reiterated that her daughter Alejandrina was spinning black alpaca for an overskirt (which were still made at the time). Natividad emphasized that Alejandrina soon would marry and needed to finish the overskirt by then. "It's so hard to get alpaca fleece — black, especially," Natividad sighed. She had not obtained any alpaca fleece all year. Then she added that she needed black fleece for herself. By the way, she needed white to weave a coca leaf carrying-cloth, and she knew that her sister-in-law Regoria was looking for a certain shade of brown to weave a food carrying-cloth. And on, and on, and on. I felt so awful that I could barely think, let alone get excited about anything, but my *comadre* was keen to not lose an opportunity to get raw materials.[13]

In the "traditional" textile system, no person can clothe herself or himself without the labor of a member of the opposite sex. Adult dress expresses gendered complementarity in cloth production. An individual Taquilean man or woman wears some garments made by himself or herself or by another person of the same sex, and some made by a relative of the opposite sex. Who makes what for whom varies locally and regionally. On Taquile, a recently married young woman may weave a coca leaf purse for her father-in-law, but in other areas in Puno, this is considered inappropriate, almost incestuous.

While most items of dress are uniquely and clearly associated with only one sex, some textiles cross gender boundaries. The carrying-cloth/mantle (*awayu* in Aymara or *lliqlla* in Quechua), although considered quintessentially female, is also used by men but worn differently. To carry burdens in a mantle, the mantle is laid down and what will be carried (food, a baby, a case of soft drinks, and so on) is placed in the center and two opposite corners are folded over the contents. The remaining two opposite corners are used to tie the mantle for wear. Women carry a mantle by placing it on the back, bringing the two free corners over the shoulders, then knotting or pinning the corners together at the upper chest. Men also carry the mantle on the back, but they commonly pass one of the free corners over one shoulder and the other corner under the opposite arm, before knotting or pinning the corners together. The gendered use of coca leaf bags varies regionally. In Taquile, men carry coca leaf in purses (*ch'uspa*) and women, in small carrying cloths (*istalla*). In a few areas in Peru and Bolivia, women also use purses.

In Taquile, all people wear elaborately patterned belts (*chumpi*). The belts are not differentiated by gender but only for individuals. Young people tend to wear wider belts. Men may wrap a long white scarf around their waist, over or instead of a belt, which women do not do. The terms for the component parts of belts, however, are gendered. The outer, woven belt is called a *chumpi*. The underbelt, to which it is sewn, is called a *mama chumpi* (Quechua, "mother belt"), or *tayka wak'a* (Aymara, "mother belt").[14] (In figure 3, the underbelt is visible as alternating black and white squares at the bottom of the belts worn by Natividad Machaca and Pancho Huatta.)

Cloth production, perhaps more than garment use, is gendered on Taquile. The associations between cloth and the earth mother enhance connections with human women's fertility, fecundity, and productivity. Taquileans value weaving as proof of productive and aesthetic abilities, and believe a person (female or male) who does not weave well is lazy and undesirable as a potential spouse. Men admire women's weaving for its combination of art, skill, and knowledge, as well as because it represents productive fertility. Taquilean women, in turn, are justifiably proud of their weaving and of the respect from both women and men it generates. Men and women in Taquile not only believe that men are not competent to learn, much less to perfect, the technical skills of warp-patterned weaving, but that misfortune is sure to befall a man who tries it. Such beliefs reinforce gendered boundaries, in this case women's dominance of the technology and symbolic language of cloth. Women's income from selling textiles has had additional, positive effects, as I show in chapters 4 and 5.

Females master the technology of weaving as teenagers, and some even leave school to weave. They may delay marriage, or even chose not to marry, in order to devote more time to weaving (when not farming or herding). While the demands of marriage, children, farming, herding, and community service make it very hard to find time to weave fancy textiles in the early years of marriage, later, as children grow, marry, and leave home, women find more time, and some excel in the art. Many women continue to weave and spin for most of their lives, ceasing only in extreme old age, when poor eyesight, a lifetime of hard work, and strain during weaving make weaving too painful to pursue.

Female *runa* adolescents generally have considerable personal and, in some communities but not Taquile, sexual freedom, as well as creative freedom in public singing. They may lose some of that freedom and creativity, and thus lose power, when they marry and, in highland Bolivia at least, stop singing. Thus, after marriage, when women's fertility is socially controlled, they shift to "speaking" and "singing" metaphorically through the visual language of cloth (cf. Harris 1980). As Taquilean women have become more publicly vocal, speaking up during political events, for example, this freedom of expression may connect to a decline in weaving.

The unique imagery in Taquilean cloth clearly illustrates the importance of gender distinction. In particular, a flower, the most common image in Taquilean textiles, is the only one traditionally shared by men and women. This image, a hexagon composed of six triangles (as seen in figure 9), women call "roses" (*rosas*), and men "six sectors" (six *suyus*). The latter symbolizes Taquile's system of crop rotation and thus is a miniature representation of the island. Taquilean men weave another flower of eight triangles attached to a stepped-fret "staircase." While both are flowers, the male-produced image is only identified as a flower, while the female-produced image symbolizes both flowers and Taquile itself.

Some of these gendered distinctions are changing. Starting in the 1980s, as both men and women invented new images, which are representational and naturalistic (rather than women's primarily abstract images), they have begun to share some motifs. Examples of images that sometimes appear in both men's knit caps and vests and women's woven belts are cows, altars, and butterflies. This shared imagery may be a result of commercialization of textiles (new images may sell better) or of more women attending school (schoolbooks can be a source of motifs). Nonetheless, overall Taquilean females and males still command distinctive repertoires of images in the textiles they create.

Changes in the realm of cloth-making have affected both male and female *runa*, although because of the *machismo* of Andean countries, men have had more to do with urban Hispanic society than women and are more likely to stop making ethnic cloth. In turn, this may create openings for women to expand their symbolic and economic importance as culture bearers and brokers. The dominant society can nostalgically consider Andean women who spin as charming, admirably productive figures at the same time it insults men who take up the spindle as *maricones*, queers. Because of homophobia and racism, few men are willing to spin beyond the boundaries of their home or community. These factors continue to make the practice of culture in cloth more strongly female in southern Peru and Bolivia.

Even more substantial gender differences have occurred regarding the wearing of ethnic dress. In the Andes, as elsewhere, women tend to retain ethnic dress longer than men (see also Barnes and Eicher 1992; Weiner and Schneider 1989).[15] Here again, Taquile is unusual since both females and males continue to make and wear ethnic dress.

CONCLUSION

The unique importance of cloth, weaving, and wearing ethnic dress is changing for many Andeans. Each year fewer *runa* create and use handmade clothing. Nonetheless, producing handmade clothing persists as a major focus for Taquileans, even though doing so requires substantial investments of materials, money, labor, and time.

Many *runa* have stopped weaving due to migrations, economic crises, the loss of most handmade heirloom textiles to the ethnic arts market, the civil war in Peru, and destruction of the regional agro-pastoral economy. Changes and disruptions of this order are not, unfortunately, strangers to the Andes, but the intersection of these phenomena with national transformations of the past forty years, including increased access to education, urbanization, and greater integration of rural Andeans into their still-racist national societies, has hit some "traditional" practices, such as weaving, particularly hard.

Though some Taquileans who migrate seasonally for work have returned to their communities to farm, herd, and weave, in southern Peru more generally, not many urban *runa* who attend school more than a few years still weave for themselves or for their families. Beyond the dominant racist values that *runa* learn in school, which generally denigrates Andean cultural practices such as cloth, time spent in school is time not spent learning to weave.

However, renewed cultural pride in these nations' pre-Hispanic past and the strategic value that wearing ethnic dress sometimes conveys have contributed to countervailing pressures on Peruvians, across gulfs of class, to be more aware of the positive value of cloth making. Ironically, such renewed interest comes when the Andean agro-pastoral economy is no longer oriented toward supplying the raw materials needed to produce fine cloth.

Dress, whether made by hand, in cottage industries, or industrially, remains important in expressing identity at multiple levels, though certain components of dress, which are encoded in handmade cloth, are being lost as fewer *runa* weave. Taquileans cohere as an *ayllu* in part by wearing a distinctive identifiable style of clothing, which proclaims their identity to those who can read the codes, such as the audience at the major Puno folklore events I noted earlier and the Peruvian in New York City who recognized his compatriots by their dress. Symbolizing the wearers' varied experiences, dress codes mark and help construct their social positions in modern Peruvian society, including their relationship to other neighboring ethnic groups. Not all Taquileans, however, wear Taquilean dress all the time. As this chapter details, they wear and strategically deploy several styles of clothing.

Taquilean weavers selectively incorporate images and sometimes alter textiles to produce cloth they consider modern, fashionable, and beautiful — as well as marketable, such as the musician's vest. Their new textiles, along with the experiences that caused the change, help construct new forms of identity in their communities, regionally, nationally, and internationally.

Finally, gender remains significant to cloth production and use. In most of southern Peru and Bolivia, handmade cloth is gendered as female, and women weave the most complex, meaningful, and valuable textiles. Even in Taquile, however, the pressures to weave faster to sell more textiles, which I analyze in chapter 4, and to attend school and operate tourism-related businesses, which I examine in chapter 5, are leaving less time for women to weave traditional textiles. Taquile is one of the few communities where *runa,* so far, generally have been able to balance the pressures destroying contemporary Andean cloth production with the countervailing openings for preserving it. In great part, this has been due to Taquileans' ability to seize the rare opportunity to directly market their textiles, which I consider in the next chapter.

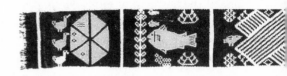

4 TRANSFORMING VALUE
BY COMMODITIZING CLOTH

Novelty is no less novel for being able to dress up easily as antiquity. . . .
[Yet] where the old ways are alive, traditions need be neither revived
nor invented.
— Eric Hobsbawm (1983: 5, 8)

[We] made the calendar, that is, I made it . . . in order to go to England.[1]
— Alejandro Flores Huatta, July 1991

NEW TRADITIONAL TEXTILES

María Huatta, one of Taquile's most promising young weavers, has
followed the example of her mother, Alejandrina Huatta (my *compadre*'s daughter, and my first weaving teacher). María's new belts are
unmistakably Taquilean yet uniquely her own. In one belt (fig. 22),
the overall organization of space into five patterned stripes, predominant use of red, and super-tight weave are as characteristically Taquilean as those her mother has woven for decades. But the way
María uses color is strikingly different. First, her belt includes bright,
or "happy" (Spanish, *alegre*), colors such as royal blue and grass
green, and the light-colored narrow stripes flanking the outer bands
further brighten the effect. Second, it is novel in using many different colors plus white in the narrow stripes flanking the central area.
A subtle, thin royal blue line also flanks that band, which visually lifts
it off the red field. Third, María uses images innovatively. Older belts
have numerous, widely spaced images on the central band. Her belt's
central band, woven in double cloth, is replete with representational,
naturalistic images. The cows, houses, and flowers are packed so
closely together that there is almost no space between them. In addition, María wove writing into her textile. The Spanish words *amor*
(love) and *nido* (nest) appear between two facing birds, demonstrat-
ing her competence as both a literate Spanish-speaker and an expert
Taquilean weaver (though she reversed the letter *n* in *nido* to better fit

22. *Detail of a belt woven by María Huatta featuring new color arrangements and tightly packed representational images in the center band, which is woven in double cloth. The weaver added writing (amor [love] and nido [nest]) to the woven symbol seen in the center. This was especially hard to do because belts are woven on the back (opposite) face, so she had to weave the words sideways and reversed. Her interpretation of Taquile's "roses/6 divisions" image is to the left, and the Peruvian national seal to the right. 2002. Belt in the collection of the author.*

the design). María's new belt is a tour-de-force — *alegre* indeed, and indisputably very well woven. María did not want to talk about her belt with me in 2002, however, other than to tell me that the bright colors are *alegre* (happy), because she was more interested in discussing the gifts I had brought from her godmother.

María is a member of the first generation of Taquileans who have lived all their lives with tourism. Like other young weavers, she wove a belt that she planned to sell, but one that aesthetically and technically satisfied her tastes (such as, for "happy" colors), which resonate with those of her generation. In this, she joins artisans worldwide struggling to reconcile individual, personal, and communal standards with the demands of a market that pays little for the objects they make. Changing traditional colors and motifs in ways that both conform to and rupture cultural norms has become a constant factor in their lives. While examining the innovations on one belt obviously prompts questions about design influences on all Taquilean textiles, the implications of design change extend far beyond the objects themselves. María's gendered, generational, ethnic, and national identity, like those of other Taquileans her age, have all been transformed through changes in textiles and dress. Yet her place in the island community depends on the heritage bequeathed by her mother, not only the weaving skills but also attachment to the values in which cloth is embedded.

In this chapter, I explain those changes and their impact on community members like María and Alejandrina Huatta. Only thirty-five years ago, Taquilean weavers did not consider the outside market. They made textiles primarily for themselves and their families and rarely sold them, in nearby Puno, though they occasionally bartered textiles.

Today Taquileans sell to tourists on their island, in Lima craft stores and galleries, and in U.S. museum shops, and, unlike other Andean communities, they do so without the mediation of a nongovernmental organization (NGO). The finely woven belts that Taquileans wear contrast markedly with many loosely woven textiles that I saw sold in their cooperative store in 2002, which raises a question: Is the overall quality of Taquilean weaving declining? That is, if most textiles are now made for sale, does commercialization dictate lower standards? The primary modifications in the process are faster

production and innovation of new items. The disparity between objects for use and for sale, however, is far from absolute. This chapter
also attends to the paradoxes that commoditization has propelled.
Art works, many now in museum collections, have also emerged
from the commercialization process. New forms of Taquilean textiles, based on but departing from their traditional antecedents, are
spectacular examples of the "arts of the contact zones," in Mary
Louise Pratt's (1995) phrase.[2]

Alejandrina was a little girl learning how to weave when Taquileans first started selling their textiles in 1968 and was María's age
when tourism to their island community started in 1976. In contrast,
weaving for sale and managing tourists have been part of María's entire life.

I argue that transformations caused by the commoditization of
textiles need to be understood in terms of broad regional, national,
and international processes of changes and, at the local level, individuals and communities actively responding to particular circumstances. I show this by examining the Taquileans' thirty-five years of
experiences and actions marketing their textiles. I argue, too, that
commoditization has both negative and positive experiences that
also must be understood in terms of local agency, as people interact
with and try to shape broader processes of change. In particular, Taquileans' experience selling textiles to nonislanders and the money
earned from textile sales were key to islanders' ability to build community-based tourism businesses and services, largely independ-
ently of outsiders, at the critical moment in the late 1970s when
tourists began to come to their island.

TEXTILE COMMODITIZATION AND THE
TRANSFORMATION OF TRADITION

Recent changes to the "traditional" textile system, which has been
transformed repeatedly over the course of Andean history, rival the
massive upheavals of the colonial period. The complex Andean system that provided resources for textile producers at both household
and state levels was destroyed, and Andeans were forced to weave for
tribute and work in sweatshops to meet colonial demands. (Andeans
also wove for the Inca state but used fleece given them by the Empire
and did not labor in sweatshops.) During the colonial period house-

hold production did continue, insofar as Andeans were able to survive as communities. Some peoples, such as the Otavalos of Ecuador, were particularly successful at producing textiles for sale in markets, as their modern descendants do today. Others, such as Taquileans, produced textiles for themselves and engaged in only the most limited trade or sale. As the economic anthropologist Enrique Mayer shows, "things" become "commodities" as people move beyond the household from "barter to ever-increasing degrees of market-dominated purchase and sale" (2002: xv). It was not until 1968 that Taquileans first produced textiles for the market in any quantity.

From about 1900 to 1960, Taquilean cloth was a commodity in only an extremely limited sense. Taquileans produced cloth almost exclusively for family use, not exchange. While herders had long exchanged household textiles, especially ropes and sacks, with lower-altitude people, other textiles rarely circulated in the Taquileans' regional Andean ethnic economy. Only a few Taquileans bartered or sold small textiles to Puno market vendors. They did, however, trade food (primarily potatoes) for weaving materials (especially sheep wool and alpaca fleece and fiber), for tools, and occasionally for Western-style clothes. Yet rarely did they have a surplus of agricultural produce. However, they did have a reputation for excellent weaving, so some Taquileans traded their labor as weavers. Master boat builder Alejandro Huatta, born in 1960, told me his parents worked off-island as weavers in exchange for food; by living as a child in Socca (on the shore of Lake Titicaca), he learned to speak Aymara.

In addition to earning cash by selling produce or textiles, until the late 1960s some Taquileans worked for wages in Puno or neighboring communities as stonecutters or miners, and others as seasonal migrant laborers in coastal agriculture or chicken farming. In Lima, a few worked in the service sector (Matos Mar 1986). Increasingly, they needed cash, especially when crops failed, for food, seeds, factory-made goods, and civil expenses such as birth certificates, permits, and licenses. To produce textiles, they had to buy wool, dyes, and yarn. Even limited improvement in economic circumstances helped their children receive an education. In addition, the off-island seasonal migration, despite unfavorable labor conditions, low pay, and discrimination, enabled men to learn Spanish.

During the 1960s, the United States Peace Corps maintained an active presence in Peru, especially in rural, highland development. One project established an artisan cooperative in Cusco. Although no Peace Corps volunteers were stationed on Taquile, several worked nearby. One such volunteer, Kevin Healy, became friendly with several Taquileans. In 1968, Healy suggested that weavers consign several textiles to the Cusco cooperative (Zorn 1983). Taquileans were doubtful that anything positive would result, as they were all too aware that the *mestizo* world disparaged them. Why, they wondered, would anyone want to buy their textiles?

However, after Healy helped Taquileans combat a problem with rats in their storehouses, two traditional community authorities—José Huatta and Dionisio Quispe—invited him to the island to discuss the matter in a community assembly. The islanders decided to organize a cooperative to market their weavings and, with trepidation, collected new and used weavings, entrusting them to Healy to take to Cusco to consign in the Peace Corps' cooperative store.

The textiles did sell, and Healy returned with money. Approximately U.S.$150 was earned from about 70 percent of the consigned items and distributed among seventy Taquileans. That sale changed the islanders' lives forever. Once the initial shock wore off, they realized their products could be commercialized outside their community. Islanders assumed responsibility for the cooperative and several men started commuting to Cusco—a day away by train or bus—on community-authorized sales trips.

Their enthusiasm was enough to weather a catastrophe: the Cusco cooperative collapsed after its president embezzled funds, leaving producers throughout southern Peru in the lurch. Taquileans lost approximately U.S.$1,000, which was a huge sum of money for poor peasants. Four Taquilean men took the initiative and started selling their own and their extended families' textiles once or twice a month in Cusco and Lima. Francisco "Pancho" Huatta, Pedro Willi, and two other men sold both to established contacts and on the streets. All vendors active in that period claim they initially made no profit. In their absence, family members worked their fields and looked after their animals in the reciprocal labor exchange called *ayni*. In this *ayni*, however, different kinds of labor were exchanged, although the amount of labor was usually the same, a week's work.

By all accounts, selling textiles very quickly became the best way to obtain cash. Manuel Huatta, then *teniente* of the island, recalled selling a coca leaf purse for José Huatta that brought s/.100, at a time when a twenty-five-pound sack of potatoes cost s/.4. Not only could they earn more money than through other forms of work, but also most people could stay home with their families and tend their fields. Many Taquileans stressed to me that earning money at home was a rare, and welcome, opportunity.

Starting in the 1970s, crafts fairs in Lima became another common sales venue. Some Taquilean men made contacts with foreign exporters from Europe and the United States based in Peru who sometimes bought in bulk (de Solari 1983). These vendors, too, say that they made no profits from these fairs, at least initially. Pancho Huatta reminisced to me about how he and Julio Quispe went hungry in 1975 after their supplies from home ran out during their first fair (they hadn't sold anything yet, so had no money to buy food), eating only when the Lima-based exporter Gertrudis de Solari realized their plight and brought them food. Despite the initial difficulties, these men formed the island's new elite.

In the Peruvian cities of Lima, Cusco, and Arequipa, male intermediaries sold new and used textiles woven by themselves and the women, men, and youths in their nuclear and extended families. Sellers adopted multiple strategies, selling wherever and whenever they could, though "requests" from established exporters typically included a mix of fine, large pieces (the woman's marriage shawl) and smaller, cheaper items (narrow belts and knitted caps). One intermediary's sales records I saw in the 1970s showed that he typically sold several hundred dollars worth of textiles per trip.

Tourism sparked an economic boom (chapter 5). By 1978, earnings from textile sales reached unprecedented levels and the islanders' reliance on intermediaries diminished as the market literally came to Taquileans' doorsteps. Every day, boats full of tourists landed at the dock and made their way to the village square. By 1981, in a move that was significant because it represented a change in the market, Taquileans established a community-run artisan cooperative retail outlet (fig. 23), called the Manco Capac Taquilean Crafts Association (*Asociación Artesanal "Manco Capac" Taquile*, named after the legendary first Inca) (Zorn 1983: 150 ff.). They consolidated their two buildings

23. *Tourists (center and right) tally purchases in Taquile's first community cooperative store. Dario Huatta Huatta (far left) and Sebastián Quispe (left) serve their monthly rotative turns as clerks. 1978.*

into one in 1982, located in the center of the plaza. Eventually all islanders became members (*socios*) of the cooperative, pledging 2 percent of textiles sold to the association's fund. Records I examined show that from 1981 to 1983 monthly sales in the cooperative averaged US$2,500, reaching nearly $6,000 during the peak tourist months of July and August (ibid.: 149 ff.). As the textiles' value soared, Taquileans and their children living in Lima even considered returning home to make a living by weaving. Alicia Huatta, a young woman born in Lima to Taquilean parents, lamented her ignorance: "I would like to live on Taquile, but I don't know how to weave like the Taquileans there do." Perhaps, she thought, she might work instead in tourism (Matos Mar 1986: 459).

The process of learning to sell textiles was not without pitfalls. Even in the early 1980s during the height of the tourist boom, textiles consigned to the community cooperative store sometimes sat for weeks before they were sold. Numerous individuals sold textiles at the island's dock or, more commonly, in the privacy of their homes, which bypassed the cooperative. People say they do so because only

24. *Children make textiles. One boy (left) learns how to use his father's knitting machine. Some Taquileans started using machines in the 1980s to knit panels for their recently created textile the "musician's vest," though they kept this quiet because tourists expect hand-knit garments, such as the cap being knitted by the boy in the center. 1989.*

those who are "lucky" sell textiles on any given day, and the tourist in their home is a captive audience. This undercuts community-established prices, since islanders often lowered prices to make a sale, and undermines community solidarity.

Production methods changed to accommodate demand (Zorn 1983). The islanders adopted strategies to produce faster and increase earnings. They eliminated the most time-consuming steps, increased the use of factory-spun yarn, purchased objects from neighboring groups and resold them, and began "putting out" the production of yardage to other communities. A few wealthier families bought knitting machines to speed up production (fig. 24). For example, they bought coca leaf purses from Amantani, a neighboring island, and sold them in their stores (ibid.). They especially put out, as well as bought outright, yardage from peasant weavers outside Taquile. People were very secretive about the existence of knitting machines, fearing that tourists might object to machine-knit textiles, even though the machines were foot-operated, not electric.

Most "new" items were modifications of existing garments and household textiles, and the lion's share were still woven and knitted by Taquileans. The polychrome "musician's vest" (*chaleco músico*) has a knit front with multiple rows of figural and geometric designs and woven sides and back. Other new knitted items include several kinds of caps, with earflaps (*ch'ullo oreja*, earflap cap) and without earflaps (*ch'ullo damas*, ladies' cap), headbands (*ganchos* or *winchas*), and knitted coin purses (*monederos*).

The majority of textiles sold during the 1970s, made initially for personal use, were worn and then sold. A few people occasionally wove specifically for sale. One elderly lady, a prodigious weaver in her youth, told me that she began to weave again because she "might die" and wanted to leave her family money for funeral expenses.

I made detailed lists in 1976–1977 of textiles that one intermediary took to sell, and copied the 1980–1984 sales records of the community's cooperative store. In 1977, belts dominated textile sales. Intermediaries also sold to exporters many knit caps and smaller numbers of carrying cloths, coca leaf purses, ponchos, and mantles. Some were higher quality and so higher priced. Women wove almost all of these items. Men only knit caps and wove yardage incorporated into shirts, pants, skirts, and vests. Thus, the majority of items sold and those with the highest values were woven by women. Questions of ownership, gifts, and allocation of earnings became increasingly troublesome over the decades, and continue to account for considerable gender conflict.

As farmers, Taquileans greatly prized land. From 1968 to 1976, aggregate family income from textile sales was generally used to purchase household items, agricultural inputs (fertilizer and pesticides), corrugated iron roofs, sewing machines, consumer items such as radios, and clothes.[3] Most Taquileans wanted to buy land with that money but, people repeatedly lamented to me, "there's no more land to buy." They continued to purchase materials for ongoing textile production.

After 1976, with tourism-derived income, they invested in tourism-related infrastructure and services, particularly boats and motors, lodgings and furnishings, and restaurants (see chapter 5). Buying food for the tourists and gasoline for boats was costly but increasingly necessary. The data I collected on textile sales and hundreds of conversations with Taquileans clearly show that it was the textile-derived income that enabled them to develop tourist services. This was key to the Taquileans' relative independence to develop community-controlled tourism, as I show in chapter 5.

The decade of the eighties brought a "boom" in the international sale of antique handwoven cloth from the Andes as well as other world regions (Zorn 1991). While few such antique textiles came from Taquile, the growth of this market nevertheless had two effects there.[4] First, it stimulated the sale of antique textiles to tourists and collectors. Although Andean textiles fetched lower prices in this market than those of other world regions, any amount probably seemed high to poor farmers devastated by floods and drought, and old textiles usually garnered more money than new ones. Second, the existing market for new textiles expanded greatly. Higher-quality new cloth, weavers and dealers learned, could, in some markets, command high prices and, simultaneously, allow precious heirlooms to remain in the community. Overall, however, it has been very difficult to create a market that pays high prices for new Andean textiles, since buyers generally prefer antique weavings, and even in 2002, tourists still could find mounds of cheap used textiles on the streets and in the shops of cities such as La Paz and Cusco.

Despite tourism's importance to Peru as a key source of foreign exchange, the violence of Peru's undeclared civil war during the 1980s and first half of the 1990s scared away tourists. In the late 1990s, tourism rebounded and Peru, like other low-income nations, promoted crafts as a source of income, for both peasants trying to survive in rural areas and migrants to Peruvian cities. This was especially important during that period's hyperinflation and repeated economic crises. Decades after Mexico, in 1985, Peru first passed the Law for Promoting Crafts (Ley de Promoción Artesanal), which authorized national expenditures to promote crafts, particularly in relation to tourism.

In the early 1990s the Ministry of Industry, Tourism, and Commerce (MITINCI), in coordination with other institutions, established three award programs for craftsmen, in media that included tinsmithing, ceramics, *retablos* (altar pieces), pyro-engraving of gourds (*mates burilados*) and, of course, textiles. The awards are the Inti Raymi National Crafts Prize (Premio Nacional Inti Raymi de

Artesanía, named after Cusco's Inti Raymi festival), the National Grand Prize Amautas of Peruvian Crafts (Gran Premio Nacional Amautas de la Artesanía Peruana, named after the Amautas, or poet-philosophers, of the Inca court), and the national prize for Grand Master of Peruvian Crafts (Gran Maestro de la Artesanía Peruana).

In 1996, the Peruvian nation officially recognized the importance of Taquilean textiles by giving to Francisco "Pancho" Huatta its highest annual award for crafts, the national prize for Grand Master of Peruvian Crafts (figs. 3 and 25). Recognizing him as a "popular artist in the area of textiles," the diploma was signed by, among others, the Minister of Industry, Tourism, and Commerce. Other artisans so honored include Peru's renowned artisans Jesús Urbano Rojas (*retablo* maker) and Ambrosio Sulca Pérez (tapestry weaver).

The award, which continues to be granted, demonstrates official awareness that crafts are important to the nation, economically and symbolically, as they help attract foreign visitors and currency, but it is not without irony. First, Taquile was recognized for the quality of its textiles at the same time fewer Taquileans were making fine cloth. Second, the award went to a single artist, but textiles depicted in award publicity were also made by other community members. In particular, most of the fabrics were woven by women, who received no recognition. Beyond its importance for Taquile, the award helped Huatta personally; he has since been reelected to important positions of community authority.

Today, elderly Taquileans are generally much more distressed than the young by the selling of old textiles. Some who initially opposed sale later accepted the practice. After thirty-five years, middle-aged and elderly weavers are often resigned but some are rueful. A few elderly Taquileans still believe that it is "wrong" or "a sin" to sell any textiles. Older people who remember earlier styles lament the passing of particular kinds of textiles or images. Yet it is precisely the elderly who are unable to make new textiles for sale, due to poor eyesight and less physical stamina, so they sometimes resort to selling older textiles. Young people, while intensely interested in contemporary and future weaving, are generally unconcerned about the loss of old textiles or the discontinuation of specific kinds of textiles. Because of the huge traffic in antique handwoven textiles, few remain in the Andes today. Taquileans are trying to keep more of their

25. Publicity announcing Francisco "Pancho" Huatta's 1996 Peruvian award as Grand Master of Peruvian Crafts. More than half of the textiles were woven by women. 1996.

heritage at home and to encourage young people to recognize the value of the old. They established a small museum on their island in the late 1970s, where they displayed and archived several old, especially well-woven textiles. Although a few fine pieces "disappeared" (i.e., were sold to visitors), they were replaced and Taquileans subsequently organized other museums in the community (see chapter 5).

Commoditization has changed life drastically, but not all effects are negative. The most positive impacts are increased income, rising monetary value for textiles, and greater personal and community prestige. Negative impacts include the loss of heirloom textiles, decline in quality, increased competition, and decreased time to produce personal and family textiles. Declining quality, signaled by synthetic fibers, coarser weaves, and nontraditional novelties, often accompanies commoditization. Yet, questions of Andean fashions and tastes for neon colors, synthetic fibers, and crowded imagery speak of aesthetic choices (cf. Bourdieu 1984; Femenías 2004; Zorn 1991, 1995, 1999). It is inappropriate, I believe, for outsiders to criticize them. However, these choices are, no doubt, influenced by changes in the materials and dyes available and the ease of use of different materials, which are linked to commoditization in ways that transcend tourism per se.

GENDERED TRANSFORMATION

Gender and textiles are linked with money and power. As Fortunato Huatta Flores observed: "Women there were not important. . . . Neither in assemblies nor in community reunions did they speak. . . . Now that they earn their own money, it seems that in assemblies they decide issues regarding the sales of their textiles; that is the change from tourism" (Matos Mar 1986: 392).

Women weave most of the traditional, elaborate textiles that fetched higher prices. In order to increase their share of money from textile sales, men began to make textiles that are more elaborate. Over the years, they created more new textiles than women (Zorn 1983) and modified textiles traditionally made by women, such as weaving a poncho on a treadle loom instead of the staked ground (horizontal) loom women use (Prochaska 1988: 50). In 2002, approximately half of the textiles available for sale in the cooperative store were made by men, including the musician's vest, and all other knitted items. Men, long in charge of yardage, were the ones who put it out, while both men and women bought and resold textiles from elsewhere. Men make vests and shirts, large items that sell for the same prices as women's belts, which, though smaller, take much longer to make. Thus, initially women earned more money from textile sales than men, but over the years, men created more new items and put-out components of male-created textiles, thereby increasing their share of earnings.

Today a single weaver, over the course of his or her lifetime, moves in and out of the market, sometimes producing primarily for personal and/or family use, at other times primarily for sale. Women commonly sell garments they have made (and wear), and men increasingly sell garments made for them by women in their family. The wide belts worn by all adults concisely illustrate how these patterns caused gendered conflicts.

At each island festival, Taquileans show off exquisite new belts and other creations, drawing the admiration and, inevitably, the critique of the community.[5] Ideally, Taquileans maintain, one should wear a new belt for each of the six annual festivals. Practically, this is impossible but nearly all weavers complete two new belts annually, one for the first festival, the Virgin of Candlemas (Candelaria) on February 2, and another for Taquile's patronal Festival of St. James (Santiago) on July 25 (fig. 26). After a person wears the new belt to one or two more festivals, it is no longer new and enters the category of "good daily wear." If used daily, it eventually becomes worn and shabby. If not, it is retired and stored as wealth and future inheritance. All Taquileans wear belts, but men are more likely than women both to wear them daily and to sell them. When her husband wears a beautiful belt once at a fiesta and then sells it, many a wife complained to me that he then "requires" another new belt for the next festival—but did he give her the money from the first one? Women must spend more time weaving but they do not always receive the money paid for their work. If they gave textiles such as belts and coca leaf purses to their husbands before sale, the men feel entitled to the money. Thus, tourism has exacerbated tensions between men and women, as gendered perceptions differ about property and rights over allocation of textiles.

26. *Festival of Saint James (Santiago), Taquile's patronal saint, on July 25. 1976.*

CREATING TRADITION FOR THE MARKET:
TAQUILE'S CALENDAR BELT

Weavers have created many new kinds of textiles for sale, expecting these inventions to be more appealing to outsiders. The most spectacular example is the "calendar belt" (*chumpi calendario*, Quechua and Spanish, or *faja calendario* in Spanish), which represents their effort to enter the art market as well as the souvenir market (fig. 27). Over the past twenty years, this higher-priced item (compared to similarly sized weavings) has become popular for foreign museums to collect, according to Taquileans.[6]

The calendar belt has three notable features. First, it is sold accompanied by a text on paper, which has written commentary and drawings of motifs (the version created by the "Natives of Taquile" Folklore Association is shown in Figure 28). Second, its central stripe has twelve nonrepeating images. Third, all calendar belts follow one of two potential sets of design motifs, or "models."

To my knowledge, this is the first case of newly literate indigenous Andeans authoring a text that presents written interpretations of their cloth. Such a meta-discourse offers a rare opportunity to explore the relationship between visual and textual "literacies."

The calendar belt also is interesting to people concerned about

27. *Taquilean calendar belt* (chumpi calendario, *or* faja calendario), *developed during the 1980s and based on an older type of textile. Folklore Association – type belt (top), woven by Terencia Marca Willi in 1991. Close-up of January, February, and March images (left to right, bottom). 1991. Belt in the collection of the author.*

ENERO — WATA KALLARiy —

Mes de alegria y se vestin,como sus campos,con
ropas nuevas lás que tienen el simbolo de la
FLOR DE ROSAS"SOJTA SUYO" La Isla Taquile esta
dividido en 6 suyos,las, los puntos que está en
la figura,significan sembrado de papa,despues de
papa sembrado de Oca,despues de estos vienen a
sembrar cebada,avas,trigo,y maíz.

Los tres espacios que quedan en la figura,sig-
nifica: son las tierras que descansan pasto pa
ra los animales.

Así socesivamente rotación de agricultura en -
los 6 suyos.

Los tres pájaros que significan la ley de Inca
ama suwa, mama llolla, ama Kella.

FEBRERO — TTICAy quiLLA.

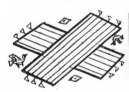

Mes de las flores del campo.- El pescado suchi
demuestra su significado por su cambio de color
cuanto cambia color negro es para que caiga llo
via,cuanto es color Gres es para que caiga granisada (triste)cuanto sus niditos son muchos es
para buena cosecha.- Altar bandera.-significa -
la fiesta de la virgen Candelaria,los poblador
de la isla danzan el vaile LOS GALLITOS y hacen
vendecir las primeras papas de sus cultivos por
la Virgen de la Candelaria,tambien recuerdan -
los sufremientos que les imponian los antiguas
capataces obligandoles con pena de quetarle sus terrenitos a trabaja
gratuitamente: De la misma manera de muestra su alegria simbolizando
la con bande ras blancas, hoy diá libre y paz.

MARZO — PACHA MAMA yuyARil ꓷuiLLA.

Mes del recuerdo a la madre tierra,donde los
pobladores pagan a la madre tierra "pacha Mama" Con mucho arrepentemiento por los males-
que hayan hecho durante el año.
Reunin toda la comunidad en la plaza y entran
a la iglesia hacen oraciones,entre ellos dando
un abrazo piden perdon de Dios por los males
que hayan hecho.
En siguida suben al cerro Mulsina cerro mas
alto de todos para pagar a la Santa tierra -
Pacha Mama" llivando coca,llanp'o k'owa,vino
Ch'uwa,ñawichatos,encencios,mustasilla para-
adornar la misa de la tierra. Suven haciendo
oraciones en los 12 estaciones. Los ancianos "Pakos"que pagan partin
en dos en la sexta estación a otro cerro llamado Ttaquile pata en -
hay paga a la madre tierra.Y el resto y toda la comunidad vá al cerro
Mulsina mas apu de todos¿Llegando a la misa de pago comiensa la ce-
libración orando,pediendo perdon para todos y ruegos a los apus ce-
rros mas altos,para que no caiga granisada,helada,ni sequea,ni haya
granizada ninguna clace de plagas,pediendo para que hayga mas produc-
cíon de la cosécha.

ABRIL — CoseCHAy ꓷuiLLA -

Mes de la cosecha,Los Taquileños recogen los
productos de sus cultivos como la papa,Oca,ce-
bada,trigo,maiź y avas.Tambien recogen las pa
plantas medécinales y tintes naturales.

La pareja llamado pechitanca trayé buena suir-
te,cuanto pone buevo en las papas es buena suir
te, ase mismo cuanto pone buevo en escondido
o dentro de las rocas es para que cayga

granisada

28. Calendar text created by the "Natives of Taquile" Folklore Association
(January–April). 1994. Used by permission.

issues of authenticity, invented tradition, and the relationship of "tourist" art to traditional arts. The calendar belt, apparently an "invented tradition," cross-cuts these categories (cf. Appadurai 1986; Babcock, Monthan, and Monthan 1986; Hobsbawm and Ranger 1983; Jules-Rosette 1984). When I first wrote about the calendar belt in 1987 in a chapter that is part of a catalogue on Andean textiles (Zorn 1987a), I was preoccupied with the question of whether or not the calendar belt was ancient or newly created, and whether it was "tourist art" or "traditional art." My concerns do not seem to be shared by most consumers or by Taquileans in the form expressed in scholarly debates. The consumers I spoke with believed in the authenticity of the calendar belt, and the Taquileans clearly followed a plan in creating them (Jeffrey H. Cohen, personal communication, 2003).

Calendar belts feature in their central stripe twelve large, distinct images. Each symbolizes a month of the Gregorian calendar by depicting one or more representative events or features. The calendar belt in Figure 27 symbolizes the month of February (bottom, center) with flowers (which grow abundantly that month during the summer rainy season), catfish (whose color and nests Taquileans watch to predict weather and harvest), and an altar with flags (for Taquile's Festival of the Virgin of Candlemas (Candelaria). July is symbolized by stars (which appear clearest when they appear that month during midwinter) and an altar with flags (for Taquile's patronal Festival of Saint James Santiago).

The belts have several other stripes, some with geometric motifs. Apart from the contents of the central stripe, however, the calendar belt is similar to all Taquilean belts in color and striped organization, and thus it remains part of the Taquilean visual language. The current version appears to be based on an older model of Taquilean belt woven with symbols that recorded family and community events, functioning in part as a historical record (Prochaska 1983; Zorn 1997a). What is now called a calendar belt is, however, more like an almanac (and indeed Taquileans used that term to describe it in the early 1980s), since the textile does not record past events, but instead serves as a general predictive calendar (January, February, and so on).

There are two general models of what is now called the calendar belt. The first was woven by Agustina Huatta Flores, according to the written and drawn text created and sold with it by her husband, Sebastián Marca (Zorn 1987a: 74, 78). The second model was invented collectively by the "Natives of Taquile" Folklore Association, with the belts woven by wives of Association members, starting with Teodosia Marca Willi.[7] The two models differ in several significant ways, including symbols used for each month and the organization of the drawn-and-written text and the information contained in it.

Interpretations of textile images derive from an oral tradition, ongoing and evolving since the colonial period. Only recently have such interpretations been oriented to outsiders, including non-Taquilean Andeans. These calendars, I believe, are based in part on Taquileans' analysis of how Westerners "read" their textiles, though no one said that to me in such explicit terms. Some of the information was recorded by non-Taquilean textile scholars, including myself, based on oral interviews with Taquileans (Prochaska 1983; de Solari 1983; Zorn 1979, 1983). Several of the resulting publications have circulated in Taquile, including many archived in Taquile's museum (discussed in chapter 5), and the interpretations in them have become part of the discourse of some Taquileans, especially male textile sellers, about textiles.

Calendar belts are marketed as containing traditional, ancient knowledge but presented in a format more easily grasped by non-Taquileans. The two-part calendar (woven belt and drawn-and-written text), which interprets Taquilean culture and society for those who are "illiterate" in the visual language of Andean cloth, was influenced by published scholarship. Nevertheless, the written text interprets the calendar belt not just for collectors and tourists but for young Taquileans as well. The young may not be learning the oral tradition in school or while escorting tourists on boats, the elders fear. Writing down an oral tradition, therefore, is also a new form of intellectual representation for Taquileans themselves. Although the impetus to create the calendars-with-texts may have come from tourism, ultimately they also serve to continue Taquilean traditions. As "autoethnographic texts . . . in which people undertake to describe themselves in ways that engage with representations others have made of them" (Pratt 1995: 182–83), these belts embody the physical and conceptual "contact zones" of the island and its people's ethnic status. The written commentaries, in particular, illustrate how Andeans respond to others' views of them (cf. Boone and Mignolo, 1994).

Calendar belts illustrate changing relationships among gender, weaving, and writing. The texts are written and drawn on paper in Spanish or mixed Spanish-and-Quechua. The two general calendar-belt models are interpreted in this way, and the pages are photocopied. The women who weave the belts are, almost without exception, alphabetically illiterate. Far more men are literate, and it was a few such men who began to write and draw the texts about twenty years ago. Sebastián Marca authored the first text ca. 1980. Group authorship also has occurred. In 1985, the first international exhibition of Taquilean art abroad was held in London (Fini 1985). Alejandro Flores, seen in figure 29, told me that for that exhibition he and other male members of the "Natives of Taquile" Folklore Association collectively created a written-and-drawn text. They also claimed at that time that they had invented a new art object. The two models of calendar belts (the Huatta-Marca model and the Association's) continue to be woven; I am not aware of other, competing models.

Marca states in his text that only his wife's family and several other families have exclusive knowledge to create this kind of belt. (The Folklore Association's text does not state this.) The text for December in Marca's belt reads, in part, "Weaver Agustina Huatta [this belt] was the secret inheritance of her ancestors. . . . Check the textile, there might be imitations. Thank you."[8]

The male-authored texts are models, which men expect women weavers to copy. However, one rarely meets an Andean woman who lets a man tell her what to weave (Gary Urton, personal communication, 1997) — or, at least, who admits it. The calendar belts, therefore, exemplify conflicts between women and men over dominance of the symbolic language of cloth, as well as collaboration to both preserve Taquilean history and increase income. Taquilean women dominate the language of cloth, which historically has been of enormous importance in Andean society, but the calendar belt is "designed" by men in the form of the written calendar. Although women weave all the belts, they initially accepted men's incursions into the realm of weaving because sales brought income. The women, in turn, altered the belts in response to the paper "translations," e.g., by adjusting an

29. *Alejandro Flores Huatta displays a calendar belt at the Smithsonian Institution American Folklife Festival, explaining the meaning of the woven images for visitors to the festival. 1991. Photograph by Ron Weber. Courtesy Inter-American Foundation.*

image's proportions. Each weaver also created her own, individual variations. In creating the calendar belt, therefore, women simultaneously collaborated with men and reclaimed an aesthetic space that previously belonged to them alone. Today, increasing numbers of women are learning to read and write, in part stimulated by these texts, and men create more textiles with images, especially caps and vests. Still, the gendered literacy gap remains large, and women continue to weave the most symbolically meaningful textiles.

The new belt simultaneously "mythifies" the Andean past, by presenting Taquileans' self-identification as Incas (the Association's text states that the three birds in the symbol for January "signify the Inca's law: don't steal, don't lie, don't be lazy"), and embodies contemporary social changes. Previously, belts provided a historical, mnemonic record of family and community events. The record was composed of images including a hexagon, signifying roses and/or the land-tenure division for crop rotation (*suyus*) of Taquile (see fig. 9 and fig. 27, bottom left); a diamond, meaning Venus (*ch'aska*), the morning or evening "star," and/or July; and birds of many species. For example, a woman who has sown three crops in her fields would weave the hexagon symbol with one, two, or three dots in three of the hexagon's triangles to show this, or weave an altar with flags to mark a community festival or a child's wedding. In contrast, the new calendar belt does not record past events but rather provides a general model of typical natural and social annual events. More than half its images are new in the Taquilean repertoire, especially flowering plants, houses, and altars. Its organization is linear, to be read from left to right; each segment is different, and none is repeated. In non-calendar belts, half or more of the images typically are variations of Taquile's hexagon. Again, I believe this reorganization and elimination of apparent redudancy resulted from Taquileans' understanding of non-Andean ways of reading cloth.

Images are important to consumers, following a Euro-American aesthetic that privileges images over color and organization of space in reading. I have observed this focus on images when listening to numerous conversations between consumers and sellers in Taquile and elsewhere in the Andes, as potential buyers asked, "What does this (pointing to a motif) mean?" I have been asked the same question when I have shown Taquilean textiles to non-Andeans.

Research by textile scholars and my apprenticeship as a weaver show that color choice and the organization of the textile space, however, are more significant than images (Cereceda 1990, 1992; Dávalos, Cereceda, and Martínez 1992; Cereceda, Dávalos, and Mejía 1993). Cereceda and Torrico have shown how color in plain and patterned areas encodes various types of information, including ethnic identity, kinship relations, and gender. Almost all Taquilean belts have red as the predominant color (which helps identify them as Taquilean), with certain exceptions (brown for a *paqo*, or ritual specialist, and all colors used as the predominant color in belts woven for sale). The tone of red differs (clear, medium, blood, burgundy, and so on), ideally indicating the festival and time for which the belt was woven (clear red for St. James; cf. Prochaska 1990: 80).

The calendar belts and texts provide the Andean people's interpretations of Andean cultural practices and beliefs, on topics including festivals, the calendar (cf. Aveni 1995), and astronomy (cf. Urton 1981). They are not only symbols, but also comments on symbols. Through the creation and sale of this object, Taquileans have tapped the rich potential of their traditions, and thus living women and men have adapted to new challenges and opportunities. By drawing on traditional textile knowledge, social organization, and community identity, they have creatively responded to new events. This process bolsters internal social cohesion even as it masks gender inequality. Such flexibility and contradictions have long been important in the continued, but highly conflicted, survival of Andean highland societies.

COMMODITIZATION IN THE WORLD MARKET

The shift to producing textiles for sale in addition to family use or barter that has altered Taquilean life is part of a growing worldwide phenomenon: the commoditization of crafts from areas that once were largely outside the cash economy. For many centuries, goods flowed from industrial centers to the colonies. Today there is "a reverse flow as consumers seek the exotic and unique objects of handicraft production in Third World countries" (J. Nash, 1993: 1–2).

The "commodity status of artisan production" (Bourdieu 1977) varies considerably by both time and place. While Taquileans are relatively new players, other Andeans, such as the Otavalo of Ecuador, have sold artisan products for centuries and probably exchanged them long before the colonial period (Colloredo-Mansfeld 1999; Meisch 1987a, 2002; Salomon 1979). Moreover, the impact of increased commercialization and new forms of exchange differs considerably at the local level, even within the same ethnic group. Indisputably, most artisans are dependent on distant markets over which they exert no control. Artisans maneuver within narrow constraints and thus have limited choices, creating almost unlimited potential for new forms of dependence. The production of cloth, among other handmade crafts, "is influenced, even dictated, by local, national, and international factors" as Carlsen (1993: 200) has noted of Guatemala; J. H. Cohen found this to be the case in Mexico as well, though he shows that success is limited to particular families in the community (1998), as is mostly true for Taquile. Nevertheless, local people can, and do, modify crafts according to their own standards. Many indigenous producers have continued to produce fine crafts to meet international demand for their products. While the common lament that crafts are debased when sold in tourist markets is well founded, in many instances they have instead, or simultaneously, improved. "In this postmodern world of amalgamated cultures and the search for identity through consumerism, the strange alliance of a politically conscious consuming elite . . . and culturally rooted producing communities may continue to generate new and beautiful forms and textures in artisan products" (J. Nash 1993: 20).

The widespread changes have compelled national governments to create policies and sometimes bureaucratic units to assist and regulate peasant artisans. The Mexican government, for example, has provided direct support to artisans by creating cooperatives to buy raw materials for artisans and to sell finished crafts products, through the Mexican National Foundation for the Development of Folk Art (FONART) and other governmental agencies. No comparable system in the Andean countries provides a state-run network of stores and export services. Nevertheless, thousands of crafts cooperatives exist in the Andean countries, set up by national and foreign governments and NGOs, and a great deal of money has been spent promoting them. The few that encourage very high standards and successfully return a good price to weavers include, in Cusco, Peru, the Center for Traditional Textiles (CTTC) and in Sucre, Bolivia,

Antropólogos del Surandino — ASUR (Anthropologists of the Southern Andes, the Foundation for Anthropological Investigation and Ethno Development) (Cereceda, Dávalos and Mejía 1993; Dávalos, Cereceda and Martínez 1992; Healy 2001). Taquile is apparently unique because tourists pay fairly high prices for textiles there, yet sales operate independent of NGO assistance. Thus, all profits (except for the 2 percent cooperative fund fee) go directly to the producers, increasing their earnings and making it more likely they will continue to produce textiles. Taquileans also interact with their market daily, which gives them up-to-the-minute information on international market preferences.

The collectors and scholars who for many decades have lamented declining quality were apparently premature in predicting the demise of craft production in the Americas. But why have crafts increased under capitalist expansion? In Mexico, Bauer noted that in 1980 there were more craftsmen — and women — than ever, with 10 percent of the Mexican population producing arts and crafts (2001: 215). More recently, increasing poverty in rural Mexico, caused by neoliberal policies, including changing agrarian policies in 1992 and loss of *ejido* lands (Otero 1999), have made arts and crafts increasingly important as a source of income. Increasing globalization and its consequent uniformity of production does not contradict localized artisan production but rather requires it, Néstor García Canclini argues convincingly (1982, 1990, 1993). Such products "fit into the overall picture of capitalist hegemony because they contribute to social cohesion and the ability of the society to reproduce itself" (Bauer 2001: 216). With population growth and land scarcity, poor rural inhabitants must seek additional income, "so they turn to work deep in their tradition" (ibid.: 215), though the primary change was increased migration to the cities. The Mexican state, in fact, encouraged artisanal production as early as the 1940s in a policy intended to stem rural-to-urban migration (García Canclini 1993). Contemporary Peruvian efforts likewise recognize the importance of crafts in the subsistence of millions of low-income Peruvians, and policies aim to promote crafts production in close relation to tourism.

Increased commercialization has substantially affected gender roles, due primarily to women's increased autonomy and leadership in cooperatives.[9] Money earned from selling crafts and the experience of exercising leadership have permitted a degree of independence previously impossible, which threatens patriarchal family structures.

Consumption trends strongly influence not only who produces what. In order to purchase Taquilean textiles for the Brooklyn Museum, the curator Nancy Rosoff had to determine what would make the textiles desirable to the museum. We wanted to buy only contemporary textiles, directly from the creator(s). But how should the objects be chosen? And by whom? How should they be valued and priced? Would those questions (let alone the answers) affect the categorization of the object as "craft" or "art"? Such ideas about authenticity and aesthetics shape both the creation and marketing of crafts. Politics, the social system, and art intersect as objects receive the "final seal of approval" in elite venues such as museum exhibits and shops (Kaplan 1993; J. Nash 1993a: 19). Both new and redesigned forms must fit the worldview of the receivers (Schneider 1987).

In this "art-culture system," objects move from the category of craft to art most often if they are understood as unique masterpieces (Myers 2001, Myers, ed. 2001; Phillips and Steiner, eds. 1999; Steiner 1994, 2001), or even if displayed in an institution (the museum) categorized as the proper home of art. Now Taquileans not only sell in Peru, to museum curators who go there explicitly to collect, but also travel abroad and sell to museums there, which has influenced their efforts to produce work that will be considered more art than craft. For the new styles of women's belts, which take longer to make, and the calendar belt with its paper exegesis, they charge higher prices. However, it is difficult to produce textiles at the same outstanding level of quality that was the norm a century ago. As I have shown, high-quality raw materials have become scarce, weavers' time is taken up with other tasks and interests, and other things are valued.

Consumption, of course, is the other face of the cloth. Increased income from craft sales and involvement in global capitalism turns the producers into bigger consumers. As artisans produce more goods for consumption by tourists, in turn they consume more manufactured products such as easier-to-wash factory-made garments or unbreakable plastic or metal dishes, which may be cheaper or desirable for other practical reasons. The "allure of the foreign" (Orlove 1997), too, is a large factor in the relationship between globalizing capitalism and traditional arts and crafts (Bauer 2001: 217), whether for Taquileans or for me.

CONCLUSION

In this chapter, by examining almost four decades in the lives of Taquileans, I have sought to demonstrate how changes brought about by commoditization can be understood in relationship to Taquileans' unflagging flexibility and capacity for invention. Since the 1970s, Taquileans have interacted with and studied tens of thousands of tourists who visited the island. The islanders maneuver, often quite skillfully, within their encounters with global phenomena, including international tourism, the market for ethnic art, and neoliberal Peruvian politics.

The impacts of the commoditization of their textiles on the lives of Taquileans have been, perhaps not surprisingly, both positive and negative. Taquile has experienced profound changes during the past decades, and textile sales and the rise of tourism occurred within broader changes brought by modernization and globalization as they took shape within particular regional and national contexts. Taquilean peoples' experiences of commoditization share certain features with people in other communities worldwide, but local circumstances, especially the agency of individual Taquileans, meant that larger processes were experienced and shaped in particular ways.

Commoditization of Taquilean textiles has affected women and men in some ways that are the same, and others that are distinctively gendered. Earning money is linked to power worldwide. On Taquile, where women do not have a tradition of working as marketwomen, and rarely migrate seasonally to work off-island, commoditizing textiles provided Taquilean females with their first source of income. This has resulted in some gendered conflicts as women have become more assertive. Other conflicts are based on disagreements over ownership of textiles and subsequent earnings from their sale and on men's efforts (as in the case of the calendar belt) to try to dominate women's domain of the symbolic language of cloth.

The calendar belt, in particular, reveals how Taquileans have drawn on community identity to negotiate modernity. The woven textile, the drawing on paper, and the written commentary all are meaningful to the Taquilean community who made them. The calendar belts provide a unique set of information about Andean cultural practices and beliefs about festivals, astronomy, and symbolism as represented and interpreted by Andeans. The belt and its text document and interpret practices that some community members fear are being lost.

Commoditization is not a fall from grace but rather one of many strategies that Andean peasants use to respond to global and local circumstances. Both commoditization and the dichotomy traditional/modern imply that there is no turning back. Taquileans, however, attempt to balance traditional demands with modern opportunities. Some of their moves in and out of the market are gradual, others precipitous. Is there, in fact, no turning back? Were traditional Taquilean weavers forever "corrupted" the first time they sold their textiles? It seems not. Taquileans continue to weave, both for themselves, as they always have, and now for the market as well. Their active efforts to produce and sell textiles have brought gains to individual residents and to the community as a whole in ways undreamed of in the early 1970s. It was a long road for Pancho Huatta, from going hungry at a Lima crafts fair in 1973 to receiving Peru's highest prize for crafts, and the distance he traveled symbolizes some of the gains that some Taquileans, at least, have made in the intervening two decades.

In the next chapter, I show how and why the Taquileans' diverse experiences marketing their textiles, and the money earned from doing so, is interwoven with, and key to, their unprecedented success controlling tourism to their community during the 1970s and 1980s.

5 VISIT TAQUILE – ISLE OF PEACE AND ENCHANTMENT

Make your decision and escape to be in contact with nature,
do not forget to visit Taquile, the isle of peace and enchantment....
— Gamaliel de Amat (1984: 22)

Nobody goes there anymore; it's too crowded.
— Yogi Berra

JOURNEY TO TAQUILE, 1984

The early morning boat trip out from the frigid Puno mainland, captained and crewed by indigenous Taquileans, transports travelers across the ever-changing and varied blues of enormous, sparkling Lake Titicaca, which, at nearly 13,000 feet above sea level, looks more like a sea than a lake (fig. 13). Glacier-capped Andean peaks tower over the lake to the northeast and southwest. After a trip of about three hours, if the weather is favorable, the small, rocky, and extensively terraced island comes into view. Its carefully built stone dock, Inca roads, stone arches, and stone-paved plaza present a view of tidiness and order. Its people wear beautiful handwoven clothing in dramatic colors of blood red, white, and black, adorned with stunning belts, caps, and purses emblazoned with intricate symbols.

Having survived the forty-five-minute climb from the dock, which starts at nearly two and a half miles above sea level, leaving even the fittest travelers gasping for oxygen,[1] tourists meet other Taquileans. The peasant reception committee registers them by age, duration of stay, and nationality. Committee members describe the physical layout of the island and its principal attractions, and assign accommodations. The host family, often represented by a female family member who is not attending school or traveling, escorts the visitor to her home. In contrast to the poor peasants and urban beggars most travelers encounter (or avoid) during a visit to Peru, Taquile and its residents seem perfect, almost too perfect. On Taquile, the lake is serene, the inhabitants are visually stunning and appear healthy and self-confident.

INTRODUCTION

The final decades of the twentieth century brought intensified articulation between peasant communities and "the outside" world; while this process has been a constant since the Spanish invasion, the intensity of contact has varied over the centuries, and has differed regionally and even by community. In the past twenty-five years Taquile, far more than the communities surrounding it, has had accelerated contact with the world outside that has profoundly impacted and shaped it.

This chapter analyzes how, through a combination of fortuitous timing, control of access to the island, and the ability of islanders to mobilize at different levels of social organization, Taquileans were able to take advantage of an opportunity rare in the impoverished *altiplano* to earn cash at home. Taquileans' success from late 1970s through the mid-1990s in managing key aspects of its tourism-related enterprises, relative to so many other peasant communities, reinforces recent anthropological research that shows how, under certain circumstances, indigenous or small communities can benefit from mass tourism. However, my research also shows that this success is extremely fragile, though to some extent the Taquileans continue to benefit.

Taquile's type of tourism is probably best described as ecotourism, though ethnic tourism and cultural tourism also drive it since a major goal of visitors is to see people described as "ethnic." By 1982, Taquileans had received tourists from North and South America, Australia, New Zealand, Japan, Israel, and most countries in Western Europe. An average of seven hundred and fifty tourists visited monthly, usually staying two to three days. Despite the substantial dip in numbers during Peru's civil war from the early-1980s to the mid-1990s, by 2000 the tourists were back and their numbers had quintupled over 1982, reaching three thousand five hundred tourists a month. No longer was Taquile the peaceful and tranquil island it had once been (Gartner and Morton 2000).

Like Conrad Phillip Kottak (1999), I came to the study of tourism accidentally. When the first tourists began to arrive in numbers on Taquile in 1976, I quickly incorporated studying tourism as well as cloth into my ongoing endeavors, reversing the usual social science project of preparing a research plan based on theory used by prior generations of anthropologists. Consequently, the early anthropological studies of tourism did not inform my first writings about Taquilean tourism (Healy and Zorn 1982–1983, 1983), which were "data," not "theory," driven.

Since many tourist areas are former colonies and are in low-income regions, it has been difficult for social analysts to differentiate between the effects of tourism in particular and those related to other aspects of development, modernization, and globalization (Crick 1989). Generally, anthropological writing on tourism shows how initial anxieties and pessimism about the destructive effects of mass tourism have shifted towards a more nuanced understanding. In 1990, I could have written that Taquile was an exception to the adage that tourism inevitably destroys local community organization, forms of cultural performance, and so on, but more recent work has shown that other exceptions exist as well (see, for example, Boissevain 1996, Boissevain, ed. 1996; Gmelch, ed. 2004).

Sometimes a small event can bring unexpected changes. That certainly was the case for Taquileans, whose lives and fortunes were altered because of a note written by a tourist in the 1976 edition of the well-known travel guide *South American Handbook*. Tristan Jones described Taquile in glowing terms as "the most interesting island to visit" in Lake Titicaca near Puno. He continued:

The Jefe de Comunidad, a Quechua named Quispe, on the island, will arrange sleeping accommodations in the schoolroom. There are numerous pre- and Inca ruins on the island, but the most interesting thing of all is the way the islanders are completely self-sufficient — one of the very few remaining places on the Lake where this is true. Everyone wears home-spun clothes and makes beautiful cummerbunds and woven belts, trousers and shirts. . . . None of the houses are locked at night. The north side of the island is the warmest part of Lake Titicaca, and there is a waterfall where you can take a shower; also here, and only here, you will see small green birds that look like budgerigars fluttering about, and butterflies. (Brooks 1977: 556–57)

What adventurous, "off the beaten path" tourist would not want to go? It's inexpensive, "exotic," and beautiful. The report provides a fairly useful orientation to the island in the mid-1970s and gives the overall impression that Taquile is an entrancing place to visit. And visiting Taquile is, of course, precisely what happened.

Taquile is exceptional in facing a double set of ecological problems that are compounded by tourism, since it is both a small island and in a mountainous region (cf. WTO 2001a, 2001b). Each of these environments brings its own challenges and, combined, these effects are multiplied. Taquile shares characteristics with other small islands throughout the world, facing similar problems and possessing the same particular advantages (cf. Apostolopoulos and Gayle 2002b; WTO 2001a).[2]

The rest of this chapter examines how Taquile achieved its success, remarkable both for degree and suddenness. One moment Taquile was a forgotten rocky island, and the next it was a world model for tourism.

MANAGING LOCAL TOURISM

Taquileans manage local tourism by trying to continue into the twenty-first century the ongoing traditional social and political structures based on extended family and community-wide reciprocal labor exchanges, such as the community-wide "work party" seen in figure 30. Tourism has affected these structures, and Taquileans wonder how far and for how long these traditional systems, which functioned to fulfill community responsibilities and earn individual and family prestige, can be stretched?

During the 1970s, key people, particularly Francisco "Pancho" Huatta, the Belgian priest Padre "Pepe" Loits (on nearby Capachica), and Peace Corps volunteer Kevin Healy, "persuaded [Taquile] residents of tourism's economic advantages" (Mitchell and Reid 2001: 123). While tourism's growth was propelled by these individuals, it has, in significant ways, been built on Taquile's strong communal spirit and tradition of participation, management, and fairly equitable distribution of benefits. Participation was key right from the

30. *Taquilean men quarry stone and build a new municipal building as part of a community-wide* faena *(work party) in Taquile's central plaza. Participation is starting to decline as wealthier islanders say they are too busy with tourism-related businesses to fulfill such responsibilities. 1981.*

beginning, although nearly half the islanders cannot remember the formulation of a tourism plan in the 1970s. Others "mentioned that a tourism 'dialogue' was conceived and established through public discussions and entrenched by community laws" (ibid.: 124).

This participatory tradition reflects deeply held Andean cultural and economic values of reciprocity and redistribution. Reciprocity in areas of society as diverse as dual political organization, male-female gender relations, and aesthetics was fundamental to pre-Conquest societies, and continues today in many rural social groups.

Reciprocity can, however, be hierarchical; Janaq Ladu moiety on Taquile is ranked first/higher than Uray Ladu, and in gendered relations male generally is ranked more highly than female. Similarly, reciprocity does not necessarily mean equality; the Inca state took in far more than it gave back under the ethos of reciprocity. Furthermore, individual conflicts and factionalism within communities is just as present in the Andean region as communalism (see, for example, Albó, Godínez, and Pifarré 1989). Nonetheless, Taquile is a community that until recently has been particularly successful in maintaining strong communal institutions. Santa Ana del Valle, Oaxaca, Mexico, known for its production of woolen textiles, is another example of a village where cooperation and reciprocity remain central to the creation and maintenance (reproduction) of household and community social life even as Santañeros have become increasingly involved in capitalism (J. H. Cohen 1999).

In Taquile, strong communal spirit also reflects the necessity of acting communally to allay the shared scarcity and the mistreatment by Creoles and *mestizos* that the indigenous people in Peru have suffered since the Spanish Conquest. To buy the island from its landowners in the 1940s and 1950s, islanders had to pool capital and act collectively. Similarly, in the 1950s no individual commanded the necessary capital and labor to operate a sailboat, so families joined together and formalized rules to protect individual rights within groups.

Extended family kinship forms the basis of all group organizations on Taquile. An example is found in Taquile's folklore associations, which crosscut and closely parallel boat groups in particular. While these associations existed before the advent of tourism, they have expanded in number with increased opportunities to perform and travel abroad (fig. 31). These opportunities reinforce family obligations; reciprocity obliges performers to sell textiles for relatives who stay behind, tending fields, homes, and children. The choice of who will travel to perform, not surprisingly, also put strains on familial relationships and leads to both individual and gendered conflicts.

All officials on Taquile, both governmental and those on committees, are elected to their post for one year and are unpaid. In cases of gross incompetence, elections can be held as needed. All adults can vote; however to date, only men have held elected community offices. It is important to note that so far none of the candidates or elected officials have been associated with political parties. Elections are held at weekly community assemblies, or on a special as-needed basis. Mitchell and Reid found that "for men at least, there is a strong tradition of consensual, democratic decision-making in the community" (2001: 124).

Men also monopolize all offices on committees and in associations. Women are, however, increasingly active in the work of committees in terms of the tasks they perform, such as serving turns in

31. *Taquileans on their first trip to Lima to participate in a Peruvian folklore festival in the early 1960s pose with their non-Taquilean sponsors, Dr. Mariano Cornejo (center) and three unidentified women standing behind him. Photographer unknown. Photograph in possession of Francisco Huatta; used by permission.*

the cooperative store and collecting information from boat passengers. This change reflects both increased assertiveness as well as improvements in women's education and literacy. In 2002, men as well as women were anticipating the election of women to committees and community offices.

The Tourism Committee oversees and coordinates sub-committees to manage the business of tourism: Housing, Crafts, Food (Restaurants), and Boats, as well as sub-committees formed for particular tasks. Special tasks such as construction or public maintenance are handled by volunteer work groups set up by the committees, based on *faenas*, traditional public work parties (see figs. 10, 30). In other cases, individuals carry out the actual work through rotating responsibilities.

At times, the Tourism Committee has existed more in name than in activity. Sometimes leaders have been unwilling or unable to oversee Taquile's diverse and increasingly time-consuming tourism-related enterprises, which have the effect of drawing them away from other responsibilities. As the issues and problems generated by tourism become progressively complex, the unpaid positions have become more difficult for many to manage. Internal divisions among committee members have existed between what can be called accommodationist versus activist community members, who disagree on how to handle problems generated by tourism.

Mitchell and Reid found that "Taquileans have a very high level of individual involvement in tourism service administration (79 percent of respondents) and community tourism meetings (96 percent)" (ibid.: 125), though the authors noted that participation can mean simple attendance rather than active engagement. It comes as no surprise that Taquileans were almost unanimous (93 percent) in believing that they should retain control of tourism on their island (ibid.: 130). In terms of the impact of tourism on community cohesion, Mitchell and Reid note that Taquileans felt a "high solidarity until recently, which interestingly has paralleled a perceived decrease in control over tourism" (ibid.: 127).

BOATS

The first tourists who arrived in June 1976 came as individuals, but very soon thereafter groups began to arrive, attempting to book passage to Taquile from Puno's dock. In those days, Taquile was overshadowed by the area's main attraction: the floating reed islands a twenty-minute motorboat ride from Puno, populated by people who call themselves Urus. Few travelers were adventurous enough to spend twelve or more hours sailing to Taquile overnight on a cold, windswept lake (Healy and Zorn 1983: 8).

Several private Puno motorboat owners, and a few Urus, soon added the island to their tourist run, operating either directly to Taquile or as part of a package tour around the lake. By the end of 1976, employees in Puno's Ministerio de Industrias y Turismo (Ministry of Industries and Tourism, or MIT) complained that tourists only wanted information about Taquile, about which the employees knew nothing.

By taking turns, members of Taquile's sailboat groups pooled their savings to buy gasoline-fueled truck engines to power their boats. Most of the motors were second or even third hand and of very poor quality (the first they bought from the Urus lasted only six months), and Taquileans had to learn to properly operate and maintain them.

But the shorter trip of three and a half hours meant the tourist boom to Taquile was on.

By December 1977, a group of Taquileans had formed a cooperative Motorboat Committee (Comité Lanchero) with seventy-five *socios*, or members (almost all were male heads of households), whose goal was to centralize the administration of boat transportation. Most of the new organization's members belonged to one of Taquile's five existing sailboat cooperatives, though some were new to boating. According to my *compadre* Pancho Huatta, who was elected president, until the tourists came, Taquileans had not been motivated to spend their very limited cash on improving their boats.

By March 1978, Taquileans had organized yet another Committee, called the Comité de Turismo y Desarrollo (Tourism and Development Committee) which applied for $16,000 in funds for boat parts, repair, and motors from the U.S.-government-funded development agency the Inter-American Foundation (IAF).[3] The project was approved in December 1978 "to enable the community to exercise control over tourism" (IAF document, in Zorn 1983).

Taquileans used the funds to form additional boat cooperatives, mostly as splinters from existing sailboat groups, in some cases due to conflicts between Catholics and Adventists. The new cooperatives, comprising twenty to forty families each, ordered new vessels designed specifically for motorized travel, which were built by Taquile's own boatwrights. These include Toribio Huatta Cruz (fig. 32), son of Santiago Huatta, who was one of Taquile's first master boat builders. Although still rustic, the new boats had cabins and were safer, more attractive, and could comfortably carry as many as twenty tourists at a time.

By 1978, Peruvian officials began to intervene in the transport process by issuing boat licenses, establishing regulations, and setting tariffs. The formidable paperwork this created forced Taquileans to spend more time and money in Puno, reinforcing the rising power of new Taquilean leaders, primarily men in their thirties who were literate and who spoke Spanish.

By 1980, Taquilean boats were competitive with the private boat owners based in Puno. Eventually the Taquileans displaced the Puno operators, and even obtained a government sanctioned transport monopoly to the island on the basis of rights granted to *campesino*

32. *Master boat builder Toribio Huatta Cruz (left), helped by his apprentices, uses hand tools to build the Taquilean motorboat* Corsario. *1984.*

communities officially recognized by the Peruvian government. The growing competition for tourists caused conflict with unionized Urus boatmen, forcing Taquileans to navigate outside the reed islands and forego stopovers there. This lengthened transport time and reduced what had been long-term trade between people from the Urus and Taquile. The antagonism dissipated during the 1990s when the growing role of outside tour agencies led young Urus and Taquilean leaders to join forces.

In April 1981, Taquile's Motorboat Committee incorporated and managed ten motorboats (*lanchas*) (Zuñiga 1980). By 1982, the number of cooperative transport groups in Taquile expanded to a total of thirteen, up from four in 1978, which meant that nearly every Taquilean family had at least one member in a boat group.

By 1982, 435 people (of a total population of about one thousand two hundred) shared ownership and management responsibility for boats. Traditionally Taquileans slept in their boats at the Puno dock, but during 1981, the ten boat groups in Taquile's Empresa de Transporte pooled earnings to buy land in Puno and construct a community house for overnight cooking and sleeping. By 2002, this building, located on 508 Titicaca Avenue (the main avenue going down from the center of Puno to its port) housed multiple tiny rooms and an intermittently functioning tour agency, which Taquileans set up during the late 1990s (fig. 38).

In 1983, based on interviews and figures in the boat groups' account books, I determined that overall the boats were operating perilously close to the breakeven point. Sometimes the boat groups made small profits, but other times fares were not enough to even cover gasoline (which is very expensive in Peru). Nevertheless, there were significant nonfinancial benefits: the wages paid to those working on the boats, the free transportation for island residents, and the convenience of far more frequent trips to the mainland (Zorn 1983).

By the 1990s, several of the wealthier extended families were able to raise the money to build their own boats, outside the extended-family boat associations. They did so believing that they could make more money by going it alone.

FOOD AND LODGING

Taquileans made the decision to billet tourists in their individual homes, though other arrangements also were tried.[4] Tourists pay lodging charges directly to the family and initially most tourists also ate meals with their hosts. In early 1983, an overnight stay cost US30¢, and a fish dinner US50¢. In comparison, a stay in a low-quality hostel in the city of Puno cost US$1–$2. The setting of minimum standards early on by the Tourism Committee improved the quality of visitors' lodging but was a barrier to the participation of the poorest Taquileans, who could not afford the items required, which included a bed, blankets, sheets, a washbasin, a table, a chair, and a mirror. In 1978, local authorities authorized 68 families to take in overnight guests; by August 1982, the number of approved family lodgings rose to 207, or nearly all of the 235 families on the island (207 of 235). However, Mitchell and Reid (2001) found that by 2001, only 30 families hosted most of the lodgers.

Potential and actual tourist income encouraged the household improvements, which were approved by an island lodging commission. An increasing number of tiny stores furnish toilet paper, beer, soft drinks, and, more recently, postcards and film. In the early 1980s, these products were generally considered the maximum allowable comforts consistent with an "authentic Andean experience." (In 2002, some stores were also selling cassettes and CDs of Taquilean music.)

During the first tourist season, two privately owned restaurants were opened by Taquileans who had returned to the island after having lived for many years in Lima. Seven more restaurants opened in 1982, and more than a dozen existed by 2002. The first restaurants were owned and managed by groups of families, though more recently, individual families have built and operated them. They offer food that is more varied than peasant fare—omelettes, white rice, fish, and pancakes—in addition to potatoes, soup, and herbal teas.

Prior to tourism, most islanders were not active fishermen, but the tourist demand for fish, especially trout rather than the locally preferred native species (the tiny *ispi* and the fat *carachi*), stimulated the 1981 formation of two fishing cooperatives, with twenty-one and fifty members respectively. Fishing is a relatively expensive operation, since techniques differ by species, and nets (especially those for trout) are costly and often hard to come by. These cooperatives sought and used Taquile's international contacts to facilitate the flow of international development agency support.[5] Fish also is bartered for or purchased from fisherfolk from nearby Amantani and Capachica.

During the 1990s, the members of the folklore association that traveled to Washington, D.C., to perform in the 1991 and 1994 Smithsonian Institution Festivals of American Folklife bought solar panels for electricity for their homes and restaurants; notably, they financed these panels by selling their textiles. Subsequently, other Taquilean families purchased panels and batteries with materials supplied and underwritten by a multilateral agreement among two Peruvian governmental agencies, the local Peruvian university, and a nonprofit organization called Inti Luz (Light of the Sun) (Horn n.d.). The Peruvian agencies were PAE-MEM (Energy Saving Project of the Ministry of Energy and Mines; Proyecto Para Ahorro de Energía del Ministerio de Energía y Minas) and CER-UNI (Center for Renewable Energies, National Engineering University; Centro de Energías Renovables, Universidad Nacional de Ingeniería).

Taquile has virtually none of the standard tourist services: excursions, shops, motor vehicles, regular medical facilities, potable water, plumbing, or consistent electricity. "Rustic" in Taquile can mean rugged. The hilltops of the island are more than 4,000 meters above sea level, an altitude to which few visitors are accustomed.

PERFORMANCE AND EXHIBITIONS; STORES AND MUSEUMS

A key moment in Taquilean tourism occurred in 1975 when two Taquilean men participated for the first time in an agricultural and crafts fair in Lima. A short article with photographs about them appeared in the Peruvian magazine *7 días* (7 Days), which led Gertrudis de Solari, the German exporter living in Lima, to meet them. As noted earlier, Pancho Huatta recalled decades later, with obvious affection, how "Sra. Solari" brought them food when their own ran out. After providing several meals, she bought all their textiles, beginning a long relationship involving the purchase of textiles Huatta brought to Lima.[6]

In subsequent years, Taquileans exhibited, sold textiles, and won prizes in numerous fairs all over Peru and subsequently in other countries, bringing publicity to themselves, their region, and their nation. Their increasing expertise at such events has enhanced their regional and national prestige, evidenced by Pancho Huatta's 1996 national craftsman award. Fairs also have led to increased sales of textiles and yet more tourism to the island, including visits by Peruvians.

There have been sustained gender differences in these experiences. Taquilean women have taught a few weaving courses and participated in dance and music exhibitions, but primarily men travel outside Taquile, though this is changing. Most of the textiles illustrated in publicity for Huatta's award were woven by Taquilean women, but they were not credited. Outside the island Taquilean women's creativity and production was "erased." This award did, however, provide some increased status for women in Taquile itself.

Taquilean men and women have also participated in traveling dance and music groups. During the 1960s, Dr. Mariano Cornejo organized a group of men and women from Taquile to go to Lima to perform at a folklore festival (fig. 31). Taquileans also sent dance groups to folklore competitions in Puno. As Turino (1991, 1993) has pointed out, in these circumstances, music and dance become "folklorized" in ways that enhance the Peruvian nation-state. Yet, both

Mendoza (2000) and Meisch (2002) also show how local people interpret these processes as they construct agency and seek to use these spaces to their advantage.

The extended-family folklore associations compete for opportunities to perform away from the island, primarily by networking with other Peruvians and, since the growth of tourism, with foreigners as well. Sometimes the actual amount of money earned from performance is minimal, since the investment in maintaining costumes and instruments is substantial, but many people, not surprisingly, are eager for the opportunity to travel and perform away from the island. When association members travel away from Taquile, they partly repay their families' *ayni* by selling textiles, and are under great pressure to do so.

One group, "Natives of Taquile" Folklore Association, authored one of the two calendar belt texts described in chapter 4 and has performed at folklore events in Lima, Puno, the United States, and Europe. Members of this association were in residence at the 1991 and 1994 Smithsonian Institution's Festivals of American Folklife (fig. 33), as part of international programs focused on land in the Americas, and grassroots development (Vance and Weber 1992; Zorn 1994, n.d.f). I worked both times as the group's translator and presenter at their request and, in 1994, did the same at the American Museum of Natural History in New York City, during a week-long residence I helped arrange. At least one folklore association has branched out from performance and invested in recording their own string band CD (*Conjunto Las Nuevas Ondas*, The New Waves Band), which they sell on the island. In addition, Taquileans have traveled to France to participate in a festival and have been recorded by an ethnomusicologist (Bellenger 1992).

Various groups of young Taquilean men now practice and perform at restaurants on the island, similar to the performance of music at *peñas* (folk music clubs) in all the Andean countries and abroad. Enthusiastic young men play popular Andean *waynos* (the most popular song and dance form) and, rarely, versions of traditional Taquilean music. Clearly performing music for tourists has become a usual part of life and a convenient way to combine practice with income generation.

*33. Taquilean participants at the Smithsonian Institution of American Folklife.
While the author (upper left) narrates, Paula Quispe Cruz (center) and Terencia
Marca Willi (right) demonstrate weaving for visitors to the festival. 1991.
Photograph by Ron Weber. Courtesy Inter-American Foundation.*

As tourism grew, Taquileans invented their Festival Fair that takes
place during the first two weeks of August, at the end of their annual
festival cycle. In their central plaza, islanders perform music and
dance from their annual festival cycle and set up booths to sell textiles. Since the Festival Fair is the first community event created
solely for the purpose of tourism, it is not surprising that it has
generated considerable discussion on Taquile, and beyond, about
whether Taquileans are "selling out" by extracting music and dance
from the traditional cycle to stage it solely for tourists.

Taquile's community cooperative association and store had almost three hundred and fifty members in 2002. The store still is over-
seen by the Handicraft Committee and is located on one side of the
central plaza. Taquileans moved the store in 2002 from one side of
the plaza to another, adding a second story with stairs and painting
an enormous mural across its top (fig. 34). As discussed in chapter 4,
since the cooperative's inventory is huge and relatively few textiles
sell on any given day, people sell textiles individually, which though

34. *Taquile's new, larger two-story cooperative store, in its central plaza. Note painted mural of Taquileans at top, and tourists sitting on benches. 2002.*

understandable, undermines the cooperative, and in turn community solidarity.

Unlike Taquile's other tourism services, which were all initiated by Taquileans, the idea of building a local museum was, I believe, initially suggested by outsiders, including myself. The first museum was funded from the initial IAF grant, but the museum itself wasn't constructed until years after the grant disbursement, at some distance from the plaza. The delays were due to other priorities taking precedence (motors for boats were considered more important), the community's initial lack of understanding of what a museum is, and the high cost and complexities of building, equipping, and maintaining a site museum in a rural community such as Taquile. Finally, a building was constructed and filled with mannequins, creatively made from wire with ceramic faces, illustrating Taquile's varied and impressive dance costumes. However, since Taquileans are full-time farmers and artisans, it remains a problem for the community to maintain regular hours for the relatively isolated museum.

When Taquileans performed in museums in Lima, and then abroad in England, France, and the United States, they began to appreciate the preservation and (they hoped) commercial value of mu-

35. *Juan Quispe (left) and Félix Quispe Quispe (2002 Mayor) inside Taquile's museum just off its central plaza. Juan is a member of the generation born in the 1970s that is growing up taller than their parents. 2002.*

seums. This led to building another museum located on the central plaza on land donated by the family of Alejandro Flores (fig. 29), who has traveled to Europe and the United States (Flores and Quispe 1994). Taquileans hoped this museum would be more manageable and receive more visitors, given its location on the plaza (fig. 35). Most of the items on display in 2002 were tools, foodstuffs, textiles, a *khipu* made by Taquile's *khipu* master Nieves Yucra, and photographs of local authorities; the entryway displays publications about Taquile. Other Latin American peasants also have created local museums, as Jeffrey Cohen reports from Mexico (2000).

TOURIST-TAQUILEAN INTERACTIONS

Taquileans interact, literally on their own doorsteps, with people of different regions, classes, languages, and races, most of whom are wealthier than islanders. Some relationships last only long enough to take a name on a boat list, sell a textile, or take a photograph (fig. 36). Others (such as mine) persist over decades. These relationships have

36. *A tourist photographs Taquilean authorities Fortunato Cruz Machaca (center) and Sebastián Marca (right) in Taquile's central plaza. Sabina Huatta Cruz, seated in shade (left), appears amused. 1989.*

had profound effects on Taquile and Taquileans' lives because of their novelty, consequences, and numbers.

These interactions brought both problems (such as garbage, thieves, outside prostitutes, disruptive behavior) and benefits (including exchanges of goods, subsidy of motorboat costs, new ideas and experiences, prestige, friendships, logistical and financial assistance, respect), though not yet marriages or HIV infection (cf. Meisch 1995). From the points of view of outsiders, non-Taquileans have had the opportunity to interact with *runa*, who they might otherwise never have met; for many Peruvians at least, these interactions helped humanize *runa* who still remain Peru's "exotic Others." For Taquileans, the constant stream of visitors has oftentimes been wearying, but they say they have benefited overall from these interactions.

Travelers seeking "ethnic tourism" often are looking for a world where human relationships are most important and strong communal bonds appear to exist. However, the reality is that the social relationships between tourists and local people typically are short-term and superficial, and great disparities of class and wealth typify these relationships. In low-income countries, these disparities are found even with hippie or backpacking tourists. Relationships on both sides can be marked by self-interest and exploitation. Lynn Meisch's long-term studies of Otavalo people in Ecuador provide great insight into the complexities, as well as the banalities, of such interactions (1995, 2002).

As I think about interactions between Taquileans and visitors, myself included, or reread field notes, I am struck by the variety of experiences, which range from mutual cultural incomprehension to warmth and compassion. Some could happen anywhere, not necessarily in "ethnic tourism" contexts. An example of a misunderstanding occurred when my *comadre* Natividad Machaca was extremely distressed to find that the fish soup (*ispi caldo*) she had carefully prepared for a tourist was greeted with disgust by the visitor, who stared in horror at the tiny dried fish heads poking out of the bowl, saying "They're looking at me."

As an example of a transnational connection, I recall the message I received soon after September 11, 2001, from Juan Quispe, who had traveled by boat to an Internet café to send me an e-mail: "Please we want to know that you are well. We cry and suffer because of so many disappeared people in New York and in Washington. Please tell us that you are well."[7] Because of tourism to their community, Juan and other Taquileans felt connected to people in the United States, through direct experiences not mediated either by Taquilean migration or through mass media.

Host-guest interactions typically occur between people who differ in terms of class, language, gender, nationality, and so on, and such interactions of course are permeated by mutual stereotypes (see Gmelch, ed. 2004).

On Taquile, where outsiders (anthropologists, medical personnel) have lived for a year or more at a time, and where hundreds or even thousands of people have been invited to become *compadres* (fictive kin), some, even many, of the tourist-Taquilean interactions did indeed typify the types of person-to-person contact that ethnic tourists seek.

However, I observed the enormous increase in tourism since the 1970s and Taquileans' loss of control of transportation since the 1990s, and it has become clear from talking with numerous Taqui-

37. *Taquileans and tourists, distinguishable by dress, sit on the stone steps in front of Taquile's municipal building in Taquile's urbanizing central plaza.* 2002.

leans and tourists that positive interactions have diminished. This, I believe, is due to the combined effect of these two interrelated phenomena. Most visitors now arrive in groups led by non-Taquilean guides, and nearly all tour agencies hurry visitors through a day trip. In contrast to earlier years when I typically saw tourists during the day out on paths around the island or with Taquileans, in 2002 I saw masses of tourists congregating in Taquile's central plaza, wearily resting on the broad stone steps in front of public buildings, applying sunscreen, and chatting with one another (not Taquileans) during the visitors' very brief lunchtime stay (fig. 37).

On the other hand, Taquileans recently have started participating in an international youth program they call Mosoq Wayra (New Wind), by means of which Taquileans have traveled to several cities in Peru and to Scandinavian countries, and "interns" have come to the island as well. This is signaled by a sign I saw outside a house where Taquileans and visitors were rehearsing panpipe music. The sign said "Welcome to Taquile, Dinamarca (Denmark), Noruega (Norway), Bolivia, Lima, and Cusco."

Nevertheless, as a result of mass tourism controlled by outside tour agencies, Taquilean-tourist interactions appear to primarily consist now of service — taking orders and serving in restaurants, tallying sales in the crafts cooperative, or carrying backpacks up the island's steep hills. Though I did not collect records for the 1990s, nearly all Taquileans I asked about tourism in 2002 told me that rising rates of tourism has not meant increasing profits. Taquileans are well aware that not only are they earning less money from tourists today (most visitors do not travel on Taquilean boats or lodge in Taquilean homes), but that the very interactions that so many tourists seek no longer occur. This is the case because the tourists' stay of a few hours, mediated by non-Taquilean guides (some of whom demand a cut for escorting tourists to restaurants), severely restricts the opportunities for visitors and Taquileans to interact in Taquilean homes.

RELATIONSHIP WITH THE PERUVIAN GOVERNMENT

The development of Taquilean tourism owes little to the Peruvian nation, even though many Taquileans have become adept both at dealing with an impressive number of Peruvian national agencies, regional bureaucracies, and individual agencies and at playing off local and regional interests against national Peruvian policies. Whenever possible, Taquileans learned how to find favorably inclined bureaucrats who would help them confront the Peruvian state's formidable bureaucracy.

Taquileans, like the people of Otavalo, Ecuador (Colloredo-Mansfield 1999; Meisch 1987a, 2002), or the Zapotec weavers in Mexico (Wood 2000), have mostly looked not to Peruvian or Ecuadorian metropolitan centers for assistance, but directly to places such as Tokyo, London, and New York, bypassing creole elites in favor of relationships with *gringos* in private organizations and nongovernmental agencies.

In the 1970s and early 1980s, the island community and the Puno branch of Peru's Ministry of Industry and Tourism (MIT) "discovered" one another, in a mutual process based primarily on self-interest. The MIT wanted to "help" Taquile and the islanders wanted almost any sort of assistance they could get, but especially with publicity. The Ministry (now reorganized as MITINCI — the Ministry of Industry, Tourism, and Commerce) theoretically serves "all" Peruvians, but the legacy of racism made it exceptionally difficult for Taquilean organizations to work with MITINCI. It has been even more difficult for them to work through the MITINCI with the kinds of regional business organizations the ministry traditionally has served.

Not surprisingly, the tour agencies outside Taquile were better positioned to seek favorable interpretations of Peruvian laws and work with state agencies than were the islanders. The MITINCI is accustomed to working with mainland and generally middle-class tour agencies, such as those grouped in the Puno branch of APAVIT, the Peruvian Association of Travel Agencies, not with peasant organizations such as Taquile's Tourism Committee.

1990S: OUTSIDE TOUR AGENCIES AND LOSING CONTROL

The Puno-based association of tour agencies understandably has been concerned to bolster Puno as a tourist destination on the popular transit route between Cusco (north of Puno) and La Paz, Bolivia (south of Puno). Puno is the second most visited city and region in Peru, after Cusco; in 1999, it received 83 thousand tourists (compared with Cusco, which received 330 thousand) (Contorno and Tamayo n.d.). Though regional pride designates Puno as "folklore capital of the Americas," the city itself is off-putting to many tourists because of its frigid climate and lack of spectacular urban and archaeological sites of the type Cusco and La Paz offer. Taquile, according to a report by Peruvian government officials, is the prime attraction that draws visitors to Puno, followed by the floating Urus islands and the larger island of Amantani (ibid.).

Over half of Puno's thirty-seven travel agencies take tourists to Taquile and make considerable profits doing so. Not only do they have the advantage of using modern means of attracting tourists, they also have faster boats. They charge far more than Taquileans for their services but are much better positioned to capture a far larger share of the market (Mitchell and Reid 2001: 129). By 2002, non-Taquileans used Taquile's docks (which they did not build and do not maintain) and set the travel schedules that determine how many tourists visit. Almost without exception, they offer only day trips that allow tourists a scant half hour of free time on the island (the day is taken up with the return trip across the lake, the arduous trek up to Taquile's plaza and down to the dock, and lunch in a restaurant). These one-day visitors have little time to even look at the cooperative store, and sales have declined, resulting in benefits neither for individuals nor for the community.

In the 1990s, with the Fujimori administration's adoption of an antimonopoly law, the Peruvian government cut the Taquilean monopoly over transportation. The government agreed that, instead, a fee of less than US50¢ per person should be paid to the Taquile municipality for each tourist arriving on the island. However, collecting the users' fees for docking on the island has been almost impossible. Despite a decree from the regional Puno port authority, Taquileans have had no assistance from regional authorities in ensuring that they receive the fees.

Many Taquileans, busy as they are with subsistence agriculture in one of the most challenging environments on earth, feel they do not have the time, energy, skills, or money to challenge outside agencies. Other Taquileans, particularly young men, have fought the agencies through island committees seeking to regain a state-supported transportation system, formerly available to legally recognized peasant communities such as Taquile.

Taquileans have also solicited NGOs and other institutions, including the local office of the Catholic Church, to pressure national and paranational Peruvian government agencies. While NGOs have assisted in the preparation and presentation of the multitudinous documents so beloved in Peruvian courts, Taquileans have not found any redress from the state for the tour operators' refusal to pay the community.

Taquileans have been extremely reluctant to physically block docking by the tour agencies. Taquileans are generally not physically aggressive people, and the tour guides often wheedle their way onto the island by saying the agency did not give them any money to pay the fees.

The sole exception was a *huelga* (strike) in 1989, when a group of Taquilean women linked arms to physically stop what they considered the most arrogant tour agency from docking. The women, according to Taquilean men, "shamed" the men and spurred them on to try harder to prevent non-Taquilean boats from using the dock.

Despite the formal training of guides in Peru at tourism institutes and universities, many guides to Taquile appear poorly informed and disrespectful of the islanders, and to date, there are no formally trained Taquilean guides. One of the inaccuracies that most stings Taquileans is that guides, they say, tell younger Taquileans as well as tourists that tour agencies developed tourism on Taquile, thereby erasing Taquilean agency and reinforcing Taquileans' inferior status, since in this account they appear as little more than subjects decorating the island's plaza. Taquileans told me that guides increasingly demand kickbacks in order to steer tour groups to particular restaurants for meals. In a 2003 e-mail, Juan Quispe told me that restaurants were "taking turns" (that is, rotating service) in an attempt to reduce the "high percentage" demanded by guides.

Some Taquileans have tried to make arrangements with the agencies. Families rented their boats to agencies, especially during the mid- to late 1990s, but the continued failure by tour agencies to pay wages and rental fees led them to end virtually all arrangements with Puno-based tour agencies by 2002. Some islanders continue to try to recover the money they claim the agencies still owe them.

By the late 1990s resurgence of tourism, Taquileans had pretty much lost the battle to control transporting tourists to and from their community. In 2000, they appealed to the top, sending a delegation to President Alberto Fujimori asking for an investigation of conflicts and what Taquileans termed abuses by tour agencies and guides on the island.

A team of high-ranking Peruvian women was dispatched to the island (Contorno and Tamayo n.d.). In their report, they criticized abuses by tour operators, while also pointing out that internal competition between Taquilean family groups was causing some of the difficulties. While the authors appear somewhat sympathetic to Taquileans, arguing that the Peruvian state should "communicate" directly with Taquile as a peasant community (ibid., 13), they firmly point out that the neo-liberal business climate of the Fujimori regime (presumably continued today under Alejandro Toledo) will not grant special or exclusive rights to Taquile. Free enterprise is encouraged, with the state merely serving to remind tour agencies to pay local fees and to discourage the poor behavior of guides.

Taquileans have tried to compete directly by setting up their own travel agency in Puno, built in the front of land they bought long ago near the dock to house boat crews staying overnight (fig. 38). Taqui-

38. *Francisca Huatta Cruz (far left), Julio Quispe Huatta, Juana Marca Huatta, and Juan Quispe Huatta in front of their Puno travel agency. 2002.*

leans have spent time and money fixing up the building, buying office furniture, decorating the interior, and painting murals to increase its appeal, as seen in figure 8. In 2002 and 2003 their agency functioned intermittently. In addition to the difficulty of competing with other agencies with far deeper pockets and much greater experience and networks, staffing has been a challenge. Taquileans are busy farming, weaving, and attending to tourists, so it has been difficult to get Taquileans to staff the office all day, every day, as required by a travel agency, since workers in the office are volunteers serving rotative turns. Taquilean students in Puno such as Juana Marca are helping, as can be seen in figure 38.

Another strategy to attempt recapturing more control of tourism has been instituted by a handful of younger Taquileans (in their twenties and thirties), who are literate in Spanish and can speak a bit of other languages. They have started to work with a few sympathetic international ecotourism agencies, guiding prearranged groups around the island. Taquileans say they are seeking relationships with alternative tour agencies, similar to alternative trade organizations (ATOs) that return a greater percentage of profits to local people. Some of the Taquilean families whose children were studying in Puno in 2002 say that their children are considering working in tourism, "for the island." Other strategies include increasing literacy, developing a presence on the Internet, expanding transnational contacts, and hosting special tourists, such as students in international education programs.

As gender roles on Taquile are changing and young Taquilean women are less shy, it appears that these new guides and tourism workers increasingly will include both men and women, like Juana Marca, one of two Taquileans working at the community's Puno tour agency office in 2002.

POSITIVE IMPACTS OF TOURISM FOR TAQUILEANS

On Taquile, despite intense individual and family competitiveness, the islanders were generally able to successfully submerge their differences enough to use their strong communal organizational skills to obtain benefits from tourism. Compared to other communities and projects worldwide, Taquile's growing tourist industry has been and remains strikingly equitable. Mitchell and Reid's study (2001) found a high level of integration on Taquile and reported an exceptionally high degree of community planning and management of tourism.

Taquileans, mostly working on their own, with minimum assistance from outsiders at certain moments, developed the core of their community-control model of tourism during a scant two-year period (1976–1978). This brought them an increase in cash income along with increased dependence on the cash economy for expenses such as boat parts and food for tourists (ibid.: 127).

Yet, despite their quick responsiveness to a market opportunity and their subsequent willingness to experiment with technology and cultural practices, Taquileans have been remarkably conservative in accepting changes in their annual fiesta cycle, in their daily dress, and in their personal lives. Their strong traditions are why Taquileans have been able to manage changing markets. Taquileans can fall back on their cultural roots, or creatively deploy them as needed to make sense of their work in changing circumstances, in ways similar to what Jeffrey Cohen (personal communication, 2003) and June Nash (1993: 2) found for Mesoamerican indigenous crafts producers. Taquilean control over all tourist enterprises on the island still makes them a model for other low-income communities, although their experience since the mid-1990s is more of a cautionary tale as their model has had serious problems withstanding the onslaught from outside tour agencies.

The economic and social benefits, as well as costs, of tourism are complex and vary according to time, the situation of individuals (in terms of gender, socioeconomic status, and generation), and distance from Taquile's urbanizing center. However, Mitchell and Reid found that 89 percent of Taquile's families report some benefit from tourism, almost all are members of the island's cooperative store (there were 336 members in 2002), and almost all belong to one (or more) boat groups (ibid.: 130). Beyond increased income, benefits include the chance to learn Spanish, to become literate, to interact with outsiders, to travel nationally and internationally, as well as to acquire increased prestige, recognition, and self-confidence.

Income from tourism has led to improved infrastructure: new roads, an expanded paved plaza, new buildings, and modernized houses with outhouses (though the island still does not have sanitation or running water). Compared to the Taquile I first saw in 1976, the island appears prosperous, and most people appear to be in better health, taller and less gaunt. Nevertheless, when contrasted to Peru's GNP per capita, Taquileans are still poor, though doing better overall than their immediate neighbors.

Without the IAF grant, early textile sales, and the tourist development they made possible, many more people would have had to migrate and look for work elsewhere. In contrast, unlike most other parts of the world, in Taquile migrants can actually return to live on the island.

Increased boat traffic meant that every family on the island had access to inexpensive, faster, and generally safer transportation, which substantially improved trade and communications with the mainland. It also provided a new source of personal income and "on-the-job" learning. The three crewmembers needed for each round trip to Puno received payment, at least in theory if not always in practice. New boats meant a demand for hulls and fittings, produced by the island's growing number of boat builders. In the first five years of motorboat operation, crewmembers acquired valuable skills in engine repair and maintenance, though sometimes at the expense of tourists and islanders when they fixed mechanical breakdowns in the middle of Lake Titicaca. Taquilean boat builders developed a well-deserved reputation for excellence and in 2002 were sought out by people all around the Peruvian side of the lake to build boats. They have accomplished all of this using only hand tools, but they long for generators and electric equipment.

While some impacts of tourism are decidedly positive, and others negative, some consequences have both positive and negative aspects. For example, while increasing income may be positive, it also can increase dependence on outsiders and make low-income people more vulnerable to downturns in the economy. Clearly an increased presence of outsiders in a community can also have positive and negative consequences — bringing new ideas and skills on the one hand, while potentially increasing exploitation on the other. In Taquile's case, perhaps the clearest example of both positive and negative impacts of tourism can be found in examining its impact on identity and dress.

Taquileans generally wear their own dress, unlike most rural people in highland Peru and in the *altiplano* of Peru and Bolivia, who increasingly wear manufactured clothing (though in ethnically specific styles). Men often wear cosmopolitan-style shirts and pants at home, changing into Taquilean dress for public meetings (sort of like dressing up to go to work). This may be because they prefer Taquilean dress, or because tourism is reinforcing the imperative to wear their clothing, both positively in terms of pride in the value of their dress and negatively in terms of the "need" to appear Taquilean in tourist contexts. Simply put, tourists expect Taquileans to conform to their expectations about how the islanders should look, based on either generalized images about highland Indians or specific images of the island represented on the Internet, in tourist brochures, and at hotels. Similarly, tourists who lodge in Taquilean homes prefer handmade ceramic dishes to plastic. This may mean that the islanders buy handmade dishes for tourists, while using plastic ones themselves. At this point handmade ceramic bowls in the Puno area are still cheaper than plastic ones, but ceramics break more easily, so I suspect that indeed Taquileans may find that their tastes increasingly contradict those of tourists.

Taquileans repeatedly told me that their increased regional, national, and international recognition has improved their treatment by Peruvians who consider themselves *mestizo* or white (*blanco*). During the late 1970s when I lived on Taquile, and during the 1980s when I visited regularly, Indians generally were treated with contempt or at best with condescension (though there always were exceptions, such as people in Puno who suggested an exhibit of Taquilean textiles at the Municipal Library in 1977). Taquileans were not allowed past the front door of Puno hotels, even when they had appointments, except in a few hotels run by expatriates. In restaurants, Taquileans were seated in the worst places and received poor service. The same was true in banks or any other public locale, whether a government office or a store. When I accompanied Taquileans, staff in offices, hotels, or restaurants always talked to me, not to the Taquileans.

Their experience back in 1978 in accessing the funds transferred to them by the IAF through a Puno bank reflects much of the deepseated racism and mistreatment they experienced. They repeatedly had to "prove" to the bank officials that they were the designated authorities and the true intended recipients of the rather large sum of dollars. It seemed beyond most officials' comprehension that Taquileans, whom they saw as backward and ignorant Indians, should receive so much money. Nonetheless, eventually the money was disbursed, though it cost Taquileans considerable time and expense.

By Taquilean accounts, things have changed. In Puno, they no longer regularly are chased out of hotels or restaurants, perhaps because of their international prestige, or perhaps because tourism-related businesses feel that Taquileans add to the ambience and "color." For example, a Puno hotel, run by an expatriate European, prominently displays a photo of a Taquilean in its lobby. That is another form of exploitation, but Taquileans certainly prefer it to being treated, as they say, "like dogs." Without much difficulty, they can now purchase materials such as boat parts and wood, transact busi-

ness in Western Union, banks, or Internet cafés, and even send Taquilean kids to high school.

I believe the baseline difference is money. Taquileans were poor
Indians. Now they're not so poor, and represent the possibility of
more wealth because of their status as a tourist attraction. However,
their success has also generated *envidia* (envy) both on and off the island because tourism has accentuated status differences on the island, as well as competition with other *runa* communities.

Taquileans have become the poster children for successful Indians
in Peru. Organizations on opposing sides of Peru's political spectrum
have used Taquile as a staging ground to try to gain political capital, though Taquileans continue to be reluctant to join any political
parties.

Over twenty-five years, I have seen significant changes in how Taquileans, and especially young people, behave outside their communities. Early on, I preferred visiting *runa* friends in their homes and
communities because they acted so differently there than in towns
and cities. In town, they transformed themselves from confident
and competent people into people I hardly recognized: passive, almost cringing. The increased ability of Taquileans to not conform to
stereotypical submissive behavior is one limited but important consequence of their success in managing tourism to their island.

NEGATIVE IMPACTS OF TOURISM FOR TAQUILE

"Modernization" and tourism have not brought equal benefits to
all Taquileans. The poorest Taquileans could not afford to upgrade
their homes enough to lodge visitors, nor could they spare an extra
person to await tourists registering at Taquile's mid-island check-
point for an overnight stay, and thus they have not been able to gain
income from lodging visitors and selling textiles to them. The Peruvian anthropologist José Matos Mar noted that differences between
well-off, average, and poor Taquileans in 1950 were based on access
to land and labor (Matos Mar 1951a, 1951b, 1960, 1964). Now these divisions are based on the commercialization of textiles, development
of new enterprises, and, not surprisingly, transnational contacts.

With new economic opportunities, social stratification has increased. Even by 1983, when I wrote my M.A. thesis, it was clear that
restaurant and storeowners, some individual boat owners, and textile

middlemen, all of whom come from wealthier families, had increased their incomes more than their neighbors. Mitchell and Reid found that 10 percent of the island's population made US$1000 or more from tourism, while most of the adult population made US$400 or less (2001: 130).

At the beginnings of tourism, some of the same wealthier people held important positions in the committees overseeing grants and tourism services. From 1979 to 1981, many islanders complained that elite members of the tourism and boat committees monopolized both knowledge and funds from the island's first foundation grant.

The problem was solved through special elections that put new leaders in place that ensured more equitable distribution of benefits. Nonetheless, as the new elites continued to prosper, their needs and opportunities tended to diverge from the rest of the community. Rudi Colloredo-Mansfeld explores a more advanced but related process in Otavalo, Ecuador, also based on wealth from selling textiles, which has led to what he calls a "native leisure class" (Colloredo-Mansfeld 1999). In Taquile, owners of restaurants and boats captured 74 percent of all tourism income on Taquile (Mitchell and Reid 2001: 130).

Even though the number of tourists staying overnight is declining as a percentage of total visitors, most tourists eat at least one meal on Taquile, making restaurants the island's current most-lucrative enterprise. Through the mid-1990s, most boats were owned by associations composed of many families, in contrast to restaurants, owned by nuclear or, sometimes, extended families. Once expenses have been met, any restaurant profits are divided among a small number of people, who thus receive higher shares, though running a restaurant is a far more time-consuming business than taking turns to run a boat and other community enterprises, such as the handicrafts cooperative store. Mitchell and Reid note that "certain families earn more than others and there is a growing disregard for local customs and reciprocal sharing systems" (ibid.: 131).

Some Taquileans are constructing larger buildings that can house small tourist groups. This has the obvious advantage of keeping a group together, and thus increasing income. However, this new system clearly places less-well-off islanders at a disadvantage as they cannot afford to build and equip enlarged housing, and the system will most likely exacerbate growing class divisions.

As wealth increases, communal institutions appear to be declining, as more wealthy Taquileans say they are "too busy" to attend assemblies, serve rotative turns, and otherwise participate in community activities. This breakdown in the social fabric is especially critical since Taquile's ability to overcome individual and family differences to act collectively has been key to their impressive social gains. Mitchell and Reid conclude that "community solidarity has declined in recent years due to a trend towards individualism, consumerism and globalization" (ibid.: 134). They also note that this has impacted communal ownership as well; presently only four boats are still considered cooperative (ibid.: 130).

Tourism on Taquile suffers from the classic problem of "leakage." The vast majority of money made in tourism does not go to the source destination, as numerous studies of tourism attest (Gmelch 2004: 10). Furthermore, an increasing percentage of the inputs for restaurant meals (soft drinks, beer, trout, oil for frying, flour, etc.), as well as construction materials for building or improving a restaurant, must be bought off-island. These are common problems in regions that experience mass tourism, but they are exacerbated in impoverished regions and, especially, on islands. Mitchell and Reid roughly estimate that less than 10 percent of all income from tourism to Taquile actually stays on the island (2001: 132).

The presence of tourists seems to require Taquileans to "freeze" their culture to conform to visitor expectations. Communities involved in ethnic tourism may cease to "evolve naturally" (MacCannell 1992: 178) since they come to think of themselves as representatives of something — of Incas, of Indians, of the authentic Peru — rather than as people. Every decision that was previously determined by other criteria now has potential economic repercussions. Virtually every aspect of daily life is potentially commodified. "The tourist requirement that a group internalize an 'authentic' ethnic identity, even if the promoted image is widely held to be a positive one, is no less a constraint than the earlier form of negative ethnic stereotyping" (ibid.: 179).

Income from tourism has provided a material support for continuing textile traditions that probably would have vanished when Taquileans migrated outside the community for work, but it has also created pressures to weave more quickly and produce work of lower quality for the market. At peak times, Taquileans bought textiles from nearby Amantani and marketed them as Taquilean. Some Taquileans have become so busy with tourism-related businesses that they are producing few textiles, but this probably would have occurred even without tourism, for they would have had to migrate off-island to make ends meet.

Other negative aspects of tourism include environmental degradation, increased garbage, the sale of the community's antique textiles and artifacts, theft, prostitutes arriving from the mainland (during a brief period in the late 1970s), begging by Taquilean children, and crop damage by tourists tramping through fields. Non-Taquilean guides as well as tourists are accused of improper behavior, especially drunkenness. Residents in tourist regions understandably tire of guests, especially those who must be attended to year round, and this too has strained Taquileans' traditional and well-known hospitality.

Tourism has increased tensions between the generations. This process is one that is undergone in every community where the younger generation attains more education and greater ability to speak the dominant language of the country than their parents, but the rapid arrival and intensity of tourism on Taquile has served to exacerbate the process. However, since most Andean peasants need to migrate away from their rural homes to obtain education and employment, it may be that tourism opportunities on Taquile, which allow at least some young people to study and work on the island, may mitigate some of the distance between generations.

In 1983, I felt comfortable asserting that the longstanding Andean rules of social behavior appear to have largely functioned to regulate individualism and competition, and it is true that Taquile continues to distribute economic benefits with remarkable equity. Without question, however, there is a widening gap between Taquilean verbalized behavior that favors a communal ethos of participation, management, and distribution of benefits and actual behavior that increasingly favors certain families and individuals.

IMPACT ON WOMEN

While the gender of lower-class *mestizas* (the erotic *chola*) is foregrounded in government tourist brochures, the discourse of tourism in communities such as Taquile subordinates gender to race, since the primary textual and visual message is the possibility of seeing Indians, not female Indians in particular.

I contend that overall men on Taquile have benefited more from tourism than women (Zorn 1983). When tourism went into full swing by the late 1970s, Taquilean men interacted with tourists more extensively, since men already had the role of dealing with outsiders and because more men, though still very few, spoke Spanish. Monolingual Taquilean women took turns guiding registered guests to homes and in the evenings served meals, but these interactions were far more limited. Women initially earned more than men from selling textiles to tourists, but traditional women's textiles take much longer to make, reducing the overall difference in earnings.

The gendered difference in benefits has been far more social than economic, which has implications for prestige, political power, and status. In keeping with Taquile's "traditional" pattern of public shyness and limited speech for women and of elected male authorities, Taquilean men occupied leadership positions in the new tourism enterprises. Some women were happy to avoid the additional burdens of active participation, but others told me that they, too, wanted to travel, improve their Spanish, learn how to read and write, and handle foreign currency exchange. Certainly only a small percentage of Taquileans have traveled abroad, but the composition of these groups, 75 percent men and 25 percent women, has always favored men.

By 2002, more families were sending their daughters to school than before; since the community finally has a high school, more girls can study on the island. A few are studying in Puno, and probably before too long, Taquileans of both sexes will manage to attend college in Puno or Lima. Taquilean women in their twenties and thirties are more publicly assertive, traveling regularly back and forth to Puno, and increasingly participate in the private and public aspects of tourism. In 2002, I saw women taking passengers' names on boats, and I was given a photograph of my former weaving teacher, Alejandrina Huatta, operating a motorboat out on the lake. Younger Taquilean women told me they were less "afraid" of talking in public. However, interactions with public agencies still generally occur among men, since male officials expect to deal with male Taquileans. Most recently, women have opened businesses on the island (shops and restaurants), which they run with their families' help.

While greater benefits have accrued to men, tourism has helped Taquilean women increase their options. The problem, however, is that the benefits of tourism are declining, so while women increasingly are able to take advantage of the new opportunities, these are steadily decreasing.

KEY FACTORS IN TAQUILE'S SUCCESS

Seven factors have been key to the successful development of tourism in Taquile. First, the island's geography has played a crucial role. The community is beautiful. More importantly, being an island has contributed to the preservation of Taquile's customs and, for at least the first decade of tourism, made it possible for Taquileans to have a near monopoly on transportation and so control access to the island.

Equally important is the fact that Taquileans have title to their land. Taquileans who considered selling land to outsiders for hotels were told that if they did so, they would be expelled from the community and thus lose their land-owning rights.

Third, strong communal organizations are essential in all successful community development efforts. Taquileans have preserved "Andean" forms of collective labor and social organizations, which they have effectively mobilized in taking advantage of opportunities presented by tourism.

Additionally, an expanding world trend toward adventure tourism has served Taquile well. The island's mention in a major travel guide coincided with an increase in "off the beaten track" tourism — for which Taquile is ideally suited. Its appeal is to adventurous, typically young travelers not deterred by "primitive" accommodations that lack typical Western conveniences.

Fifth, prior experience marketing handwoven cloth, which provided both income and capital, had two consequences: tourists were attracted to the island because they could buy the high-quality textiles there, and Taquileans had a ready source of cash that made possible improvements in tourist infrastructure at key moments. Most important was the capital to fund boat construction and the purchases of used motors.

Also key was the preservation of cultural practices that other communities had abandoned, including house building, road paving, weaving, music and dance, and rituals. These are an important draw for tourists seeking an "unspoiled" Andean experience.

Finally, there was an element of luck and serendipity. Taquile received a positive notice in an important guide at the very time backpacking tourism took off. Healy (2001: 416) lists this serendipity factor as one of seventeen that contribute to strong grassroots development projects.

6 CONCLUSION WEAVING A FUTURE?

In this chapter, I interweave tourism, race and identity, cloth and commoditization, and gender into a finished fabric. I begin with the meeting that took place during the winter of 2002, between officials from private business associations, Peruvian government agencies, and Taquilean officials.

TOURISM, ROOFS, AND TOURIST VILLAGES

When I visited Taquile in late July 2002, islanders were eager to tell me about a big meeting that had recently taken place on Esteves Island, location of a pricey government-built tourist resort near Puno. It was attended by representatives of all of the important players in Puno tourism: the Ministry of Industry, Tourism, and Commerce (MITINCI), the Captaincy of the Puno port (the Puno harbormaster's office), CTAR — Puno (the Puno region government office), the National Institute of Culture (INC), the Tourism Police (Policia de Turismo), and the president of APAVIT (the Peruvian Association of Travel Agencies). In preparation, Taquileans had elected (yet another) committee, called the Tourism Committee (Comité de Turismo), in an assembly like the one shown in Figure 39. The officers (all men) were a combination of the usual older leaders in their fifties and younger men.[1]

The goal of the Esteves meeting was to reach an accord that would address Taquile's ongoing problems with outside tour agencies and their guides. The outside agencies and government offices are concerned about "changes" in Taquile such as modernization of homes and increasing urbanization, which they unanimously feel were "detracting from" the quality of the "Taquile experience." They voiced concern about the appearance of the island, its homes, and the residents themselves, as well as the infrastructure (latrines, lodging,

39. *Taquileans at their Sunday community assembly. Today plaza buildings have tin roofs and multiple stories. Authorities are in the center, where Juan Cutipa (right, Western dress), visiting from a Puno organization, records the minutes in the community's* Libro de Actas, *at a time when few Taquileans were comfortably literate. Most women sit (left); men stand. 1981.*

food). These issues potentially create problems for the department of Puno, which sorely needs income and relies on tourism, however poorly executed, as a primary source of funds. Any tourist dissatisfaction could result in decreased tourism to Puno, since Taquile is, at present, the primary draw for tourists to Puno.

No matter what the long-term outcome of the gathering, such a meeting, of big-shot *mestizos* and Taquileans, would never have taken place even ten years earlier. Twenty years ago, it would have been unthinkable. Examining the meeting provides an excellent opportunity to consider some of the concerns about tourism first raised in the introduction.

For the islanders, their efforts to regain control and operation of transportation to and from the island is key, because from this most of the other conflicts stem, including profit-taking, scheduling, use of the docks and their maintenance, and regulation of guides. Some underlying issues — power, modernity versus tradition, and conflict over money — frequently became explicit. Other issues — textiles, gender, and race — were not discussed, though the issue of race, typically framed as ethnic identity, surely was present.

A paradox at the heart of contemporary ethnic tourism concerns tourist desires to see "traditional" villages, of "millennial" or "tribal" people, presumably living "untouched by the modern world." This is at the same time that mass tourism (unlike earlier "hippie backpacker" tourism), as well as health authorities, and in Taquile's case the islanders themselves increasingly demand modern infrastructure, for health, sanitation, electricity, and telephone service.

These conflicts arise, in distinctive forms, throughout the world. Should my little city of Oviedo, next to Orlando, widen a thoroughfare, thereby destroying its tiny downtown, or should it leave the road — and ever-growing congestion — as is? Should my city follow New Urbanism and build a town center, perhaps as charming as Taquile's, or at least one in New England, or should it continue giving permits to yet more subdivisions and strip malls? In our case, no outside agencies are pushing us to dress or build houses like those of Oviedo residents in the 1880s or even the 1960s. On Taquile, however, these kinds of debates crystallize issues concerning tradition, modernity, tourism, identity, and, though no one says it, race. When I arrived on Taquile in July 2002, I expected to hear about conflicts with outside tour agencies, but a lot of what I heard about was — roofs.

Taquileans told me that they had signed an agreement (*convenio*) to return to thatching their homes, though thatch is far more time-consuming to repair and replace than the manufactured corrugated iron roofs (*calamina*) that Taquileans adopted in the 1980s with income from tourism. Taquileans compromised initially by agreeing to paint the metal roofs red, so that from a distance they would look more like the colonial-style red-tiled roofs in Cusco (not typical of Puno).

Taquileans realize that the tourists probably preferred thatch houses, rather than newer looking buildings with cement facades, roofed with *calamina*. We joked about how they might need to build houses near the central plaza for the tourists that looked like "old" Taquilean homes. Maybe I would return in ten years and find the tourists living in old-style Taquilean houses, and Taquileans living in modern homes.

To complicate matters, for three years there had been a shortage of straw for thatch because of crop failure, and the Taquileans were considering buying reeds from the Urus that they could use to thatch their homes. Would they now need to earn money to buy thatch so that their homes could look like they used to when they participated in a primarily self-sufficient barter economy? That was a perfect example of postmodern irony, but the Taquileans weren't laughing.

I felt I was watching the beginning of an artificially constructed "tourist village" (cf. Tilley 1997). I was left with the nagging feeling that the only people benefiting from this would be, once again, the outside tour agencies and Peruvian officials who could pass off totora-reed thatched homes as examples of Taquile, "the island that time forgot."

I would like to write that as a result of that meeting, Taquileans were able to broker an arrangement between all parties so that island residents would regain increased control of tourism, receive money owed them for back tourist fees, and control tour guides. Unfortunately, according to an e-mail from Juan Quispe in November 2003, little had changed and conflicts continued. Taquileans remained alternately frustrated and hopeful.

RACE AND IDENTITY
People who live in thatch-roof homes in Peru are poor and, for the most part, Indian, and thus insisting on a certain "look" is to insist that Taquileans conform to stereotypes about Indians. There remain a plethora of reasons to find value in being *mestizo* rather than Indian in the Andes, even if groups such as the Taquileans have strategically deployed indigenous identity to their advantage. There are centuries of reasons why people considered Indian in Peru and neighboring Andean countries become "not-Indian" or, in this century, what the anthropologist Marisol de la Cadena reports as "indigenous mestizos" (2000). With exceptions, both the dominant class and the dominated agree that "Indians" should end, though for opposite reasons — the dominators because they see Indians as a brake on modernization and development (Albó 1999) and the dominated because

being "Indian" is to be not only the poorest but also the most discriminated against.

The voluminous and rich literature on race and ethnicity in the Andes has examined multiple aspects of the social construction of the status of Indian, as evaluated etically in terms of class and cultural beliefs and practices and, to a lesser degree, emically in terms of notion of personhood and self (Canessa 1998). While Indian status is backgrounded in a racially homogeneous community such as Taquile,[2] conflicts over social roles are fought in the most intimate spaces of people's homes and hearths.

Social status may be examined at any given moment as constitutive or at least imbricated in virtually any given action or belief but, for most people, race and ethnicity are not always considered consciously every minute. Taquileans at home sometimes think about what they do in terms of their indianness, but sometimes they do not. Given the prevailing racism in Peru, the opposite occurs when outside the community—virtually every gesture and action is interpreted and framed in terms of social identity, of being Indian, or *mestizo*, or white.

Tourism has changed the in-community/out-community consciousness of race by potentially foregrounding race on a minute-by-minute basis. Tourists and the tourism industry add more ideas and values about indianness, in addition to those of local people, regional *mestizos*, and national whites. This affects how Andeans imagine, embody, perform, and negotiate being "Indian," as tourists seek authenticity in the homes, acts, and bodies of Indians. Race, in particular indigeneity, is both foregrounded and erased in tourism. Representations of indianness are central to the attractiveness of the island of Taquile as a tourist site, and indeed of tourism to Peru and South America. Tourist brochures about the islands in Lake Titicaca code race through expressions such as "descendants of the Incas." Postcards show people wearing ethnic dress, performing ceremonies, dancing, or doing craftwork such as spinning. Tourism also leads indigenous communities into increased interactions with regional, national, and international agencies and institutions, both governmental and private, each with their own official and unofficial imaginings of indianness. Scholarship by non-Taquileans, including my writ-

40. *A tourist looks at publications, in many languages, about Taquile (including several by the author). They are displayed in the entrance of Taquile's museum. July 2002.*

ings, add additional layers of interpretations, made material in publications about Taquile (including mine), which are displayed in the plaza's museum (fig. 40).

Simultaneously, Peruvian government documents code Indians as peasants, referring to Taquile in terms of its hard-won status as an officially recognized peasant community (Comunidad Campesina Reconocida), erasing their status as Indians by using the term "peasant," which officially replaced "Indian" during the late 1960s military populist government of Velasco Alvarado. In the eyes of the Peruvian government, Taquile is one of many peasant communities fighting for its slice of Peru's tiny pie. However, as Taquile's fame has grown, it has occupied an increasingly prominent position in the Peruvian nation, becoming an icon of Peruvian indianness, a status recognized by former President Fujimori's helicopter visit to Taquile during his 2001 presidential election campaign.

The success of Taquile as a tourist destination has led Taquileans to a conundrum of ethnic and racial identity. Simply put, it has been negative to be Indian in Peru since the Conquest, but Taquileans' identity as Indian is a key component of their success with tourism. Thanks to tourism and other broader changes in Peru, there are now some small spaces where an Indian identity can potentially be positive in a way almost impossible even fifty years ago. In Bolivia and Ecuador, indianist parties and, perhaps more significantly, a few mainstream parties have successfully elected ethnically identified Indians to local, regional, and national office (Albó 2002). During a 2002 visit to the United States, Juan Quispe gave a presentation about Taquile at the Peruvian Embassy in Washington, D.C. Twenty years ago it was almost impossible to imagine such an event—a self-identified *runa*, wearing ethnic dress and speaking in flawless Spanish, talking about Taquile in the space that represents Peru in the powerful United States. Taquileans had not traveled abroad, and it was almost inconceivable that the Peruvian embassy would sponsor a formal talk by a *runa*. Many Taquileans have choices that they never did before. However, the question comes up: Indian on whose terms—their own, the government's, or tourists'?

WILL THERE STILL BE ANDEAN CLOTH IN THE TWENTY-FIRST CENTURY?

By 2002, I could see clearly that the importance of cloth in southern highland Peru and Bolivia was declining in a way that I stubbornly argued was not the case even half a decade earlier. (This is at the same time that self-identified Indian people throughout the Andean region increasingly wore ethnic dress in political mobilizations.) In earlier work, I saw the glass of water as "half full," even though the quality of handspinning and weaving steadily declined as people made poorer-quality textiles for buyers who wanted inexpensive souvenirs. I predicted that in the twenty-first century, Andeans might become like the Navajo people in the United States, among whom only a small number of people still weave. These few can do so because a market exists that will pay prices high enough to allow them to earn a living.

In the Andes, I considered the use of factory-spun (including synthetic) yarns as valuable because they allowed young weavers to weave more than before (Zorn 1995, 1999). In northern Potosí, Bolivia, I saw the young weavers' delight in the bright neon colors of factory-spun yarns that allowed them a palette otherwise impossible.

I understood increasing naturalistic and representational imagery as indicative of new aesthetic and technical challenges for a young generation of weavers who wanted to differentiate their work from that of their mothers, combined with intellectual pleasure in solving technical problems posed by learning different weave structures outside ethnic group boundaries.

I saw change as positive, while nevertheless being concerned about the loss of technical skills and symbolic meanings linked to preparing thread and weaving certain textiles. Who was I, after all, to urge weavers to spend months preparing yarns when they no longer had access to fleece, when chemical dyes ran on first washing, and a new generation of weavers and recipients (boyfriends and husbands) wanted modern weavings? My own sense of nostalgia for the lost craft traditions of my now-deceased grandmother, who fled Eastern Europe in the early part of the twentieth century, or knitting and crocheting learned from my mother, pushed me to worry about the loss of Andean textile traditions. However, I certainly was aware that, after all, it was not my tradition that was being lost. Despite my earlier collaboration with Taquileans on development projects, I probably could do no more than pose the problem as I sat with women friends on the island pondering whether their daughters should go to school or to herd. The first might let them become at least minimally literate. The latter would let them take care of their families' herds and weave beautiful textiles, but would leave them "blind" (*ñawsa*, illiterate) in contemporary Andean Quechua terms. That is, they confronted the dilemma between modernity and tradition. Which face of their two-sided belts would they choose to show, the face of modernity or the face of tradition?

Nevertheless, my 2002 trip shocked me because it appeared as if Andean weaving had, virtually, stopped. Aside from the laudable CTTC project in Cusco, few people wove, and what they did weave was coarse and poor quality.[3] I saw that weaving on the Bolivian side of the *altiplano* near La Paz had almost ended, since hundreds of thousands of Aymara-speakers had fled their rural villages for the lure of El Alto and La Paz. Middle-aged women I spoke with still possessed the technical, aesthetic, and conceptual knowledge of cloth but had neither the materials nor the time to create textiles, and their daughters, living in the capital, had even less time (and materials) to do so.[4]

During our time on Taquile, my colleague Nancy Rosoff and I initially disagreed about the current state of weaving. Perhaps fearing that little remained, I was pleased at what I saw, or chose to emphasize. In contrast, she saw people wearing textiles woven with bright synthetics and piles of loosely woven tourist items in the community store, leading her to conclude that weaving was no longer important. Instead I celebrated the tightly woven design-filled belts, coca leaf purses, and caps that most men wore, and the expertly handwoven shawls, mantles, and clothing that islanders still favored.

However, I understood Rosoff's perspective. While Taquileans still are producing high-quality weaving for their own use, they increasingly use factory-spun wool or synthetic-fiber yarns, due to lack of fleece, lower cost, and convenience. Rosoff needed to buy fine textiles handspun and handwoven from natural materials, especially alpaca, since to do otherwise was to risk rejection of the acquisitions by the Brooklyn Museum. The art market for Andean ethnic textiles favors antique objects, not recently woven ones, and Rosoff's task was hard enough without buying textiles made from kitschy-looking synthetics. We were, in short, part of how museums regulate the commodity status of objects (Phillips and Steiner, eds. 1999).

In a remarkably short time period, cloth on Taquile has gone from an object with use and exchange value that was a central focus of islanders' attention to a commodity that was a source of newfound wealth. During the 1970s and 1980s when textiles were produced both for use and for sale, they embodied two different systems of value. But as textiles moved more toward becoming handicrafts for sale (*artesanía*), people looked for ways to reduce production time. They also found other less time–consuming ways to increase income, and some or many have stopped making so many textiles. When people make textiles to sell, rather than for themselves and for their loved ones, it is not surprising that they would stop weaving when a better paying alternative can be found.

The issue, as so many have pointed out, is that making cloth may be humankind's oldest material art, but it also is one of the most labor-intensive, especially in the forms developed in the Andes. It takes a great deal of money to pay someone for all the hours that go into making a fine weaving, and crafts made by poor artisans typically sell for low prices, thus making crafts generally more suitable as an important supplement to other forms of subsistence, rather than the primary source of income. Here again, Otavalo, Ecuador, is a significant exception, as some Otavalos have been so successful marketing their textiles that crafts have provided a viable alternative to farming (Meisch 2002). Michael Chibnik (2003) found that Oaxacan wood carvers can succeed in the market, but that only the wealthy families could do so, and only as long as market demand existed.

At the beginnings of tourism, the money Taquileans earned from selling textiles brought in unprecedented earnings. Now there are easier ways to make money, but, equally if not more important, the recent form of mass day tourism appears to have led to a significant decline in crafts sales, despite the increased numbers of visitors compared to earlier decades. A post–September 11 plummet in travel led to decreased tourism and significantly lower textile sales for Taquileans as well as crafts producers in many parts of the world (Smith and Ellingwood 2001). Restaurants are turning out to be the only business on Taquile capable of generating profits, and then only depending on volume, since most items need to be imported.

At the end of my 2002 visit, as I rushed down Taquile's vertigo-inducing steps to reach the departing boat, Gerardo Huatta, eldest son of my *compadre* Pancho, caught up with me, puffing from running. He brought textiles for his *comadre* in Santa Fe, who had sent a gift with me. Somewhat abashed, because he had nothing for me, Gerardo said, "I don't dedicate myself very much to making crafts." He is one of Taquile's most successful restaurant owners, and I could believe that he rarely even knits caps anymore. I doubted that his sister Petrona, who also owns and runs a restaurant, has much time to weave.

GENDER

Considered by many policy makers the most traditional, and therefore "backward" group in the Andes, women emerge through their cloth as dynamic mediators between their community and the outside. As weavers, women are the key creators of powerful symbolic representations of an ideology that locates men's and women's places in the cosmos. This is particularly important since, among some *ayllus* in highland Bolivia, Andean women literally lose their public "voices" after marriage. Through cloth, Andean women also play an active role in the negotiation of "tradition" and "modernity" within their societies, a role often ascribed to men in general, and to male authorities in particular. Berlo (1991), focusing primarily on Maya women of Chiapas, Mexico, and highland Guatemala, makes a similar point, arguing that native women in the Americas, through the medium of textiles, are "agents of transformation."[5] Furthermore, women weave the Andean cloth that has been most heavily commercialized in the ethnic arts market, which means that the commercialization of ethnic cloth is likely to have a special effect on women and gender relations.[6]

Through the production of cloth, including recent changes in textile production, Taquilean women are active agents in development and play a key role in adapting to globalization. While the general consensus has been that women's status improves in some areas but declines in others with modernization and globalization (World Bank 2001), Taquilean women are playing a more prominent role in public life, based in part on their ability to earn more from the sale of certain textiles than do men.

Nearly all Taquileans share certain experiences of tourism, but in important ways women and men, based partly on economic status, have experienced tourism differently. Overall, control and operation of tourist resources, though not of benefits, has been dominated by male (Taquilean) intermediaries, working through male-dominated organizations. Cash from textile sales has provided women with a new source of power in their homes and their community, changing women's roles and status in myriad ways. However, in this generation, despite increased economic power, women do not yet lead collective enterprises and rarely interact with outside agencies. Nevertheless, a few Taquilean women have opened tourist-related businesses on the island (stores and restaurants), which they run with their families, and I predict that more women will do so in the future. Continued cash income combined with substantial increases in girls' education heralds an even more public role for Taquilean women in the future.

Taquilean women and men have responded in distinctive gen-

dered ways to the battle for control of transportation, with men acting through government agencies and NGOs and women acting directly—even staging a strike to prevent non-Taquilean boats from
docking. Women's and men's consistently different responses can be
understood, in part, as deriving from historical experiences of gendered relations with the Peruvian nation-state, as well as from the experience of tourism. Their responses reveal their differing attitudes
and beliefs about the Peruvian nation.

Indigenous women of Taquile clearly had little confidence that
the Peruvian government would help them in their battle to control transportation, and therefore turned to direct action, perhaps
bolstered by popularized models of fierce *cholas* and valiant indigenous women such as Micaela Bastidas, heroine of the 1780–1781 re-
volt against Spanish oppressors. The indigenous men of Taquile, who
have a long history of using typical patron-client personalistic politics to negotiate with regional and national authorities, expected they
could receive assistance from the Peruvian nation. While such efforts
brought benefits in the 1970s and 1980s, they were close to useless in
the 1990s and early twenty-first-century neoliberal Peru.

Both the sale of textiles and tourism have significantly impacted
gender relations on Taquile. As women obtained money and increased interactions with outsiders through tourists, they began to
participate in public affairs, travel abroad, and study in schools.
Women in families who left Taquile in the mid-twentieth century for
Lima (Matos 1986) experienced these changes decades earlier, but
they were very few in number. Now, such women are increasing, even
though more women than men still are monolingual Quechua speakers or illiterate.

The paths that women will take on Taquile are constrained by social status, since increasing income on Taquile has led to increased
social differentiation. As more Taquilean women assume increased
public roles, their efforts to better their lives and the lives of their
families will increasingly intersect with regional, national, and international constraints on the status of poor people, peasants, Indians,
and women within Peru.

For residents of Taquile, as for many low-income people worldwide, improving their material situation is considered in large measure to be linked to improving their access to formal education. For

all the benefits that education can bring, as Taquileans attend school and weave less, one of their challenges will be to carve out power in new areas, as so many Peruvian women have been struggling to do.

When a friend visited Taquile a few months before my 2002 visit, she brought back photos to show me how Taquile has changed. I could not identify the smiling, slender young Taquilean woman in one photo, posed in front of the museum's display case, holding a squirming baby bundled in her elaborately tasseled head shawl and standing next to a serious-looking slender young man, who wore a shirt with a designer logo and a finely knit Taquilean married-man's cap. My friend said that the young woman was looking forward to seeing me. At the Taquile museum months later, I saw this attractive young woman working behind the counter of her small shop on the plaza when I stopped in to look at postcards. She teasingly reminded me that she was Paula Quispe Cruz, "dancer and weaver" at the 1991 Smithsonian Institution Festival of American Folklife, whom I had worked with for ten intense days (Flores and Quispe 1994).

Paula represents the new generation of Taquilean women: she is a knowledgeable weaver, literate, bilingual, with experience abroad, convinced of the value of education, and making a life on Taquile. Seeing Paula again left me more optimistic about the gendered and economic changes taking place on Taquile, even though I remained concerned that eroding economic circumstances in her nation and worldwide would limit the opportunities for her and women like her.

TEXTILES AND TOURISM

Commercializing textiles has become intertwined with tourism because, despite scarcities of raw materials and time, selling textiles can produce a profit. "All" Taquileans feel that they need to wear Taquilean dress at public and communal occasions, and it appears that this also is the case when providing tourist services. It may be that those benefiting most from "modernization" and tourism are those who are weaving less. Taquileans who don't have restaurants, or live further away from the center and lodge fewer tourists, may be those most likely to continue making textiles to sell.

My prediction back in the 1970s that Andean textiles probably would take the path of Navajo cloth, with a reduced number of weavers who produce fine "art" that is well remunerated, is partly coming true. Fewer people are weaving, but few or no Andeans can yet command a high price for their cloth.

I expect to see continued differentiation in the market, though it is clear that economic privation drives people to continue to make handicrafts, as the mountains of unsold products lining the streets of Andean cities demonstrate. It remains to be seen how much the market for fine quality Andean ethnic textiles, made by living weavers, which has been developed by ASUR in Bolivia and CTTC in Peru, can expand. The challenge is to break into the art market, or extremely high-end crafts market, and persuade the buyers who pay tens of thousands of dollars for antique Andean textiles to buy contemporary masterpieces instead.

In Taquile, even though men continue to encroach upon women's traditional economic and symbolic realms, women remain at the center of the creation of new art objects and styles. A good example of this is the calendar belt, which challenges the dichotomy of tradition and modernity.

WEAVING A THIRD WAY?

Following an era of agrarian reforms, the Andean nations experienced the forceful return of "the Indian" and "indianness" at the end of the twentieth century (Albó 1999: 858). This was surprising given increased homogenization and integration of Indian communities into the nation-state and into the cash economy. By homogenization, Albó and numerous other authors mean the pressure brought by the still-prevalent belief that Indians can only obtain the benefits of modern society if they assimilate into the dominant society, that is, stop being Indian (and, at the same time, the nation-state "requires" this assimilation). In the Andean region, there has been no room for "survival for these self-designated native nations" (ibid.: 859).

Simultaneously, the dominant neoliberal economic model creates "serious crises on the local level" (ibid.), and the remedies, notably structural adjustment, cause more crises (Kohl 2002). These further "marginalize important sectors of the population, including the majority of indigenous people" (Albó 1999: 859). In the face of this marginalization, native peoples "more readily . . . look to their own traditions in search of alternative ways to survive" (ibid.). This is the "boomerang effect" of the neoliberal economic model: the more it fails at the local level, the more people who are marginalized have "reason to pursue their struggle on their own terms" (ibid.). Furthermore, "Indian citizens have no desire to lose their special way of life, and the contradictions built into the system provide good reason to affirm the advantages of their distinctive views" (ibid.).

Taquile has enjoyed certain advantages that other marginalized Indian communities have not. Its isolation, small size, and success in regaining title to community lands meant that Taquileans were spared the violence that devastated Peru during the 1980s and, overall, were less pressured to homogenize into the dominant society. Up to the 1990s, indigeneity became, through tourism, a positive social identity, at the same time that native people in Andean countries outside Peru were creating ethnic-based social and political movements. One benefit of tourism is an intangible but frequently stated pride in the value of local *costumbres* (customs). The other side of this fabric is, however, a "freezing" of practices to meet tourist expectations.

Tourism also impacted significantly on the relationship between individualism and collectivism on Taquile (and in Andean society). This delicately balanced system that has resuscitated at the end of the twentieth century, and which has helped sustain communities for thousands of years, has been altered by tourism and increasing monetization of Taquile's economy. The shift in income sources from cooperatively owned and managed boats to restaurants owned and managed by individual families has led to increased social stratification on the island. Jeffrey Cohen (1999) found that rural people in Santa Ana, Mexico, continue to develop "new ways of cooperating" and that corporateness, marked by cooperation, does not necessarily decline with increasing capitalism and personal fortune in the form of wealth. It remains to be seen on Taquile, however, whether structural factors such as localized competition in tourism-related businesses, notably restaurants, and individual and household decisions concerning what Cohen calls the framing and use of wealth, will lead to declining cooperation.

The "boom" in Taquile tourism has been followed by the sorry tale of the "bust," not in numbers of tourists, but in Taquilean loss of control. Not surprisingly, this has had negative consequences economically, socially, and psychologically. As Taquileans lose control of ownership and operation of tourist transportation, and thereby of tourism, they are increasingly changed from active agents into performing subjects. Taquile's earlier model of community control of tourism created spaces for them to practice an agency that they are losing. The Taquileans who operate boats, cook and serve meals, sell textiles, register tourists, and invite endless visitors to become godparents project agency in a way that does not occur with passive tourists brought by outside tour agencies. The change has profound implications for tourists' ideas about indianness but, more importantly, for the Taquileans' own imaginings of indianness.

The more general problem of the regulation of behavior of non-Taquileans on the island is a part of the relationship between Taquile and the Peruvian nation. (Taquileans have told me they recognize that in some cases they are competing with other poor peasants like themselves but, in general, they feel that in their own community they should control access and reap the profits.) Under neoliberalism, Taquileans can enjoy no special protection, which they and other communities coping with mass tourism require so as to realize economic benefits and also control the impact of tourism. Ironically, Taquile continues to serve as a model for community-controlled tourism to other indigenous communities, including Charazani and Coroma in Bolivia.

Globalization has led to an enormous increase in world tourism, which includes a subset of ecotourism that focuses on ethnic tourism. Ecotourists seek precisely the kind of place that Taquile was (and, to a great extent, still is): remote, beautiful, and populated by friendly native people practicing interesting customs. Local activism in controlling visits by foreigners went hand in hand with transformations in textile production, and together these played vital roles in Taquileans' struggles to not only earn income but also to assert positive aspects of Indian identity in Peru's rapidly changing political climate.

The active efforts of people from Taquile to shape their future provide an important example of agency in actively reworking the impact of larger processes at the local level, which in turn will affect these very processes at national and international levels. Taquileans made the move into the global economy in order to improve their material situation in a context that was completely disadvantageous to them and others at the lowest socio-economic levels. This context has only worsened under neoliberalism.

Albó argues that many native Andean peoples are seeking a "third approach" between that of the homogenized nation and the marginalized Indian community. They seek inclusion within the nation-state at the same time that they retain distinctive features of their ways of life. While not working in organized political movements, Taquile has been at the forefront of efforts to try to weave a future that provides them the benefits of development while minimizing the costs.

AFTERWORD TRAVELING TO TAQUILE

How can you travel to Taquile on boats captained and crewed by islanders, stay overnight (or longer), and ensure that the money you spend stays in the community? With rare exceptions (a few alternative tourism organizations work directly with Taquileans), the *only* way to do this is to book passage on a Taquilean boat at the Puno dock, not ahead of time through a travel agency or via the Internet. Trust me, it is easy to do!

Taquilean boats leave from the farthest end of the Puno dock at the end of Titicaca Avenue every morning between 8 and 9 A.M., though it's a good idea to get there about half an hour earlier. Boats from Taquile arrive at the Puno dock around 5 or 6 P.M., which makes it possible to go to the dock in the evening to book passage for the next day. Your challenge is to distinguish Taquileans and Taquilean boats from the many people who try to sell you passage as you approach the dock (or earlier, at the train station, hotel, or on the street). Some people wear Taquilean caps, and even vests, to persuade tourists they're Taquileans, but only Taquileans wear complete Taquilean outfits, and Taquilean women's dress is especially distinctive. Ask for a Taquilean boat, captained by Taquileans, and look for a boat with several islanders there.

Taquile's travel agency, depicted in figure 38, unfortunately does not operate daily. Still, stop by their office on No. 508 Titicaca Avenue on the way to the dock from the center of Puno. They might be open, and then you can be sure that your trip to Taquile from start to finish is with the people you want to visit. Thanks for supporting community-controlled tourism!

NOTES

1. INTRODUCTION: TOURISM, CLOTH, AND CULTURE

1. I have long pondered the terms I should use in English to describe the people I am writing about and have found all the possible terms dissatisfying for one reason or another. The terms "indigenous," "Indian," "indian," "native," "*runa*" (the latter a Quechua term), or "peasant" are all used in daily life and in publications for the people living on Taquile Island. All of these terms have, of course, histories of denotations and connotations, many of which reflect racial and ethnic, caste, or class discrimination. The 1968 Peruvian nationalist revolution of Juan Velasco Alvarado officially substituted the term peasant (*campesino*) for "Indian" (*indio*), but "peasant" then acquired the racist overtones that "Indian" had. While "Indian" has been revived or reclaimed on the Bolivian side of Lake Titicaca by Aymara-speaking peoples, this reversal has not been widespread in southern Peru. Some social scientists have returned to using the term "indian" (with a lowercase *i*), in part to emphasize the historical and political aspects of ethnic and racial politics in the Andes. Yet "Indian," whether capitalized or not, is a word not used by most community members to describe themselves, though this is changing among younger Taquileans. People often refer to themselves as Taquile *runa*, or "people from Taquile," and as *campo runa*, or "people from the countryside," somewhat akin to "peasant." As Ben Orlove (2002) points out, *runa* is gender-neutral, and thus a reasonable translation is "Taquile people." I use the term Taquileans since I am writing in English, but sometimes use *runa* when speaking of how Taquileans refer to themselves, or Taquileños/as, which is Spanish for "people from Taquile" and is used by Taquileans when they speak Spanish.

2. Throughout Latin America, it has long been the case that artisans also are farmers, and successful farmers often become successful crafts people (Jeffrey H. Cohen, personal communication 2003). This is documented in J. H. Cohen (1999), Colloredo-Mansfeld (1999), and Meisch (2002), but see Chibnik, who argues that Oaxacan woodcarvers are better understood as "people who pursue multiple livelihoods" (2003: 93), whether farming or wage-labor.

3. Taquileans set up this type of loom (technically a horizontal staked-out ground loom) by placing the back loom bar behind two stakes pounded into the ground (fig. 18). Taquileans visiting New York City in 1994 adapted their loom for indoor use by developing a frame with holes for pegs, which makes it

possible to set up this type of loom anywhere. On weaving technology, including loom types, see Zorn (1979, 1983, 1997a), and chapter 3.

4. As an outsider, I was intervening by encouraging the women to move to the center of the field near the textiles, but I felt I had lived long enough on Taquile to be ignored if people did not like my suggestion. I did not realize until later that some of the women who were present had woven several of the textiles that would be evaluated, which might have contributed to their reluctance to join the group.

5. The *ayllu*, a form of Andean social organization, can be translated as "family," "lineage," or "kin group"; more recently, as "rural social group" (Abercrombie 1998b), or "ethnic group." *Ayllus* have been extensively studied by Andeanists; see, for example, Abercrombie (ibid.) and Isbell (1978) among others. *Ayllus* have been somewhat perplexing to characterize, in part because Andeans apply the same term to groups at nested levels of social organization, from very small (a family of five) to very large (a rural social group of more than twenty thousand).

6. *Mestizo* is a Spanish word that during the colonial period meant people of "mixed blood," specifically racial mixing between Spaniards (whites) and Indians. *Mestizaje*, or "mixing," is conceptualized in racial terms, but the differences between Indians and whites, and by extension, Indians and *mestizos*, are cultural, not biological. People in Peru frequently say that all Peruvians are *mestizos*, but this egalitarian ideology masks social differences, including those of race. *Mestizos* are urbanized, higher-status people who generally wear Western clothing, speak Spanish, and do not consider themselves *runa*. Recent scholarship, such as Weismantel (2001), is exploring the gendered violence associated with *mestizaje*. Cadena's study of what she calls "de-Indianization" (2000: 6) shows how poor people from Cuzco, Peru, both resist and "leave room for racism to persist" (ibid.: 7) by defining themselves as non-Indians who nonetheless do not reject indigenous culture.

7. Catherine Allen's ethnographic play *Condor Qatay* (1997) presents the *qatay* (son-in-law) transformed from a *cholo* (urban Indian) driver back to an *ayllu* member. The struggle by indigenous people who seek the benefits of modernization, yet also wish to retain aspects of their culture, is one of the recurrent themes in the film *Transnational Fiesta: 1992*, by Paul Gelles and Wilton Martínez. On why the younger generation of Songo, Peru, no longer consider themselves *indios* (Indians), see the Afterword in Allen 2002.

8. Commoditization refers to the process of selling something (or someone) that previously was not exchanged for money; commodification refers to changes in meaning and values that accompany that process. Social scientists sometimes use these terms interchangeably.

9. For the "classical" definition of the commodity as something produced to be exchanged, see Marx (1977: 953–55). On recent approaches to the relationship between art and commodity, including issues of authenticity that are central to commoditized forms of production of handmade, "ethnic" arts, see the extensive collection of essays in Phillips and Steiner, eds. (1999).

10. Commercialization's potentially positive impact on local traditions has been shown in recent research on cloth in other Andean regions (Ackerman 1991; Femenías 1991, 1997, 2004; Meisch 1991, 2002; Zorn 1991, 1999) and other parts of the Americas. Rowe and Schelling (1991) summarize divergent approaches to popular culture/folklore, including those that see degeneration in all change; these authors also examine cultural production in postmodern Latin America, which they characterize as a place where postmodernity predates a modernity that never arrived.

11. Andeans have, of course, been articulated into a global market system since the sixteenth-century Spanish invasion, with varying degrees of success and failure at making the system work for them, even in some small way (Larson, Harris, and Tandeter 1995). For example, it seems quite likely that Indians in Chayanta, Bolivia, due to successful sales of wheat, were far wealthier in the late 1800s than they are now (Grieshaber 1977, cited in Platt 1982: 24). *Runa* in Taquile participated mostly in an "ethnic" subsistence economy (Harris 1987) before 1968, but primarily through seasonal migration they earned the cash required to make the all-important purchase of their community lands and to buy materials to build wooden sailboats.

12. My fieldwork on Taquile has consisted of residences of nearly a year in 1976 and in 1980–1981 and shorter stays ranging from a few days to a few weeks in 1977, 1978, 1983, 1984, 1986, 1987–1989, and 2002. I also traveled with Taquileans repeatedly to the city of Puno, as well as to Cusco and Lima. When away from the island, I stay in contact intermittently through letters delivered by travelers and, recently, through irregular e-mails and cell phone calls.

13. See the Code of Ethics of the American Anthropological Association and the Case Studies and proposed solutions on its website: http://www .aaanet.org.

14. Guillermo Pulido, a Mexican friend who traveled with me to Taquile during 1976, and I may be the "first tourists" referred to by Agustín Machaca Huatta: "It began with a pair of tourists who went periodically, they returned after a month, some went for a year to carry out studies" (Matos Mar 1986: 393). My return after a month's absence marked an important turn in my relations with Taquileans, who, to my surprise, became friendlier and more open thereafter.

15. During 1980–1981, I also helped other peasant communities in the Puno

area, including Amantani Island, Ccota, and Chichillapi, write grants; a grant I helped Taquileans write for fishing cooperatives was only partly funded.

16. My *compadre* Pancho Huatta told me that a German nurse, "Amay," who lived on Taquile for several months, had started to learn to weave.

17. Men know about female symbols, just as women know about male symbols, and, at least in the Andes, men and women know a great deal about each other's work — certainly enough to take over in a pinch, though preferably not too skillfully (to maintain gendered boundaries). This gender division of labor is shifting as indigenous Latin American women move into occupations previously held by men.

2. TAQUILE ISLAND IN LAKE TITICACA

1. This text appears in Bayle's edition of the Loyola ms. version of Murúa's *Historia del origen y geneaología real de los reyes incas del Perú* (1946). The Wellington ms. version does not contain references to any Lake Titicaca island. I am grateful to Catherine Julien, who long ago provided me with a copy of these pages from the Bayle edition, and answered my questions about Murúa's manuscripts and Lake Titicaca island names.

2. James Clifford (1988) shows how early anthropologists, notably Bronislaw Malinowski, used various literary devices to help establish the anthropologist's authority to report a truth that he had observed.

3. Infant and child mortality is very high in the *altiplano*, though Taquile fares somewhat better than average, probably due to better nutrition. By 2002, it appeared that young people were marrying at a later age.

4. Describing these pre-Conquest polities as nations, federations, or kingdoms depends, of course, on a historically situated reading of the polity's structure. I use the term "federation" (and "confederation") for my writing, but "nation" or "kingdom" when quoting from a source that uses those terms. See Choque Canqui (1993: 15–16) on the problem of using the term *reino* (kingdom), a characterization based on European monarchies, to refer to pre-Conquest Aymara polities.

5. The Aymara "kingdoms" were divided conceptually into Urqusuyu and Umasuyu, which referred to a human relationship with space (Bouysse-Cassagne 1986: 202; Choque Canqui 1993: 14).

6. *Mitmaq*, from *mit'a*, Quechua for "labor rotation," were populations moved by the Inca state, including colonists sent by the Inca to settle rebellious or far-flung areas of the Empire.

7. Knowing of female authorities in some Aymara-speaking communities, in July 2002 I asked some Taquilean men and women whether Taquile had yet

had female officeholders. Several people told me that they would not be surprised if Taquile had a *tenienta* (female governor) before long.

8. This term is an example of assigning a different meaning to a Spanish word taken into Quechua; *cesante* in Spanish means unemployed, but in Taquilean Quechua it refers to people holding high public office.

9. De la Cadena (1995) discusses the growing importance for Indians near Cusco, Peru, of knowing how to make one's way outside the community; her discussion is based on the definition of "work" and its implications for hierarchical differences between men and women.

10. The study of gendered images of *runa* males, and men, awaits research. De la Cadena (1995) argues that Indians, in general, are gendered as more "female" or "feminine," which in contemporary Peruvian Hispanic society connotes inferiority; furthermore, not only are Indians "feminized" in general, but women are "more Indian."

11. When I did long-term fieldwork, I did not have a child. My condition was, overall, pitied, but after heartfelt expression of concern, many *runa* (both men and women) asked me how I had accomplished this, desiring information about birth control.

12. The Andean colonial chronicler Guaman Poma de Ayala represents the earliest humans, who appear to wear leaves, practicing this gendered division of labor for planting.

13. Taquileans sometimes introduced me to other *runa* by saying that I ate *ch'uñu*, meaning that I accepted (even enjoyed) their food, and therefore wasn't a racist.

14. After a comment in a professional meeting by the Peruvianist anthropologist William Stein reminding me that "*mestizos* always are cast as the bad guys," I realized I had indeed unthinkingly adopted the Taquilean viewpoint. I had used the term *mestizo* in a way that was too facile, and in fact, however unintentionally, was racist in its own right.

3. THE CLOTH OF CONTEMPORARY INCAS

1. *Qumpi* (Quechua, also *qompi* and, in Spanish sources, *cumbi*) may refer to tapestry weaving or perhaps to any kind of very fine cloth; early Spanish sources are ambiguous (Phipps 1996: 155 n. 27; also Murra 1962; A. Rowe 1978; J. Rowe 1946: 242).

2. Davis may be usefully contrasted with Turner (1980), on the structures integral to meaning in Kayapo dress, and with Guss (1989). See also Rubinstein (1995); Ash and Wilson (1992), on U.S. and global fashion; Garber (1992), on cross-dressing; and Steele (1996), on fetish.

3. Probably one hundred textiles were stolen from Coroma and sold through a chain of middlemen until they reached the United States. They included pre-Inca, Inca, and early and late colonial period weavings. After Bolivian anthropologist Cristina Bubba and Coroma authorities denounced a San Francisco exhibit of colonial textiles, the United States Customs Service seized them. Eventually, the United States returned forty-eight handwoven textiles to Coroma, a landmark victory for textiles as patrimony (Bomberry 1993, 1994; Bubba et al. 1990; Healy 2001: 115; Lobo 1991). In a related case in Canada, textiles also were repatriated to Bolivia.

4. On weaving technology, see A. Rowe (1975, 1977, 1978); Zorn (1983) reviews technical literature on southern Andean textile structures, weaving techniques, and dress.

5. Some *vicuña* are raised in national projects in Peru and sheared for legal export; by the late twentieth century, several Andean communities were experimenting with using round-ups (*chaku*) rather than slaughter to obtain wool, which was a sustainable Inca period practice (FWS [U.S. Fish and Wildlife Service] n.d.).

6. The sexual division of labor in cloth production varies regionally. In central and southern Peru and in Bolivia women weave plain and patterned cloth on the Andean loom, and men weave yardage on the European-type loom. In Cusco, both women and men in some communities weave patterned cloth on a backstrap loom, and in Puno a few men weave blankets on a ground loom. In Ecuador both men and women spin, and men weave patterned cloth (Meisch 1986, 1987a, 1987b, 1991). Generally, men are the weavers in northern Peru and Ecuador (Meisch 1987a).

7. The *wich'uña* is made from a llama's foreleg bone (*wich'u*), carefully split, cleaned, and extensively (and lovingly) polished. Split bones are sold in markets. The *wich'u* is a prized specialty item of herders.

8. The latter involves simple spinning (*mismiy*) on a stick (*mismina*), rather than spinning (*pushkay*) on a spindle, which has a whorl (*pushka*) (Zorn 1986, 1987b).

9. Andeans may pass through different stages of gender identification and gender importance in the life cycle, with all babies perhaps considered female (Isbell, n.d.a). *Runa* personhood is actively created, not achieved merely through growth, as Canessa (1999) shows for residents of Pocobaya, Bolivia.

10. Such choices and transformations are virtually impossible for the very poorest consumers, who have only one set of clothes (Campbell 1996). Taquileans, while poor indeed, have more choice in part because they produce their own clothes.

11. In an apparent worldwide "special relationship" with cloth (Barber 1994; Weiner and Schneider 1989), women make most of the cloth used, and cloth itself is generally gendered as female. Many pre-Columbian burials of women, and occasionally men, include spindles and weaving implements, indicating diversity in the ancient sexual division of labor in cloth production. See, among others, Bruhns (1994).

12. Women may manipulate cloth-making to express a "traditional" discourse stressing women's centrality in kinship and *ayllu* formation, as Arnold argues for the Qaqachaka of Bolivia (1988).

13. The patronal festival of Saints Peter and Paul is the occasion for an important regional wool market, when peasant herders of llamas and alpacas descend from their distant mountain homes to trade fiber for food (especially corn), which farmers bring. Taquileans rarely go to this market, but my *comadre* thought that with a preestablished contact through me, she could risk the trouble and expense of taking potatoes and *ch'uñu* to that unfamiliar festival-fair.

14. *Mama*, "mother," is used as a general, respectful term of address for adult *runa* women (for example, Mama Natividad). *Mama* also refers to the womb (de Lucca 1983), and is used for objects considered enclosing and generative, such as the *mama q'epi*, "mother bundle," in which herders store ritual paraphernalia (Zorn 1986, 1987b). Women weave the linguistically unmarked, gender-neutral belt (*chumpi*), while men make the *mama chumpi*, which is gender-marked as female, mother, and generative.

15. One consequence of the decline of women's handweaving has been the concomitant rise of regional, semi-specialized cloth producers, usually males, who create ethnic dress principally for women. This can be seen in the spectacular embroidered dress of the Colca Canyon region of Arequipa, Peru, worn only by women (Femenías 1994, 1996, 1997, 2004; Gelles and Martínez 1992), and in urban women's Indian *cholita* dress, most notable for its elegance and cost in La Paz, Bolivia.

4. TRANSFORMING VALUE BY COMMODITIZING CLOTH

1. "Calendariotaq ruwarqayku, o sea que, noqa ruwarqani, o sea que, Inglaterra rinaypaq, no?" Flores was the first Taquilean to travel abroad, to participate in the opening of an exhibition of Peruvian textiles (Fini 1985). "We" refers to other members of the "Natives of Taquile" Folklore Association.

2. Research on the paradoxes wrought by commoditization is well established. See Graburn (1976, 1993, 1999) on tourist arts and Appadurai (1986) and other contributions to Appadurai, ed. (1986) on categorization of objects.

Weiner (1992) offers perspectives on the sacred character of objects, which renders them inalienable from their culture of production. See also Kopytoff on commoditization as a process (1986); Myers, ed. (2001) on recent perspectives on material culture, and Phillips and Steiner, eds. (1999) on art and craft as commodity.

3. Numerous studies, including Benería and Feldman 1992, Deere 1990, and World Bank 2001, show that money earned by peasant women usually goes to family expenses and that earned by men to individual expenses. In Taquile, with low rates of alcoholism, this aspect of gender disparity is rarely a problem.

4. Most antique textiles probably came from Cusco, other parts of Puno, and Bolivia, but those in collections are often undocumented and unprovenanced (see chapter 3, also Zorn 1991). It is impossible to estimate accurately how many textiles have been removed. Dealers occasionally provide information, for example, on prices in *Art in Auction* and in exhibition catalogues (Adelson and Takami n.d. [1978]; Siegal 1991; Wasserman and Hill 1981; Yorke 1980).

5. Young weavers especially pride themselves on creating tightly woven textiles, said to be like "leather" (*cuero*, Spanish), which not only require skill in designing but strength in weaving, as beating the weft requires force.

6. Taquilean calendar belts are in the collection of the Elvehjem Museum of Art, University of Wisconsin–Madison (1986.8.1, in Zorn 1987a: 74 [figure 43], 78 [figure 43]); the Brooklyn Museum (2002.62.15); and according to Pancho Huatta, at least one museum in Germany, which I have not yet identified.

7. Nancy Rosoff purchased this belt for the Brooklyn Museum during our 2002 trip to Taquile (chapter 1). The weaver and her husband Alejandro Flores told us that they had been keeping the belt (made of perfectly handspun sheep wool and alpaca fleece yarn, carefully and expertly woven) for themselves, but decided to sell it because they were pleased that it would be in a museum collection.

8. Some of the words are misspelled, which often happens when Quechua speakers write Spanish, and vice versa. "Tejedora Agustina Huatta acedo irincia secreto de sus tatara abuelos. . . . Fijese el tejido puede haver imitación *Gracías.*"

9. Women's opportunities are still limited in cooperatives. In a highly regarded crafts cooperative, San Jolobil in Chiapas, Mexico, which produces impressively high-quality textiles, men still dominate control over the profits and decision-making. In another Mexican case, the female leader of a potter's cooperative was murdered (J. Nash 1993: 11).

5. VISIT TAQUILE – ISLE OF PEACE AND ENCHANTMENT

1. Everything brought to the island must be hauled up the stone paths on some Taquilean's back.

2. A "small island" is generally defined as one with a population of less than one million, which makes Taquile tiny indeed (McElroy and de Albuquerque 2002: 17).

3. The Taquileans learned of the IAF because Kevin Healy, who had first helped the community sell their textiles, was working there. I helped the community write the grant. Healy and I are examples of the importance of transnational contacts for Taquile's development. Similar examples can be found worldwide (Grimes and Milgram 2000).

4. In 1996 Peru's FONCODES (Peruvian Social Investment Fund) built two "tourist inns" (*albergues turísticos*), on Taquile and on Amantani. Taquile's inn, located in its central square, still wasn't functioning when I visited in 2002. Former president Fujimori had promised to send funds to finish construction, which had not arrived, and islanders were debating what to do with the building.

5. For a much fuller discussion of fishing and fisherfolk in Lake Titicaca, see Orlove (2002).

6. That relationship was important for me, too, because I ended up going to Taquile as a result of Gertrudis de Solari's suggestion that Taquile would be a good place to look for weavers; I was given her name by the Andeanist anthropologist Billie Jean Isbell, who ten years later became my professor when I studied for a Ph.D. at Cornell University.

7. Partial transcription of the e-mail, dated September 21, 2001, in Spanish: "[Salutation] Nosotros estamos muy preucupado de ustedes pues las notecias por television nos hacen sufrir mucho. por favor queremos saber que estan bien. Lloramos y sufrimos de tantas personas desparicidas en nueva york. y en washinton. por favor avisarnos que estan bien."

6. CONCLUSION: WEAVING A FUTURE?

1. Though the meeting took place in June 2002, the new slate of officers wasn't legalized by the community until the election of a new set of traditional authorities in November, which shows how conflicts within a community affect relations with outsiders. I heard from several Taquileans in 2003 that conflicts continued to inhibit the committee's full functioning, but in 2004 Taquileans agreed on a new law to regulate tourism.

2. Several Taquilean families migrated to Lima, where they, or their children, have become *mestizo*.

3. The CTTC (Center for Traditional Textiles of Cusco) was founded by Nilda Callañaupa, as a Cultural Survival project; they have battled for eight years to help weavers in communities near Cusco regain and even surpass traditional standards of superb and inventive textiles (CTTC n.d.).

4. Elvira Espejo, a young woman I met in La Paz in 2002 who had learned to weave while growing up in her Aymara-speaking *ayllu* of Qaqachaka, Oruro, Bolivia (Espejo 1994), was resolutely determined to present new versions of fine Andean textiles to fulfill assignments in the city's fine arts university where she studied, but she has been insulted by faculty and students, and her woven assignments often have not been accepted. The situation is different around northern Potosi, Bolivia, where tens of thousands of *ayllu* members still weave. Among the communities served by ASUR, the other Andean project that successfully promotes the production of fine textiles, Cassandra Torrico reports that one ethnic group has reorganized its daily calendar to permit weaving, by having children attend school starting at 5:30 A.M., so that they have time to weave during the day (Cassandra Torrico, personal communication 2002). Nonetheless, problems remain; a weaver in the Charazani area of Bolivia, long famed for its gorgeous weavings, told me that people in her community no longer had direct access to alpaca fleece and didn't have money to buy it, so they could weave with alpaca (instead of synthetics) only when making textiles for sale to tourists.

5. Several scholars have observed that Andean women historically have assumed the role of preserving what local people feel is most Andean about their culture and society. See, for example, Silverblatt (1987), on the importance of women herders who preserved Andean religion in the face of Spanish pressure to convert to Catholicism, and de la Cadena (1995), on how women preserve ethnicity. Catherine Allen (2002) shows how women's continued weaving and wearing of handmade dress "saves" the men of Sonqo, who (perhaps) remain Inca despite male use of items of factory-made dress. In many parts of the world, women continue to wear ethnic dress long after men have switched to Western-style dress (Eicher 1995; Eicher and Roach-Higgins 1992a, 1992b). Why women rather than men are viewed as more capable of representing continuity, ethnicity, and tradition, or are required to represent (literally, embody) them, deserves further research.

6. Though women weave the patterned cloth that collectors and tourists seek, women weave not just for themselves but for others, so some or many of the textiles sold in the ethnic arts market belong to men.

GLOSSARY

In this book, all translations from Spanish and Quechua are by me unless otherwise noted. I follow Cusihuamán (1976a, 1976b) for writing Quechua according to Peru's official Quechua alphabet, adopted in 1969, though I write Quechua names from maps, colonial documents, or other written sources as they appear in the original, and I spell Inca with a "c," as this is more common than Inka. When writing Aymara, I follow Briggs (1993) and Yapita (1994).

(A)=Aymara, (M)=Maya, (Q)=Quechua, (S)=Spanish

agente municipal	(S) municipal agent
ahijado(a)	(S) godson (goddaughter)
albergue	(S) inn
alcalde	(S) mayor
alcalde mayor	(S) "elder," (principal) mayor
alcalde varayoq	(S, Q) mayor, "staff-bearer"
alegre	(S) happy, cheerful
altiplano	(S) high plain or plateau, surrounding Lake Titicaca
aqsu	(A) woman's overskirt; formerly, overdress
artesanía	(S) crafts, handicrafts
awana	(Q) loom, lit., a-thing-for-weaving, from (Q) *away*, to weave
awasqa	(Q) woven; (colonial) average weaving
awayu	(A) mantle, woman's shawl, carrying cloth
ayllu	(Q and A) family, lineage, kin group, rural social group, ethnic group
ayni	(Q) reciprocal aid, returned in the same way
balsa	(S) raft, float; in Andes, totora-reed boat
barrio	(S) neighborhood
bayeta	(S) thick handwoven cloth; also *wayta*
blanco(a)	(S) white, white person
cacique	(Q, S) indigenous lord; from Arawak
calamina	(S) corrugated iron
calendario	(S) calendar, almanac
campesino	(S) peasant; synonym for "indian" (Andes)
campo alcalde	(S) fields' master; also *campo suyuq*
campo runa	(Q, S) lit., country person, indigenous peasant

campo suyuq	(Q, s) fields' master; also *campo alcalde*
canchón	(s) field, from (s) *cancha*, field
Candelaria	(s) Candlemas (February 2)
capitanía	(s) harbor master, of Puno port
cargo	(s) religious-political obligation, office, position
cesante	(s) lit., unemployed, but meaning person holding high office
chaleco	(s) vest; also *chaliku*
chaleco músico	(s) musician's vest, from (s) *músico*, musician
chalina	(s) scarf; also *kufanda*
ch'aska	(Q) Venus as morning or evening star
chicha	(s) fermented corn beer; also (Q) *aqha*
ch'in	(Q) silence, emptiness
cholita	(Q, s) urban indian woman; see *chola*
cholo(a)	(s) urban indian man (woman)
chuku	(Q) woman's headshawl; also *chucu*
ch'ullu	(Q) knit cap; also *ch'ullo*
ch'ullu damas	(Q, s) woman's knit cap, from (s) *damas*, lady
chumpi	(Q) handwoven belt; also (A) *wak'a*
chumpi calendario	(Q, s) calendar belt
ch'uño, ch'uñu	(Q) Andean freeze-dried potatoes
ch'usaq	(Q) empty
ch'uspa	(Q) coca leaf purse
comadre	(s) female ritual kin (lit., co-mother)
compadrazgo	(s) ritual or spiritual kinship
compadre	(s) male ritual kin (lit., co-father)
compadres	(s) ritual kin (lit., co-parents)
comunidad	(s) community, hamlet
conjunto	(s) music group
conocido	(s) someone who is known
costumbre	(s) custom
criollo	(s) creole, born in New World; white (Peru)
cuero	(s) hide
cumbi	(Q) (colonial) very fine weaving; also *cumpi, qompi,* or *qumpi*
cumbia	(s) Colombian song-and-dance form
curaca	(A) traditional *ayllu* authority; indigenous lord; also *kuraka*
de pollera	(s) wearing the *pollera,* i.e., indian dress

de vestido	(s) wearing *vestido*, i.e., cosmopolitan dress
departamento	(s) department
dispensa	(s) storeroom
encomienda	(s) colonial grant of indian labor to a Spaniard
envidia	(s) envy
faena	(s) work party
faja	(s) belt; also (Q) *chumpi*
faja calendario	(s) calendar belt; also *chumpi calendario*
fiesta	(s) festival
fiesta-cargo	(s) festival-office, from (s) *fiesta* and (s) *cargo*
gamonal	(s) large landowner, exploiter
gancho	(s) headband, from (Q) *wincha*; (s) hook
gringo(a)	(s) foreigner, light-haired person; also *gringu(a)*
guaca	(Q) sacred, shrine, divinity; also *huaca, waka*
hacienda	(s) estate
hanan	(Q) upper, as in Hanansaya (Q) upper moiety
hombres cesantes	(s) "completed person"; person holding high office; from (s) *cesante*, unemployed
hurin	(Q) lower, as in Hurinsaya (Q) lower moiety
indio(a)	(s) indian
istalla	(Q) small carrying cloth for coca leaf
janaq	(Q) upper; also *hanaq*
Janaq Ladu	(Q, s) upper "half" or moiety
jilaqata	(Q and A) traditional *ayllu* authority; also *jilakata*
juez	(s) judge
k'anti	(Q) heavy spindle for plying (doubling) yarn
khipu	(Q) knotted cords for recording information; also *quipu*
kipu	(Q) steward, foreman (Taquile), in unpaid servitude
kuraq	(Q) senior
ladu	(s) half, moiety, from (s) *lado*, side
llaki	(Q) sad, unhappy
lliqlla	(A) mantle, woman's shawl, carrying cloth; see (A) *awayu*
machismo	(s) traditional ideal Latin masculine behavior, male domination; from (s) *macho*, male
mama chumpi	(Q) interior belt, lit., mother belt; see *tayka wak'a*
mama q'epi	(Q) herder's bundle, lit., mother bundle; also *q'ipi*
maricones	(s) homosexuals (impolite)
material noble	(s) lit., noble material; cement finish
mayordomo	(s) overseer, foreman
mestizo(a)	(s) "mixed" indian and Spaniard; non-indian

mestizaje	(s) "racial" (cultural) mixing of indian and Spanish
mismiy	(Q) stick-spinning
mit'a	(Q) rotative turn
mitimaes	(Q, s) colonists; see *mitmaq*
mitmaq	(Q) populations resettled by the Inca state
monedero	(s) coin purse
músico	(s) musician
musuq ruinas	(Q, s) new (recently built) ruins, from (Q) *musuq*, new, and (s) *ruinas*, ruins
ñawsa	(Q) blind, illiterate
obraje	(s) workshop; (colonial) textile sweatshop
oca	(Q) Andean tuber; also *uka*
paceña	(s) chromatic shading; lit., woman or object from La Paz
pacha	(Q) world; also space, time, earth
p'acha	(Q) dress, clothing
pallay	(Q) warp-patterned weave, from (Q) *pallay*, to select
pampa	(Q) field, flat plain; wide plain-weave area in textiles
pasadu runa	(s, Q) "passed" person (Taquile), who has completed the *fiesta-cargo* system
pasante	(s) festival sponsor, lit., passer
peñas	(s) folk music clubs
pica-piedras	(s) stone-cutters, from (s) *picar*, to cut stone, and (s) *piedra*, stone
pobres	(s) the poor
pollera	(s) full pleated skirt, worn by urban indian women; also *pullira*
pueblo	(s) town, village, people (collective)
puna	(Q) high grasslands, 3,500+ meters above sea level
punchu	(Q and A) poncho
pushka	(Q) Andean drop spindle; also *phushkha*
pushkay	(Q) to spin single thread; also *phushkhay*
qapaq	(Q) great, powerful
q'ara	(Q) peeled, shorn hide; non-indian (impolite)
q'ipi	(Q) ancestral textile bundle
quipu	(Q) knotted cords for recording information; also *khipu*
qumpi	(Q) (colonial) very fine weaving; also *qompi*, *cumpi*, or *cumbi*
reducción	(s) colonial district created by grouping dispersed hamlets
registro civil	(s) secretary; lit., civil registrar
reino	(s) kingdom; see *señorio*

runa	(Q) person, indigenous person, personhood
runa p'acha	(Q) handwoven clothing, indigenous dress
Rutuchiy	(Q) haircut; First Haircut ceremony; also *Uma Rutuy, Rutuchikuy, rutochico*
Santiago	(S) James; Saint James (celebrated July 25)
sargento de playa	(S) beach sargeant; port authority (Taquile); from (S) *sargento*, sargeant, and (S) *playa*, beach
segundo alcalde	(S) assistant mayor, from (S) *segunda*, second
señorio	(S) kingdom, from (S) *señor*, lord; see *reino*
sikuri	(Q and A) Andean panpipe; panpipe ensemble; from (A) *siku*, panpipes; also (S) *zampoña*
silencio	(S) silence, emptiness
sol	(Q) Peruvian money, from (S) *sol*, sun
suerte	(S) luck, good fortune
sunqu	(Q) heart; also *sonqo*
suyu, suyo	(Q) division; sector; crop rotation sectors on Taquile
Tahuantinsuyu	(Q) lit., the four quarters united; the Inca Empire; also *Tawantinsuyu*
tayka wak'a	(A) interior belt, lit., mother belt; see *mama chumpi*
teniente gobernador	(S) lieutenant governor; highest Peruvian government authority (Taquile)
tinku	(Q) ritual battle; encounter; meeting
t'ipana	(Q) overdress; lit., a-thing-for-pinning
totora	(S) reed in Lake Titicaca; cattail, bulrush
traje	(S) dress, costume, indigenous dress
traje típico	(S) characteristic indigenous dress
trueque	(S) exchange, barter
tupu	(Q) spoon-shaped mantle (shawl) pin
tzute	(M) rectangular head covering, worn by men or women
uma	(Q) head; water; Umasuyo, lower moiety
Uma Rutuy	(Q) haircut, First Haircut ceremony; also *Rutuchiy*
unkhuña	(Q) small carrying cloth
uray	(Q) lower
Uray Ladu	(Q, S) lower "half" or moiety
urqu	(Q) male; mountain; Urqusuyo, upper moiety
vestido	(S) dress, suit
wak'a	(A) handwoven belt; also (Q) *chumpi*; see *tayka wak'a*
walsa	(Q) reed boat; see *balsa*
wawa	(Q) baby
wayaqa	(Q) small carrying bag

wayno	(Q) common Andean song-and-dance form; also *huayno*, *waynu*
wayta	(Q) see *bayeta*
wayta awana	(Q) loom for weaving yardage for cloth
wich'u	(Q) foreleg
wich'uña	(Q) bone weaving pick, from (Q) *wich'u*
wincha	(Q) headband; also *gancho*

REFERENCES

SERIALS

El Diario, Lima
El Comercio, Lima
La República, Lima
New York Times, New York
Peruvian Connection Ltd., Tonganoxie, Kansas
Viajera, Puno

BOOKS, ARTICLES, AND PRESENTATIONS

Abercrombie, Thomas

1991   "To Be Indian, to Be Bolivian: Ethnic and National Discourses of
        Identity." In *Nation-States and Indians in Latin America*. G. Urban
        and J. Sherzer, eds. Pp. 95–130. Austin: University of Texas Press.

1998a   Commentary. *Journal of Latin American Anthropology* 3(2): 150–65.

1998b   *"Pathways of Memory and Power: Ethnography and History among an
        Andean People."* Madison: University of Wisconsin Press.

Ackerman, Raquel

1991   "Cloth and Identity in the Central Andes: Province of Abancay,
        Peru." In *Textile Traditions of Mesoamerica and the Andes: An
        Anthology*. M. B. Schevill, J. C. Berlo, and E. B. Dwyer, eds.
        Pp. 231–60. New York: Garland.

Adelson, Laurie, and Bruce Takami

[1978] *Weaving Traditions of Highland Bolivia*. Exhibition catalogue.
        December 19, 1978–February 4, 1979. Los Angeles: Craft & Folk
        Art Museum.

Adelson, Laurie, and Arthur Tracht

1983   *Aymara Weavings: Ceremonial Textiles of Colonial and 19th Century
        Bolivia*. Exhibition catalogue. SITES [Smithsonian Institution
        Traveling Exhibition Service]. Washington, D.C.: Smithsonian
        Institution Press.

Albó, Xavier

1999   "Andean People in the Twentieth Century." In *The Cambridge
        History of the Native Peoples of the Americas*. Vol. 3, South America,
        Part 2. F. Salomon and S. B. Schwartz, eds. Pp. 765–871.
        Cambridge: Cambridge University Press.

2002   Pueblos indios en la política. *Cuadernos de investigación CIPCA* No.
        55. La Paz: Ed. Plural/CIPCA.

Albó, Xavier, A. Godínez, and F. Pifarré, eds.

1989   *Para comprender las culturas rurales en Bolivia.* La Paz: CIPCA.

Allen, Catherine J.

1997   *Condor Qatay: Anthropology in Performance.* Prospect Heights, IL:
        Waveland Press.

2002   *The Hold Life Has: Coca and Cultural Identity in an Andean Community.*
        2nd ed. Washington, D.C.: Smithsonian Institution Press.

Altamirano, Teófilo

2000   "Transnationalization and Cultural Encounters: Catholics in
        Paterson, New Jersey, U.S.A." In *Transforming Cultures in the
        Americas.* D. Castillo and M. J. Dudley, eds. Pp. 10–20. Ithaca, NY:
        Latin American Studies Program, Cornell University.

de Amat Quiroz, Gamaliel

1981   "Taquile: Fenámeno Turístico en una isla del Lago Titicaca."
        Viajera 12: 22–25. Lima.

1984   "Descubre Puno. . . . ahora a tu alcance . . . te esperamos." *Viajera*
        26: 20–22. Lima.

Apostolopoulos, Yorghos, and Dennis J. Gayle

2002   "From MIRAB to TOURAB? Searching for Sustainable
        Development in the Maritime Caribbean, Pacific, and
        Mediterranean." In *Island Tourism and Sustainable
        Development: Caribbean, Pacific, and Mediterranean Experiences.*
        Y. Apostolopoulos and D. J. Gayle, eds. Pp. 3–14. Westport, CT:
        Praeger.

Apostolopoulos, Yorghos, and Dennis J. Gayle, eds.

2002   *Island Tourism and Sustainable Development: Caribbean, Pacific, and
        Mediterranean Experiences.* Westport, CT: Praeger.

Appadurai, Arjun

1986   "Introduction: Commodities and the Politics of Value." In *The
        Social Life of Things: Commodities in Cultural Perspective.* A.
        Appadurai, ed. Pp. 3–63. Cambridge: Cambridge University Press.

Appadurai, Arjun, ed.

1986   *The Social Life of Things: Commodities in Cultural Perspective.*
        Cambridge: Cambridge University Press.

Arnold, Denise

1988   "Matrilineal Practice in a Patrilineal Setting: Rituals and
        Metaphors of Kinship in an Andean Ayllu." Unpublished Ph.D.
        dissertation. University College. London.

1994 "Hacer al hombre a imagen de ella: Aspectos de género en los textiles de Qaqachaka." *Revista Chungará* 26(1): 79–115.

2000 *El rincón de las cabezas: Luchas textuales educación y tierras en los Andes*. La Paz: UMSA and Ed. ILCA.

Arnold, Denise, ed.

1997 *Más allá del Silencio: Las fronteras de género en Los Andes*. La Paz: Ed. ILCA/CIASE.

1998 *Gente de carne y hueso: Las tramas de parentesco en Los Andes*. La Paz: Ed. ILCA/CIASE.

Arnold, Denise, and Juan de Dios Yapita

1998 *Río de vellón, río de canto: Cantar a los animals, una poética andina de la creación*. La Paz: Ed. ILCA/HISBOL.

Arnold, Denise, and Juan de Dios Yapita, eds.

1996 *Madre Melliza y sus crías: Ispall Mama wawampi*. La Paz: Ed. HISBOL/ ILCA.

Arnold, Denise, and Juan de Dios Yapita, with Apaza M. Cipriana

1996 Mama Trama y sus crías: Analogías de la producción de la papa en los textiles de Chukiñapi, Bolivia. In *Madre Melliza y sus crías: Ispall Mama wawampi*. D. Y. Arnold and J. de D. Yapita, eds. Pp. 373–411. La Paz: Ed. HISBOL/ILCA.

Ash, Juliet, and Elizabeth Wilson, eds.

1992 *Chic Thrills: A Fashion Reader*. Berkeley: University of California Press.

Avalos de Matos, Rosalía

1951a "Changements culturels dans les îles du Lac Titicaca." *Travaux de l'Institut Français d'Études Andines* 3: 40–50.

1951b L'organisation sociale dans l'île de Taquile. *Travaux de l'Institut Français d'Études Andines* 3: 74–87.

Aveni, Anthony F.

1995 [1989] *Empires of Time: Calendars, Clocks, and Cultures*. New York: Kodansha International.

Ayres, Ron

2002 "Cultural Tourism in Small-Island States: Contradictions and Ambiguities." In *Island Tourism and Sustainable Development: Caribbean, Pacific, and Mediterranean Experiences*. Y. Apostolopoulos and D. J. Gayle, eds. Pp. 145–60. Westport, CT: Praeger.

Babb, Florence E.

1989 *Between Field and Cooking Pot: The Political Economy of Marketwomen in Peru*. Austin: University of Texas Press.

Babcock, Barbara A., G. Monthan, and D. Monthan

    1986   *The Pueblo Storyteller*. Tucson: University of Arizona Press.

Baizerman, Suzanne

    1987   "Textiles, Traditions, and Tourist Art: Hispanic Weaving in Northern New Mexico." Unpublished Ph.D. dissertation. University of Minnesota.

    1990   "Trade in Hispanic Weavings of Northern New Mexico and the Social Construction of Tradition." In *Textiles in Trade*. Proceedings of the Textile Society of America Biennial Symposium, September 14–16, 1990. Pp. 233–40. Los Angeles: Textile Society of America.

Bandelier, Adolph

    1910   *The Islands of Titicaca and Koati*. New York: Hispanic Society of America.

Barber, Elizabeth W.

    1994   *Women's Work, the First 20,000 Years: Women, Cloth, and Society in Early Times*. New York: W. W. Norton.

Barnes, Ruth, and Joanne B. Eicher, eds.

    1992   *Dress and Gender: Making and Meaning*. New York: BERG.

Barragán, Rossana

    1992   "Entre polleras, ñañacas y lliqllas: Los mestizos y cholas en la conformación de la 'tercera república'." In *Tradición y modernidad en los Andes*. H. Urbano, ed. Pp. 43–73. Cusco, Peru: Centro de Estudios Regionales Andinos, "Bartolomé de las Casas."

Bauer, Arnold J.

    2001   *Goods, Power, History: Latin America's Material Culture*. Cambridge: Cambridge University Press.

Bauman, Richard, and Patricia Sawin

    1991   "The Politics of Participation in Folklife Festivals." In *Exhibiting Cultures: The Poetics and Politics of Museum Display*. I. Karp and S. D. Levine, eds. Pp. 288–314. Washington, D.C.: Smithsonian Institution Press.

Benería, Lourdes, and Shelley Feldman, eds.

    1992   *Unequal Burden: Economic Crises, Persistent Poverty, and Women's Work*. Boulder, CO: Westview Press.

Berlo, Janet C.

    1991   "Beyond Bricolage: Women and Aesthetic Strategies in Latin American Textiles." In *Textile Traditions of Mesoamerica and the Andes: An Anthology*. M. B. Schevill, J. C. Berlo, and E. B. Dwyer, eds. Pp. 437–79. New York: Garland.

Bird, Junius B.

1968 "Handspun Yarn Production Rates in the Cuzco Region of Peru." *Textile Museum Journal* 2(3): 9–16.

Bird, Junius B., and Louisa Bellinger

1954 *Paracas Fabrics and Nasca Needlework*. Catalogue Raisonné. Washington, D.C.: The Textile Museum.

Boissevain, Jeremy

1996 "Introduction." In *Coping with Tourists: European Reactions to Mass Tourism*. J. Boissevain, ed. Pp. 1–26. Providence, RI: Berghahn Books.

Boissevain, Jeremy, ed.

1996 *Coping with Tourists: European Reactions to Mass Tourism*. Providence, RI: Berghahn Books.

Bomberry, Victoria

1993 "Text and Context: Organizing the Return of the Sacred Textiles to the Community of Coroma, Bolivia." *Akwek:kon Journal* 9(4): 2–11.

1994 "Souls of the Ancestors: Defending Cultural Property." *Akwek:kon Journal* 11(3–4): 97–8.

Boone, Elizabeth Hill, and Walter D. Mignolo, eds.

1994 *Writing without Words: Alternative Literacies in Mesoamerica and the Andes*. Durham, NC: Duke University Press.

Borden, Carla, and Peter Seitel, eds.

1994 *Festival of American Folklife, July 1–4 and July 7–10*. Catalogue. Washington, D.C.: Smithsonian Institution.

Bourdieu, Pierre

1977 *Outline of a Theory of Practice*. Cambridge: Cambridge University Press.

1984 *Distinction: A Social Critique of the Judgment of Taste*. Cambridge, MA: Harvard University Press.

Bouysse-Cassagne, Thérèse

1986 "Urco and Uma: Aymara Concepts of Space." In *Anthropological History of Andean Polities*. J. V. Murra, N. Wachtel, and J. Revel, eds. Pp. 201–27. Cambridge: Cambridge University Press.

1987 *La identidad Aymara: Aproximación histórica* (Siglo XV, Siglo XVI). La Paz, Bolivia: HISBOL.

Briggs, Lucy

1993 *El idioma Aymara: Variantes regionales y sociales*. La Paz, Ed. ILCA.

Brooks, John, ed.

1977 *The South American Handbook*. 52nd ed. Bath, England: Trade and Travel Publications.

Bruhns, Karen Olsen

1994　*Ancient South America*. Cambridge: Cambridge University Press.

Bubba Zamorra, Cristina, Pio Cruz Flores, Damian Mendieta Cruz, and Justo Romero Romero

1990　"Los textiles de Coroma." *Unitas*, no. 11 (January).

Buechler, Hans C., and Judith-Maria Buechler

1992　*Manufacturing against the Odds: Small-Scale Producers in an Andean City*. Boulder, CO: Westview Press.

Cadaval, Olivia

1991　"Knowledge and Power: Land in Native American Cultures." In *Smithsonian Institution 1991 Festival of American Folklife*. Catalogue. Pp. 76–80. Washington, D.C.: Smithsonian Institution.

de la Cadena, Marisol

1995　" 'Women Are More Indian': Ethnicity and Gender in a Community near Cuzco." In *Ethnicity, Markets, and Migration in the Andes: At the Crossroads of History and Anthropology*. B. Larson and O. Harris, with E. Tandeter, eds. Pp. 329–48. Durham, NC: Duke University Press.

2000　*Indigenous Mestizos: The Politics of Race and Culture in Cuzco, Peru, 1919–1991*. Durham, NC: Duke University Press.

Campbell, Colina

1996　"The Meaning of Objects and the Meaning of Actions: A Critical Note on the Sociology of Consumption and Theories of Clothing." *Journal of Material Culture* 1(1): 93–105.

Candler, Kay Louise

1993　"Place and Thought in a Quechua Household Ritual." Unpublished Ph.D. dissertation. Dept. of Anthropology. University of Illinois at Urbana-Champaign.

Canessa, Andrew

1999　"Making Persons, Marking Difference: Procreation in Highland Bolivia." In *Conceiving Persons: Ethnographies of Procreation, Fertility, and Growth*. P. Loizos and P. Heady, eds. Pp. 69–87. London: Athlone Press.

Carlsen, Robert S.

1993　"Textile Production in Contemporary Highland Guatemala." In *Crafts in the World Market: The Impact of Global Exchange on Middle American Artisans*. J. Nash, ed. Pp. 199–222. Albany: State University of New York Press.

Caro, Deborah A.

1985   "'Those Who Divide Us': Resistance and Change among Pastoral
Ayllus in Ulla Ulla, Bolivia." Unpublished Ph.D. dissertation.
Dept. of Anthropology. Johns Hopkins University, Baltimore.

Cason, Marjorie, and Adele Cahlander

1976   *The Art of Bolivian Highland Weaving*. New York: Watson-Guptill
Publications.

Cereceda, Verónica

1978   "Sémiologie des tissus andins." *Annales: Economies Sociétés
Civilisations* 33(5–6): 1017–35.

1986   "The Semiology of Andean Textiles: The *Talegas* of Isluga." In
Anthropological History of Andean Polities. J. V. Murra, N. Wachtel,
and J. Revel, eds. Pp. 149–73. Cambridge: Cambridge University
Press.

1987   "Aproximaciones a una estetica Andina: De la belleza al tinku."
In *Tres Reflexiones Sobre el Pensamiento Andino*. J. Medina, ed.
Pp. 133–231. La Paz: HISBOL.

1990   "A partir de los colores de un pajaro. . . ." *Boletín del Museo Chileno
de Arte Precolombino* 4: 57–104.

1992   "Notas sobre el diseño de los textiles 'Tarabuco.'" In *Textiles
Tarabuco*. J. Dávalos, V. Cereceda, and G. Martínez. Pp. 71–112.
La Paz: ASUR/CORDECH.

Cereceda, Verónica, Jhonny Dávalos, and Jaime Mejía

1993   *Una diferencia, un sentido: Los diseños de los textiles Tarabuco y Jalq'a*.
Sucre, Bolivia: ASUR.

Chambers, Erve

1997   "Introduction: Tourism's Mediators." In *Tourism and Culture:
An Applied Perspective*. E. Chambers, ed. Pp. 1–11. Albany: State
University of New York Press.

2000   *Native Tours: The Anthropology of Travel and Tourism*. Prospect
Heights, IL: Waveland Press.

Chambers, Erve, ed.

1997   *Tourism and Culture: An Applied Perspective*. Albany: State
University of New York Press.

Chibnik, Michael

2003   *Crafting Tradition: The Making and Marketing of Oaxacan Wood
Carvings*. Austin: University of Texas Press.

Choque Canqui, Roberto

1993   *Sociedad y economía colonial en el sur andino*. La Paz: HISBOL.

CISA [Consejo Indio de Sud America]

1998a CISA: Asamblea Estatutaria. E-mail sent 3/12/98.
https://www.puebloindio.org/.

1998b CISA: Convocatoria a la Asamblea Estatutaria. E-mail sent 1/8/98.
https://www.puebloindio.org/CISA/.

1998c Manifiesto de Taquile. E-mail sent 3/12/98.
https://www.puebloindio.org/CISA/.

Clark, Nikki

1993 "The Estuquiña Textile Tradition: Cultural Patterning in Late
Prehistoric Fabrics, Moquegua, Far Southern Peru." Unpublished
Ph.D. dissertation. Washington University, St. Louis.

Clifford, James

1988 *The Predicament of Culture: Twentieth-Century Ethnography,
Literature, and Art*. Cambridge, MA.: Harvard University Press.

Cohen, Jeffrey H.

1998 "Craft Production and the Challenge of the Global Market: An
Artisans' Cooperative in Oaxaca, Mexico." *Human Organization*
57(1): 74–82.

1999 *Cooperation and Community: Economy and Society in Oaxaca*. Austin:
University of Texas Press.

2000 "Textile Production in Rural Oaxaca, Mexico." In *Artisans and
Cooperatives: Developing Alternate Trade for the Global Economy*.
K. M. Grimes and B. L. Milgram, eds. Pp. 129–41. Tucson:
University of Arizona Press.

Cohen, John

1957 "An Investigation of Contemporary Weaving of the Peruvian
Indians." Unpublished M.A. thesis. Dept. of Design, Yale
University.

Colloredo-Mansfeld, Rudi

1999 *The Native Leisure Class: Consumption and Cultural Creativity in the
Andes*. Chicago: University of Chicago Press.

Conklin, William J.

1971 "Chavin Textiles and the Origins of Peruvian Weaving." *Textile
Museum Journal* 3(2): 13–19.

Contorno, Elena, and Lucia Tamayo Flores

2000 Informe de viaje a las islas Taquile y Amantaní. Email dated May
16, 2000.

Coy, Michael

1989a "From Theory." In *Apprenticeship: From Theory to Method and Back
Again*. M. Coy, ed. Pp. 1–11. Albany: State University of New York
Press.

1989b "Being What We Pretend To Be: The Usefulness of Apprenticeship as a Field Method." In *Apprenticeship: From Theory to Method and Back Again.* M. Coy, ed. Pp. 115–35. Albany: State University of New York Press.

Coy, Michael, ed.

1989 *"Apprenticeship: From Theory to Method and Back Again."* Albany: State University of New York Press.

Crick, Malcolm

1989 "Representations of International Tourism in the Social Sciences: Sun, Sex, Sights, Savings, and Servility." *Annual Review of Anthropology* 18: 307–44.

Cusihuaman G., Antonio

1976a *Diccionario Quechua Cuzco-Collao.* Lima: Ministerio de Educación / Instituto de Estudios Peruanos.

1976b *Gramatica Quechua: Cuzco-Collao.* Lima: Ministerio de Educación / Instituto de Estudios Peruanos.

DAAC [Distributed Active Archive Center]

2002 Lake Titicaca. http://daac.gsfc.nasa.gov/DAAC_DOCS/geomorphology/ GEO_7/GEO_PLATE_KL-15.HTML. Accessed September 12, 2002.

Dávalos, Jhonny, Verónica Cereceda, and Gabriel Martínez

1992 *Textiles Tarabuco.* La Paz: ASUR / CORDECH.

Davis, Fred

1992 *Fashion, Culture, and Identity.* Chicago: University of Chicago Press.

Dean, Bartholomew

1993 "Weaving Inequality: Debt-peonage and the Commodification of Inalienable Possessions in Amazonia." Paper presented at the American Ethnological Society annual meeting, Santa Fe, 1993.

Deere, Carmen Diana

1990 *Household and Class Relations: Peasants and Landlords in Northern Peru.* Berkeley: University of California Press.

De Lucca D., Manuel

1983 *Diccionario Aymara-Castellano, Castellano-Aymara.* La Paz: Comisión de Alfabetización y Literatura en Aymara (CALA).

Denby, David

2002 "Invaders." *New Yorker*, July 8, 2002.

Desforges, Luke

2000 "State Tourism Institutions and Neo-Liberal Development: A Case Study of Peru." *Tourism Geographies* 2(2): 177–92.

Desrosiers, Sophie

 1982 *Métier à Tisser et Vêtement Andins, ou le tissu comme être vivant. Du 5 November–2 December 1982*. Exhibition catalogue. Paris: Ceteclam.

 1992 "Las técnicas del tejido tienen un sentido? Una propuesta de lectura de los tejidos andinos." *Revista Andina* 10(1): 7–46.

d'Harcourt, Raoul

 1974 [1962] *Textiles of Ancient Peru and Their Techniques.* G. G. Denny and C. M. Osborne, eds; S. Brown, trans. Seattle: University of Washington Press.

Eber, Christine Engle

 2000 *Women and Alcohol in a Highland Maya Town: Water of Hope, Water of Sorrow*. Austin: University of Texas Press.

Echeandia Valledares, J. M.

 1982 "La isla Taquile: Agricultura, tejidos y diseños." *Historia Andina* 13 (April). Lima.

Eicher, Joanne B., ed.

 1995 *Dress and Ethnicity: Change across Space and Time.* Oxford: Berg.

Eicher, Joanne B., and Mary Ellen Roach-Higgins

 1992 "Introduction." In *Dress and Gender: Making and Meaning*. R. Barnes and J. B. Eicher, eds. Pp. 1–7. New York: Berg.

Eicher, Joanne B., and Mary Ellen Roach-Higgins, eds.

 1992 *Dress and Gender: Making and Meaning*. New York: Berg.

Escobar, Arturo

 1995 *Encountering Development: The Making and Unmaking of the Third World*. Princeton: Princeton University Press.

Espejo Ayka, Elvira, with Denise Y. Arnold and Juan de Dios Yapita, eds.

 1994 *Ahora les voya narrar: Jichha nä parlt'ä*. La Paz: UNICEF/Casa de las Américas.

Espinoza, Julio

 1983 *Taquile: Historia-economía-artesanía*. Puno, Peru: IIDSA [Instituto de Investigaciones para el Desarrollo Social del Altiplano].

Femenías, Blenda

 1987 "Introduction." In *Andean Aesthetics: Textiles of Peru and Bolivia*. B. Femenías, ed. Pp. 1–8. Madison: University of Wisconsin Press.

 1994 "Ethnic Artists and the Appropriation of Fashion: Embroidery and Identity in the Colca Valley, Peru." In *Contact, Crossover, Continuity: Proceedings of the Textile Society of America Biennial Symposium, September 24–26, 1994*. Pp. 331–41. Washington, D.C.: Textile Society of America.

 1996 "Regional Dress of the Colca Valley, Peru: A Dynamic Tradition." In *Textile Traditions of Mesoamerica and the Andes: An Anthology*.

M. B. Schevill, J. C. Berlo, and E. Dwyer, eds. Pp. 179–204. Austin: University of Texas Press.

1997   "Ambiguous Emblems: Gender, Clothing, and Representation in Contemporary Peru." Unpublished Ph.D. dissertation. Dept. of Anthropology, University of Wisconsin, Madison.

2004   *Ambiguous Emblems: Gender and the Boundaries of Dress in Contemporary Peru*. Austin: University of Texas Press.

Femenías, Blenda, ed.

1987   *Andean Aesthetics: Textiles of Peru and Bolivia*. Exhibition Catalogue, Elvehjem Museum. Madison: University of Wisconsin Press.

Fini, Moh

1985   *The Weavers of Ancient Peru: An Exhibition of Peruvian Textiles at the Commonwealth Institute, London, 5th September to 28th October, 1985*. London: Tumi.

Flores, Alejandro, and Paula Quispe

1994   "Preserving Our Culture." In *All Roads Are Good: Native Voices and Life and Culture*. Pp. 166–75. Washington, D.C.: Smithsonian Institution/National Museum of the American Indian.

Frame, Mary

1983   "Faugustino's Family: Knitters, Weavers, and Spinners on the Island of Taquile, Peru." In *Celebration of the Curious Mind: A Festschrift to Honor Anne Blinks on Her 80th Birthday*. Pp. 21–34. Loveland, CO: Interweave Press.

1986   "The Visual Images of Fabric Structures in Ancient Peruvian Art." In *The Junius B. Bird Conference on Andean Textiles, April 7th and 8th, 1984*. A. P. Rowe, ed. Pp. 47–80. Washington, D.C.: The Textile Museum.

1989   *A Family Affair: Making Cloth in Taquile, Peru*. Museum Note No. 26. Vancouver: U.B.C. Museum of Anthropology.

Franquemont, Christine R.

1986   "Chinchero Pallays: An Ethnic Code." In *The Junius B. Bird Conference on Andean Textiles, April 7th and 8th, 1984*. A. P. Rowe, ed. Pp. 321–29. Washington, D.C.: The Textile Museum.

Franquemont, Edward M.

1986a   "Cloth Production Rates in Chinchero, Peru." In *The Junius B. Bird Conference on Andean Textiles, April 7th and 8th, 1984*. A. P. Rowe, ed. Pp. 309–37. Washington, D.C.: The Textile Museum.

1986b   "Threads of Time: Andean Cloth and Costume." In *Costume as Communication: Ethnographic Costumes and Textiles from Middle America and the Central Andes of South America*. M. B. Schevill. Pp. 81–92. Bristol, RI: Haffenreffer Museum of Anthropology.

Franquemont, Edward M., and Christine Franquemont

1986   *Benita Gutierrez: Perfection Was Her Only Signature*. San Francisco: San Francisco Craft and Folk Art Museum.

Franquemont, Edward M., Christine Franquemont, and Billie Jean Isbell

1992   "Awaq ñawin: El Ojo del tejedor. La práctica de la cultura en el tejido." *Revista Andina* 10(1): 47–80.

FWS [U.S. Fish and Wildlife Service]

1999   *Federal Register*, September 8, 1999 (vol. 64, no. 173). Proposed Rules. Endangered and Threatened Wildlife and Plants. P. 48749. http://policy.fws.gov/library/99fr4873

Garber, Marjorie

1992   *Vested Interests: Cross-Dressing and Cultural Anxiety*. New York: HarperCollins.

García Canclini, Néstor

1982   *Las culturas populares en el capitalismo*. México, D.F.: Ed. Nueva Imagen.

1990   *Culturas híbridas: Estrategias para entrar y salir de la modernidad*. Austin: University of Texas Press.

1993   *Transforming Modernity: Popular Culture in Mexico*. México, D.F.: Ed. Grijalbo.

Gartner, William C., and Molly Morton

2000   Estrategia de desarrollo de turismo para el corredor económico del PRA: Analisis de la oferta. http://www.chemonicspe.com/ boletin2/Publicaciones/Estudio_Oferta_Turistica_Puno.pdf. Accessed November 19, 2001.

Gisbert, Teresa, Silvia Arze, and Martha Cajías

1984   *El arte textil en los Andes bolivianos*. Exhibition Notes. March 13–31, 1984. Cochabamba, Bolivia.

1987   *Arte textil y mundo andino*. La Paz: Gisbert y Cía.

Gmelch, Sharon Bohn

2004   "Why Tourism Matters." In *Tourists and Tourism: A Reader*. S. B. Gmelch, ed. Pp. 3–21. Long Grove, IL: Waveland Press.

Gmelch, Sharon Bohn, ed.

2004   *Tourists and Tourism: A Reader*. Long Grove, IL: Waveland Press.

Golte, Jürgen

1980   *Repartos y rebeliones: Túpac Amaru y las contradicciones de la economía colonial*. Lima: Instituto de Estudios Peruanos.

Goodell, Grace

1968a   "A Study of Andean Spinning in the Cuzco Region." *Textile Museum Journal* 2(3): 2–8.

1968b   "The Cloth of the Quechuas." *Natural History* 78(1): 48–55.

Graburn, Nelson H. H.

1976 *Ethnic and Tourist Arts: Cultural Expressions from the Fourth World.*
      Berkeley: University of California Press.

1993 "Ethnic Arts from the Fourth World: The View from Canada."
      In *Imagery and Creativity: Ethnoaesthetics and Art Worlds in the*
      Americas. D. S. Whitten and N. E. Whitten, eds. Pp. 171–204.
      Tucson: University of Arizona Press.

1999 "Epilogue: Ethnic and Tourist Arts Revisited." In *Unpacking*
      Culture: Art and Commodity in Colonial and Postcolonial Worlds. R. B.
      Phillips and C. B. Steiner, eds. Pp. 335–53. Berkeley: University of
      California Press.

Gramsci, Antonio

1971 *Selections from the Prison Notebook of Antonio Gramsci.* Q. Hoare and
      G. N. Smith, eds. and trans. London: Lawrence and Wishart.

Grandino, Cecilia

1997 *La faja calendario de Taquile: Descifrando los simbolos de un arte y*
      una ciencia / Del wata qhawana killa al hallp'a tikray killa. Lima:
      Ed. Minka.

Grandino, Cecilia, and Cronwell Jara Jiménez, eds.

1996 *Las ranas embajadoras de la lluvia y otros relatos: Cuatro*
      aproximaciones a la isla de Taquile. Lima: Ed. Minka.

Greenwood, Davydd J.

1989 "Culture by the Pound: An Anthropological Perspective on
      Tourism as Cultural Commoditization." In *Hosts and Guests: The*
      Anthropology of Tourism. 2nd ed. V. L. Smith, ed. Pp. 171–85.
      Philadelphia: University of Pennsylvania Press.

Greimas, Algirdas Julien

1987 *On Meaning: Selected Writings in Semiotic Theory.* P. J. Perron
      and F H. Collins, trans. Minneapolis: University of Minnesota
      Press.

Grimes, Kimberly M., and B. Lynne Milgram, eds.

2000 *Artisans and Cooperatives: Developing Alternate Trade for the Global*
      Economy. Tucson: University of Arizona Press.

Guss, David M.

1989 *To Weave and Sing: Art, Symbol, and Narrative in the South American*
      Rain Forest. Berkeley: University of California Press.

Harraway, Donna J.

1991 *Simians, Cyborgs, and Women: The Reinvention of Nature.* New York:
      Routledge.

Harris, Olivia

1978   "Complementarity and Conflict: An Andean View of Women and Men." In *Sex and Age as Principles of Social Differentiation.* J. S. La Fontaine, ed. Pp. 21–40. New York: Academic Press.

1980   "The Power of Signs: Gender, Culture and the Wild in the Bolivian Andes." In *Nature, Culture and Gender.* C. MacCormack and M. Strathern, eds. Pp. 70–94. Cambridge: Cambridge University Press.

1982   "The Dead and the Devils among the Bolivian Laymi." In *Death and the Regeneration of Life.* M. Bloch and J. Parry, eds. Pp. 45–73. Cambridge: Cambridge University Press.

1987   *Economia étnica.* (Breve biblioteca del bolsillo.) La Paz: HISBOL.

1995   "Ethnic Identity and Market Relations: Indians and Mestizos in the Andes." In *Ethnicity, Markets, and Migration in the Andes: At the Crossroads of History and Anthropology.* B. Larson and O. Harris, with E. Tandeter, eds. Pp. 351–90. Durham, NC: Duke University Press.

Healy, Kevin

1991   "Ethno-Development in Taquile." In *1991 Festival of American Folklife.* Catalogue. P. 95. Washington, D.C.: Smithsonian Institution.

2001   *Llamas, Weavings, and Organic Chocolate: Multicultural Grassroots Development in the Andes and Amazon of Bolivia.* Notre Dame, IN: University of Notre Dame Press.

Healy, Kevin, and Elayne Zorn

1982–1983 "Lake Titicaca's Campesino-controlled Tourism." *Grassroots Development: Journal of the Inter-American Foundation* 6(2)/7(1): 3–10.

1983   *Taquile's Homespun Tourism: Natural History* 92(11): 80–93.

Hendrickson, Carol

1995   *Weaving Identities: Construction of Dress and Self in a Highland Guatemala Town.* Austin: University of Texas Press.

Hitchcock, Robert K.

1997   "Cultural, Economic, and Environmental Impacts of Tourism among Kalaharin Bushmen." In *Tourism and Culture.* E. Chambers, ed. Pp. 93–128. Albany: State University of New York Press.

Hobsbawm, Eric

1983   "Introduction: Inventing Traditions." In *The Invention of Tradition.* E. Hobsbawm and T. Ranger, eds. Pp. 1–14. Cambridge: Cambridge University Press.

Hobsbawm, Eric, and Terence Ranger, eds.

1983   *The Invention of Tradition*. Cambridge: Cambridge University
        Press.

Hodder, Ian

1982a   *Symbols in Action: Ethnoarchaeological Studies of Material Culture.*
        Cambridge: Cambridge University Press.

1982b   *The Present Past: An Introduction to Anthropology for Archaeologists.*
        New York: Pica Press.

Horn, Manfred

[2002] Alumbrar las noches con la energía solar: El proyecto Taquile.
        http://quipu.uni.edu.pe/OtrosWWW/webproof/public/revistas/
        comunidad/20/h.html. Accessed October 23, 2002.

Isbell, Billie Jean

1976   "La otra mitad esencial: Un estudio de complementariedad sexual
        en los Andes." *Estudios Andinos* 5(1): 37–56.

1978   *To Defend Ourselves: Ecology and Ritual in an Andean Village.* Prospect
        Heights, IL: Waveland Press.

N.d.   "From Unripe to Petrified: The Feminine Symbols and Andean
        Gender Constructions." Ms. in author's possession.

Jacobsen, Nils

1993   *Mirages of Transition: The Peruvian Altiplano, 1780–1930.* Berkeley:
        University of California Press.

Jules-Rosette, Benetta

1984   *The Messages of Tourist Art: An African Semiotic System in Comparative
        Perspective.* New York: Plenum Press.

Julien, Catherine

1983   *Hatunqolla: A View of Inca Rule from the Lake Titicaca Region.*
        University of California Publications in Anthropology 15.
        Berkeley: University of California Press.

1993   "Finding a Fit: Archaeology and Ethnohistory of the Incas." In
        *Provincial Inca: Archaeological and Ethnohistorical Assessment of the
        Impact of the Inca State.* M. A. Malpass, ed. Pp. 177–233. Iowa City:
        University of Iowa Press.

Kaplan, Flora S.

1993   "Mexican Museums in the Creation of a National Image in World
        Tourism." In *Crafts in the World Market: The Impact of Global
        Exchange on Middle American Artisans.* J. Nash, ed. Pp. 103–25.
        Albany: State University of New York Press.

Karp, Ivan

1991 "Festivals." In *Exhibiting Cultures: The Poetics and Politics of Museum Display*. I. Karp and S. D. Levine, eds. Pp. 279–87. Washington, D.C.: Smithsonian Institution Press.

Kincaid, Jamaica

1988 *A Small Place*. New York: Farrar, Straus and Giroux.

Kohl, Benjamin

2002 "Stabilizing Neoliberalism in Bolivia: Popular Participation and Privatization." *Political Geography* 21: 449–72.

Kopytoff, Igor

1986 "The Cultural Biography of Things: Commoditization as Process." In *The Social Life of Things: Commodities in Cultural Perspective*. A. Appadurai, ed. Pp. 64–91. Cambridge: Cambridge University Press.

Kottak, Conrad Phillip

1999 *Assault on Paradise: Social Change in a Brazilian Village*. 3rd ed. New York: McGraw-Hill.

Lambert, Anne M.

1990 "Textiles in the Tourist Trade: Woollen Textile Production in Momostenango, Guatemala." In *Textiles in Trade*. Proceedings of the Textile Society of America Biennial Symposium, September 14–16, 1990. Pp. 253–61. Los Angeles: Textile Society of America.

Larrazábal, H., E. Pita, and C. Toranzo

1988 *Artesania rural boliviana*. La Paz: CEDLA / ILDIS.

Larson, Brooke, and Olivia Harris, with Enrique Tandeter, eds.

1995 *Ethnicity, Markets, and Migration in the Andes: At the Crossroads of History and Anthropology*. Durham, NC: Duke University Press.

Lauer, Mirko

1982 *Crítica de la artesanía: Plástica y sociedad en los Andes peruanos*. Lima: DESCO.

LeCount, Cynthia G.

1990 *Andean Folk Knitting: Traditions and Techniques from Peru and Bolivia*. St. Paul, MN: Dos Tejedoras Fiber Arts Publications.

Libermann, Kitula, Armando Godínez, and Xavier Albó

1989 "Mundo rural andino." In *Para comprender las culturas Rurales en Bolivia*. X. Albó, A. Godínez, and F. Pifarré, eds. Pp. 18–156. La Paz: CIPCA.

Lobo, Susan

1991 "The Fabric of Life. Repatriating the Sacred Coroma Textiles." *Cultural Survival Quarterly* 15.3 (Summer): 40–46.

Low, Linda

2002 "Managing and Sustaining Tourism in Small States: Singapore and the Pacific Islands." In *Island Tourism and Sustainable Development: Caribbean, Pacific, and Mediterranean Experiences.* Y. Apostolopoulos and D. J. Gayle, eds. Pp. 49–66. Westport, CT: Praeger.

MacCannell, Dean

1992 *Empty Meeting Grounds: The Tourist Papers.* London: Routledge.

Mackey, Carol

1990 *Nieves Yucra Huatta y la continuidad en la tradición del uso del quipu.* C. Mackey et al, eds. Pp. 157–64. Lima: CONCYTEC [Consejo Nacional de Cienca y Technological].

2002 "The Continuing Khipu Traditions: Principles and Practices." In *Narrative Threads: Accounting and Recounting in Andean Khipu.* J. Quilter and G. Urton, eds. Pp. 320–47. Austin: University of Texas Press.

Mackey, Carol, Hugo Pereyra, Carlos Radicati, Humberto Rodriguez, and Oscar Valverde

1990 *Quipu y yupana: Colección de escritos.* Lima: CONCYTEC [Consejo Nacional de Ciencia y Technologia].

Martin, Richard

1988 "Transmutations of the Tartan: Attributed Meanings to Tartan Design." In *Proceedings of the First Symposium of the Textile Society of America, September 16–18, 1988.* Pp. 51–62. Minneapolis: Textile Society of America.

Marx, Karl

1977 *Capital.* Vol. 1. Ben Fowkes, trans. New York: Vintage Books.

Mato, Daniel

1997a "Culturas indígenas y populares en yiempos de globalización." *Nueva Sociedad* 149(Mayo–Junio): 100–113.

1997b "Globalización, organizaciones indígenas de América Latina y el 'Festival of American Folklife' de la Smithsonian Institution." *Revista de Investigaciones Folklóricas* 12: 112–19.

1998 "The Transnational Making of Representations of Gender, Ethnicity, and Culture: Indigenous Peoples' Organizations at the Smithsonian Institution's Festival." *Cultural Studies* 12(2): 193–209.

Matos Mar, José

1951a "La propriedad en la isla de Taquile (Lago Titicaca)." *Revista del Museo Nacional* 26 (1951): 211–71.

1951b   "La propriété dans l'Ile Taquile." *Travaux de l'Institut Français d'Études Andines* 3: 51–73.

1960   "El trabajo en una comunidad andina." In *Etnología e Arqueoloqía. Instituto de Etnología y Arqueología 1*. Pp. 9–23. Lima: Universidad Nacional Mayor de San Marcos.

1964   "La propriedad en la isla de Taquile (Lago Titicaca)." In *Estudios sobre la cultural actual del Perú*. Pp. 66–124. Lima: Universidad Nacional Mayor de San Marcos.

1986   "Taquile en Lima. Siete familias cuentan. . . ." Lima: UNESCO/Banco Internacional del Perú.

Mayén de Castellanos, Guisela

1986   *Tzute y jerarquia en Sololá*. Guatemala City: Museo Ixchel del Traje Indígena de Guatemala.

Mayer, Enrique

1992   "Peru in Deep Trouble: Mario Vargas Llosa's 'Inquest in the Andes' Reexamined." In *Rereading Cultural Anthropology*. George E. Marcus, ed. Pp. 181–219. Durham, NC: Duke University Press.

2002   *The Articulated Peasant: Household Economies in the Andes*. Boulder, CO: Westview Press.

McElroy, Jerome L., and Klaus de Albuquerque

2002   "Managing Sustainable Tourism in Small Islands." In *Island Tourism and Sustainable Development: Caribbean, Pacific, and Mediterranean Experiences*. Y. Apostolopoulos and D. J. Gayle, eds. Pp. 15–31. Westport, CT: Praeger.

Medlin, Mary Ann

1983   "Awayqa Sumaj Calchapi: Weaving, Social Organization, and Identity in Calcha, Bolivia." Unpublished Ph.D. dissertation. University of North Carolina, Chapel Hill.

1986   "Learning to Weave in Calcha, Bolivia." In *The Junius B. Bird Conference on Andean Textiles, April 7th and 8th, 1984*. A. P. Rowe, ed. Pp. 275–87. Washington, D.C.: Textile Museum.

1987   "Calcha Pallay and the Uses of Woven Design." In *Andean Aesthetics: Textiles of Peru and Bolivia*. B. Femenías, ed. Pp. 60–66. Madison: University of Wisconsin Press.

1991   "Ethnic Dress and Calcha Festivals, Bolivia." In *Textile Traditions of Mesoamerica and the Andes: An Anthology*. M. B. Schevill, J. C. Berlo, and E. B. Dwyer, eds. Pp. 261–79. New York: Garland.

Meisch, Lynn

1980   "The Cañari People: Their Weaving and Costume." *El Palacio* 86(3): 15–26.

1986   "Weaving Styles in Tarabuco, Bolivia." In *The Junius B. Bird Conference on Andean Textiles, April 7th and 8th, 1984*. A. P. Rowe, ed. Pp. 243–74. Washington, D.C.: Textile Museum.

1987a   *Otavalo: Weaving, Costume, and the Market*. Quito: Ed. Libri Mundi.

1987b   "The Living Textiles of Tarabuco, Bolivia." In *Andean Aesthetics: Textiles of Peru and Bolivia*. B. Femenías, ed. Pp. 46–58. Madison: University of Wisconsin Press.

1991   "We Are Sons of Atahualpa and We Will Win: Traditional Dress in Otavalo and Saraguro, Ecuador." In *Textile Traditions of Mesoamerica and the Andes: An Anthology*. M. B. Schevill, J. C. Berlo, and E. B. Dwyer, eds. Pp. 145–77. New York: Garland.

1995   "Gringas and Otavaleños: Changing Tourist Relations." *Annals of Tourism Research* 22(2): 441–62.

1997   *To Honor the Ancestors: Life and Cloth in the Andean Highlands*. Exhibition catalogue. San Francisco: Fine Arts Museums of San Francisco.

2002   *Andean Entrepreneurs: Otavalo Merchants and Musicians in the Global Arena*. Austin: University of Texas Press.

Menchú Tum, Rigoberta

1991   [1984] *I, Rigoberta Menchú: An Indian Woman in Guatemala*. E. Burgos-Debray, ed.; A. Wright, trans. London: Verso.

Mendoza, Zoila S.

2000   *Shaping Society through Dance: Mestizo Ritual Performance in the Peruvian Andes*. Chicago: University of Chicago Press.

Mitchell, Ross E., and Donald G. Reid

2001   "Community Integration: Island Tourism in Peru." *Annals of Tourism Research* 28(1): 113–39.

Money, Mary

1983   *Los obrajes, el traje y el comercio de ropa en la audiencia de Charcas*. La Paz: Instituto de Estudios Bolivianos / UMSA.

Murillo Vacareza, Josermo

1982   *La pollera: Investigación social e histórica*. La Paz: Ed. ISLA.

Murra, John V.

1962   "Cloth and Its Functions in the Inka State." *American Anthropologist* 64(4): 710–28.

1972   "El 'control vertical' de un máximo de pisos ecológicos en la economía de las sociedades andinas." In *Visita de la Provincia de Leon de Huánuco en 1562: Iñigo Ortiz de Zuñiga, visitador*. Vol. 2. J. Murra, ed. Pp. 427–68. Huánuco, Peru: Universidad Nacional Hermillo Valdizán, Facultad de Letras y Educación.

1975   *Formaciones económicas y políticas del mundo andino.* Lima: Instituto
        de Estudios Peruanos.

1978   "Los límites y las limitaciones del 'archipélago vertical' en los
        Andes." *Avances* 1: 75–80.

1995   [1962] "Cloth, textile, and the Inca empire." In *The Peru Reader:
        History, Culture, Politics.* O. Starn, C. I. Degregori, and R. Kirk, eds.
        Pp. 55–69. Durham, NC: Duke University Press.

de Murúa, Father Martín

1946   [1605] *Historia del origen y geneaología Real de los reyes Incas del Perú.*
        Biblioteca Missionalia Hispanica, vol. 2. Madrid: Instituto Santo
        Toribio de Mogrovejo.

Myers, Fred R.

2001   "Introduction: The Empire of Things." In *The Empire of Things
        Regimes of Value and Material Culture.* Fred Myers, ed. Pp. 3–64.
        Santa Fe, NM, and Oxford: SAR Press/James Currey.

Myers, Fred R., ed.

2001   *The Empire of Things: Regimes of Value and Material Culture.* Santa
        Fe, NM, and Oxford: SAR Press/James Currey.

Nash, Dennison

1996   *Anthropology and Tourism.* Tarrytown, NJ: Pergamon/Elsevier
        Science.

Nash, June C.

1993   "Introduction: Traditional Arts and Changing Markets in Middle
        America." In *Crafts in the World Market: The Impact of Global
        Exchange on Middle American Artisans.* J. Nash, ed. Pp. 1–22. Albany:
        State University of New York Press.

2001   *Mayan Visions: The Quest for Autonomy in an Age of Globalization.*
        New York: Routledge.

Nash, June C., ed.

1993   *Crafts in the World Market: The Impact of Global Exchange on Middle
        American Artisans.* Albany: State University of New York Press.

Newman, Cathy

2003   "Dreamweavers." *National Geographic Magazine.* January: 50–73.

O'Brien, Jay, and William Roseberry, eds.

1991   *Golden Ages, Dark Ages: Imagining the Past in Anthropology and
        History.* Berkeley: University of California Press.

O'Neale, Lila, and Alfred Kroeber

1930   "Textile Periods in Ancient Peru." *American Archaeology and
        Ethnology* 28(2): 23–56.

Ong, Walter J.

    1982   *Orality and Literacy: The Technologizing of the Word*. London: Methuen.

Orlove, Benjamin

    1977   *Alpacas, Sheep, and Men: The Wool Export Economy and Regional Society of Southern Peru*. New York: Academic Press.

    1993   "Putting Race in Its Place: Order in Colonial and Postcolonial Peruvian Geography." *Social Research* 60(2): 301–36.

    2002   *Lines in the Water: Nature and Culture at Lake Titicaca*. Berkeley: University of California Press.

Orlove, Benjamin, ed.

    1997   *The Allure of the Foreign: Imported Goods in Postcolonial Latin America*. Ann Arbor: University of Michigan Press.

Otero, Gerardo

    1999   *Farewell to the Peasantry? Political Class Formation in Rural Mexico*. Boulder, CO: Westview Press.

Painter, Michael

    1991   "Re-Creating Peasant Economy in Southern Peru." In *Golden Ages, Dark Ages: Imagining the Past in Anthropology and History*. J. O'Brien and W. Roseberry, eds. Pp. 81–106. Berkeley: University of California Press.

Palmer, David Scott, ed.

    1992   *Shining Path of Peru*. New York: St. Martin's Press.

Parry, J, and Maurice Bloch, eds.

    1989   *Money and the Morality of Exchange*. Cambridge: Cambridge University Press.

Phillips, Ruth B.

    1990   "Moccasins into Slippers: Traditions and Transformations in Nineteenth-Century Woodlands Indian Textiles." In *Textiles in Trade: Proceedings of the Textile Society of America Biennial Symposium, September 14–16, 1990*. Pp. 262–73. Los Angeles: Textile Society of America.

Phillips, Ruth B., and Christopher B. Steiner

    1999   "Art, Authenticity, and the Baggage of Cultural Encounter." In *Unpacking Culture: Art and Commodity in Colonial and Postcolonial Worlds*. R. B. Phillips and C. B. Steiner, eds. Pp. 3–19. Berkeley: University of California Press.

Phillips, Ruth B., and Christopher B. Steiner, eds.

    1999   *Unpacking Culture: Art and Commodity in Colonial and Postcolonial Worlds*. Berkeley: University of California Press.

Phipps, Elena J.

    1996   "Textiles as Cultural Memory: Andean Garments in the Colonial Period." In *Converging Cultures: Art and Identity in Spanish America*. D. Fane, ed. Pp. 144–56. New York: Brooklyn Museum/ Harry N. Abrams.

Platt, Tristan

    1982   *Estado boliviano y ayllu andino: Tierra y tributo en el Norte de Potosí*. Lima: Instituto de Estudios Andinos.

    1986   "Mirrors and Maize: The Concept of Yanantin among the Macha of Bolivia." In *Anthropological History of Andean Polities*. J. V. Murra, N. Wachtel, and J. Revel, eds. Pp. 228–59. Cambridge: Cambridge University Press.

Poole, Deborah, ed.

    1994   *Unruly Order: Violence, Power, and Cultural Identity in the High Provinces of Southern Peru*. Boulder, CO: Westview Press.

Poole, Deborah, and Gerardo Rénique

    1991   "The New Chroniclers of Peru: U.S. Scholars and Their 'Shining Path' of Peasant Rebellion." *Bulletin of Latin American Research* 10(2): 133–91.

    1992   *Peru: Time of Fear*. London: Latin American Bureau.

Pratt, Mary Louise

    1992   *Imperial Eyes: Travel Writing and Transculturation*. London: Routledge.

    1995   "Arts of the Contact Zone." In *Reading the Lives of Others*. D. Bartholomae and A. Petrosky, eds. Pp. 180–95. Boston: Bedford Books of St. Martin's Press.

Price, Sally

    1989   *Primitive Art in Civilized Places*. Chicago: University of Chicago Press.

Prochaska, Rita

    1983   "Ethnography and Enculturation of Weaving on Taquile Island, Peru." Unpublished M.A. thesis. Dept. of Anthropology, University of California at Los Angeles.

    1988   *Taquile: Tejiendo un mundo mágico/Weavers of a Magic World*. Lima: Arius.

    1990   *Taquile y sus tejidos*. Versión Castellano-English. Lima: Arius/ CONCYTEC [Consejo Nacional de Ciencia y Tecnologica].

Rasnake, Roger N.

    1988   *Domination and Cultural Resistance: Authority and Power among an Andean People*. Durham, NC: Duke University Press.

Rénique, José Luis

    1994   "Political Violence, and State, and the Peasant Struggle for Land (Puno)." In *Unruly Order: Violence, Power, and Cultural Identity in the High Provinces of Southern Peru*. D. Poole, ed. Pp. 233–45. Boulder, CO: Westview Press.

    1998   "Apogee and the Crisis of a 'Third Path': *Mariateguismo*, 'People's War,' and Counterinsurgency in Puno, 1987–1994." In *Shining and Other Paths: War and Society in Peru, 1980–1995*. S. J. Stern, ed. Pp. 307–38. Durham, NC: Duke University Press.

Rivera Cusicanqui, Silvia, ed.

    1996   *Ser mujer indígena, chola o birlocha en la Bolivia postcolonial de los años 90*. La Paz: Plural editores.

Rockefeller, Stuart

    1998   "'There Is Culture Here': Spectacle and the Inculcation of Folklore in Highland Bolivia." *Journal of Latin American Anthropology* 3(2): 118–49.

Rogers, Mark

    1998a   "Introduction: Performing Andean Identities." *Journal of Latin American Anthropology* 3(2): 2–13.

Rogers, Mark, ed.

    1998b   "Performance, Identity, and Historical Consciousness in the Andes." Special issue of *Journal of Latin American Anthropology* 3(2).

Romero, Raúl R.

    2001   *Debating the Past: Music, Memory, and Identity in the Andes*. Oxford: Oxford University Press.

Roseberry, William

    1989   *Anthropologies and Histories: Essays in Culture, History, and Political Economy*. New Brunswick, NJ: Rutgers University Press.

Roseberry, William, and Jay O'Brien

    1991   "Introduction." In *Golden Ages, Dark Ages: Imagining the Past in Anthropology and History*. J. O'Brien and W. Roseberry, eds. Pp. 1–18. Berkeley: University of California Press.

Rowe, Ann Pollard

    1975   "Weaving Processes in the Cuzco Area of Peru." *Textile Museum Journal* 4(2): 30–46.

    1977   *Warp-Patterned Weaves of the Andes*. Washington, D.C.: Textile Museum.

    1978   "Prácticas textiles en al area de Cuzco." In *Tecnología andina*. R. Ravines, ed. Pp. 369–94. Lima: Instituto de Estudios Peruanos.

    1981   *A Century of Change in Guatemalan Textiles*. New York: Center for Inter-American Relations.

Rowe, Ann Pollard, Elizabeth P. Benson, and Anne-Louise Schaffer, eds.

1979   *The Junius B. Bird Pre-Columbian Textile Conference, May 19–20, 1973.*
Washington, D.C.: Textile Museum and Dumbarton Oaks.

Rowe, Ann Pollard, and John Cohen

2002   *Hidden Threads of Peru. Q'ero Textiles.* Washington, D.C.: Textile
Museum.

Rowe, John Howland

1946   "Inca Culture at the Time of the Spanish Conquest." In
Handbook of South American Indians. J. H. Steward, ed.
(Smithsonian Institution, Bureau of American Ethnology,
Bulletin 143.) Washington, D.C.: U.S. Government Printing
Office. 2: 183–330.

Rowe, William, and Vivian Schelling

1991   *Memory and Modernity: Popular Culture in Latin America.* London:
Verso.

Rubinstein, Ruth P.

1995   *Dress Codes: Meanings and Messages in American Culture.* Boulder,
CO: Westview Press.

de Sahonero, M. L. Canavesi

1987   *El traje de la chola paceña.* Cochabamba, Bolivia: Los Amigos del
Libro.

Salas de Coloma, Miriam

1979   *De los obrajes de Canaria y Chincheros a las comunidades indígenas de
Vilcashuaman.* Siglo XVI. Lima: SESATOR.

Salomon, Frank

1979   "Weavers of Otavalo." In *Peoples and Cultures of Native South
America.* D. R. Gross, ed. Pp. 463–92. Garden City, N.Y.:
Doubleday/Natural History Press.

1982   "Andean Ethnology in the 1970s: A Retrospective." *Latin American
Research Review* 17(2): 75–128.

Schevill, Margot Blum

1985   *Evolution in Textile Design from the Highlands of Guatemala.* The
Occasional Papers: No. 1. Berkeley: University of California.

1986   *Costume as Communication: Ethnographic Costumes and Textiles from
Middle America and the Central Andes of South America.* Bristol, RI:
Haffenreffer Museum of Anthropology.

1991   "The Communicative Power of Cloth and Its Creation." In *Textile
Traditions of Mesoamerica and the Andes: An Anthology.* M. B.
Schevill, J. C. Berlo, and E. B. Dwyer, eds. Pp. 3–15. New York:
Garland.

Schevill, Margot Blum, Janet Catherine Berlo, and Edward B. Dwyer, eds.

1991   *Textile Traditions of Mesoamerica and the Andes: An Anthology*. New York: Garland.

Schneider, Jane

1987   "The Anthropology of Cloth." *Annual Review of Anthropology* 16: 409–48.

Schneider, Jane, and Annette B. Weiner

1986   "Cloth and the Organization of Human Experience." *Current Anthropology* 27(2): 178–84.

Seligmann, Linda J., and Elayne Zorn

1981   "Visión diacrónica de la economía de la producción textil andina." *America Indígena* 41(2): 265–87.

Selwyn, Tom, ed.

1996   *The Tourist Image: Myths and Myth Making in Tourism*. Chichester, England: John Wiley and Sons.

Siegal, William

1991   *Aymara-Bolivianische Textilien/Historic Aymara Textiles. November 20, 1991–January 26, 1992*. Exhibition catalog. Krefeld: German Textile Museum.

Silva Santisteban, Fernando

1978   "Los obrajes en el virreinato del Perú." In *Tecnología andina*. R. Ravines, ed. Pp. 347–67. Lima: Instituto de Estudios Peruanos.

Silverblatt, Irene

1987   *Moon, Sun, and Witches: Gender Ideologies and Class in Inca and Colonial Peru*. Princeton: Princeton University Press.

Skomal, S. N.

1992   Retrieving the Fabric of Life. *Anthropology Newsletter* 33(8): 2.

Smith, Gavin

1991   "The Production of Culture in Local Rebellion." In *Golden Ages, Dark Ages: Imagining the Past in Anthropology and History*. J. O'Brien and W. Roseberry, eds. Pp. 180–207. Berkeley: University of California Press.

Smith, James F., and Ken Ellingwood

2001   "Sept. 11 Leaves Carpet Loomers Idle in Oaxacan Town." *Los Angeles Times*, November 28.

Smith, Valene L., ed.

1989   *Hosts and Guests: The Anthropology of Tourism*. 2nd ed. Philadelphia: University of Pennsylvania Press.

de Solari, Gertrudis B.

1983   "Una manta de Taquile: Interpretación de sus signos." *Boletín de Lima* 29(5): 57–73.

Starn, Orin, Carlos Iván Degregori, and Robin Kirk, eds.

1995   *The Peru Reader: History, Culture, Politics.* Durham, NC: Duke University Press.

Steele, Valerie

1993   "The F Word." *Annual Editions Anthropology* 93/94: 66–69.

1996   *Fetish: Fashion, Sex and Power.* Oxford: Oxford University Press.

Stein, William

2000   *Vicisitudes del discurso del desarrollo en el Peru: Una etnografía sobre la modernidad del proyecto Vicos.* Lima: Sur Casa de Estudios del Socialismo.

Steiner, Chris B.

1985   "Another Image of Africa: Toward an Ethnohistory of European Cloth Marketed in West Africa, 1873–1960." *Ethnohistory* 32(2): 91–110.

1994   *African Art in Transit.* Cambridge: Cambridge University Press.

2001   "Rights of Passage: On the Liminal Identity of Art in the Border Zone." In *The Empire of Things: Regimes of Value and Material Culture.* F. R. Myers, ed. Pp. 207–31. Santa Fe, NM, and Oxford: SAR Press/James Currey.

Stephen, Lynn

1991a   "Marketing Ethnicity." *Cultural Survival Quarterly* 16(4): 25–27.

1991b   *Zapotec Women.* Austin: University of Texas Press.

1993   "Weaving in the Fast Lane: Class, Ethnicity, and Gender in Zapotec Craft Commercialization." In *Crafts in the World Market: The Impact of Global Exchange on Middle American Artisans.* J. Nash, ed. Pp. 25–57. Albany: State University of New York Press.

Stephenson, Marcia

1999   *Gender and Modernity in Andean Bolivia.* Austin: University of Texas Press.

Stern, Steve J.

1993   *Peru's Indian Peoples and the Challenge of Spanish Conquest: Huamanga to 1640.* 2nd ed. Madison: University of Wisconsin Press.

Stern, Steve J., ed.

1998   *Shining and Other Paths: War and Society in Peru, 1980–1995.* Durham, NC: Duke University Press.

Stoll, David

1990   *Is Latin America Turning Protestant? The Politics of Evangelical Growth*. Berkeley: University of California Press.

Swain, Margaret Byrne

1989   "Gender Roles in Indigenous Tourism: Kuna *Mola*, Kuna *Yala*, and Cultural Survival." In *Hosts and Guests: The Anthropology of Tourism*. 2nd ed. V. L. Smith, ed. Pp. 83–104. Philadelphia: University of Pennsylvania Press.

Tedlock, Barbara, and Dennis Tedlock

1985   "Text and Textile: Language and Technology in the Arts of the Quiché Maya." *Journal of Anthropological Research* 41(2): 121–46.

Thomas, Nicholas

1991   *Entangled Objects: Exchange, Material Culture, and Colonialism in the Pacific*. Cambridge, MA: Harvard University Press.

Thorp, Rosemary, and Geoffrey Bertram

1978   *Peru, 1890–1977: Growth and Policy in an Open Economy*. New York: Columbia University Press.

Tilley, Christopher

1997   "Performing Culture in the Global Village." *Critique of Anthropology* 17(1): 67–89.

Tilley, Christopher, ed.

1990a   *Reading Material Culture: Structuralism, Hermeneutics and Post-Structuralism*. London: Basil Blackwell.

Titicaca [NASA Image Collection]

2002   "Lake Space Imagery." http://titicaca.ucsb.edu/chamak_pacha/docs/lake_space_imagery/index.html. Accessed September 12, 2002.

Trevor-Roper, Hugh

1983   "The Invention of Tradition: The Highland Tradition of Scotland." In *The Invention of Tradition*. E. J. Hobsbawm and T. Ranger, eds. Cambridge: Cambridge University Press.

Turino, Thomas

1991   "The State and Andean Musical Production in Peru." In *Nation-States and Indians in Latin America*. G. Urban and J. Sherzer, eds. Pp. 259–85. Austin: University of Texas Press.

1993   *Moving Away from Silence: Music of the Peruvian Altiplano and the Experience of Urban Migration*. Chicago: University of Chicago Press.

Turner, Terry S.

1980   "The Social Skin." In *Not Work Alone: A Cross-Cultural View of
        Activities Superfluous to Survival*. J. Cherfas and R. Lewin, eds.
        Pp. 112–40. Beverly Hills, CA: Sage Publications.

Urban, Greg, and Joel Sherzer, eds.

1991   *Nation-States and Indians in Latin America*. Austin: University of
        Texas Press.

Urton, Gary

1981   *At the Crossroads of the Earth and the Sky: An Andean Cosmology*.
        Austin: University of Texas Press.

1990   *The History of a Myth: Pacariqtambo and the Origin of the Inkas*.
        Austin: University of Texas Press.

1991   "The Stranger in Andean Communities." In *Cultures et Sociétés
        Andes et Méso-Amérique: Mélanges en Hommage à Pierre Duviols*.
        R. Thiercelin, ed. Vol. 2. Pp. 791–810. Aix-en-Provence:
        Publications de l'Université de Provence.

Valencia Chacon, Américo

1980   "Los sikuris de la isla de Taquile: Estudio del siku bipolar de
        Taquile." *Separata del Boletín de Lima* 8–9 (September, November):
        1–24.

Vance, Marion R., and Ron Weber

1992   "Harmony with the Earth: A Celebration of Andean Culture."
        Grassroots Development: Journal of the Inter-American Foundation
        16(1): 32–41, cover.

Wasserman, Tamara E., and Jonathan S. Hill

1981   *Bolivian Indian Textiles: Traditional Designs and Costumes*. New York:
        Dover.

Waterbury, Ronald

1989   "Embroidery for Tourists: A Contemporary Putting-Out System
        in Oaxaca, Mexico." In *Cloth and Human Experience*. A. B. Weiner
        and J. Schneider, eds. Pp. 243–71. Washington, D.C.: Smithsonian
        Institution Press.

Weiner, Annette B.

1992   *Inalienable Possessions: The Paradox of Keeping–while–giving*.
        Berkeley: University of California Press.

Weiner, Annette B., and Jane Schneider, eds.

1989   *Cloth and Human Experience*. Washington, D.C.: Smithsonian
        Institution Press.

Weismantel, Mary

1988   *Food, Gender, and Poverty in the Ecuadorian Andes*. Philadelphia:
        University of Pennsylvania Press.

2001   *Cholas and Pishtacos: Stories of Race and Sex in the Andes.* Chicago: University of Chicago Press.

Wolf, Eric

1955   "Types of Latin American Peasantries: A Preliminary Discussion." *American Anthropologist* 57: 457–71.

1957   "Closed Corporate Communities in Mesoamerica and Central Java." *Southwestern Journal of Anthropology* 13(1): 1–18.

1986   "The Vicissitudes of the Closed Corporate Peasant Community." *American Ethnologist* 13(2): 325–29.

Wood, William Warner

2000   "Flexible Production, Households, and Fieldwork: Multisited Zapotec Weavers in the Era of Late Capitalism." *Ethnology* 39(2): 133–48.

World Bank

2001   *Engendering Development: Enhancing Development through Attention to Gender.* Washington, D.C.: World Bank/New York: Oxford University Press.

WTO [World Tourism Organization]

2001a   Conference on Sustainable Development of Ecotourism in Small Island Developing States (SIDS) and Other Small Islands. Preparatory Conference for the International Year of Ecotourism. Mahé, Seychelles, 8–10 December 2001. Final Report. http://www.world-tourism.org/sustainable/IYE/Regional_Activities/Seychelles/Menu.htm. Accessed November 15, 2002.

2001b   Conference on Ecotourism in Mountain Areas: A Challenge to Sustainable Development. European Preparatory Conference for the International Year of Ecotourism and the International Year of Mountains. Co-sponsored by the United Nations Environment Programme. Final Report. Electronic document, http://www.world-tourism.org/sustainable/IYE/Regional_Activiites/Austria-proceedings. Accessed November 15, 2002.

Yapita, Juan de Dios

1994   *Aymara: Metodo Facil 1.* La Paz: Ed. ILCA.

Yorke, Roger

1980   *Woven Images: Bolivian Weaving from the 19th and 20th Centuries.* Exhibition Catalogue. 28 February–30 March, 1980. Dalhousie Art Gallery, University of Halifax, Nova Scotia.

Zorn, Elayne

1979   "Warping and Weaving on a Four-Stake Ground Loom in the Lake Titicaca Basin Community of Taquile, Peru." In *Looms and Their*

Products: Irene Emery Roundtable on Museum Textiles, 1977
Proceedings. P. Fiske and I. Emery, eds. Pp. 212–27. Washington,
D.C.: Textile Museum.

1983   "Traditions Versus Tourism in Taquile, Peru: Changes in the
        Economics of Andean Textile Production and Exchange Due
        to Market Sale." Unpublished M.A. thesis. Institute of Latin
        American Studies, University of Texas–Austin.

1986   "Textiles in Herders' Ritual Bundles of Macusani, Peru." In *The
        Junius B. Bird Conference on Andean Textiles, April 7th and 8th, 1984.*
        A. P. Rowe, ed. Pp. 289–307. Washington, D.C.: Textile Museum.

[1987] "Re-Inventing Ancient Textile Tradition? Taquile's 'Calendar
        Belt.'" Keynote paper presented at the Elvehjem Museum of Art,
        University of Wisconsin, Madison.

1987a   "Encircling Meaning: Economics and Aesthetics in Taquile, Peru."
        In *Andean Aesthetics: Textiles of Peru and Bolivia.* Exhibition
        Catalogue, Elvehjem Museum. B. Femenías, ed. Pp. 67–80.
        Madison: University of Wisconsin Press.

1987b   "Un análisis de los tejidos en los atados rituales de los pastores."
        Revista Andina 5(2): 489–526.

1991   "Modern Traditions: The Impact of the Trade in Traditional
        Textiles on the Sakaka of Northern Potosí, Bolivia." In *Textiles in
        Trade: Proceedings of the Textile Society of America Second Biennial
        Symposium.* Pp. 241–52. Los Angeles: Textile Society of America.

1993   "Textiles as a Daily Obsession in the Andes: A Day in the Life
        of an Andean Weaver." In *Textiles in Daily Life: Proceedings of the
        Textile Society of America Third Biennial Symposium.* Pp. 151–62.
        Washington, D.C.: Textile Society of America.

1994   "Taquile, Peru: Model Tourism." In *1994 Festival of American
        Folklife.* Catalogue. P. 22. Washington, D.C.: Smithsonian
        Institution.

1995   "(Re-)Fashioning Identity: Late Twentieth-Century
        Transformations in Dress and Society in Bolivia." In *Contact,
        Crossover, Continuity: Proceedings of the Textile Society of America
        Fourth Biennial Symposium.* Pp. 343–54. Toronto: Textile Society
        of America.

[1995] "Taquileños on the Mall/Washingtonians (and others) in Taquile:
        The Smithsonian Folklife Festival, International Tourism, and
        the 'Last Inkas.'" Paper presented at the 94th Annual Meeting
        of the American Anthropological Association, Washington, D.C.
        1995.

1997a   "Marketing Diversity: Global Transformations in Cloth and
         Identity in Highland Peru and Bolivia." Unpublished Ph.D.
         dissertation. Dept. of Anthropology, Cornell University, Ithaca,
         NY.

1997b   "Coca, Cash, and Cloth in Highland Bolivia: The Chapare and
         Transformations in a 'Traditional' Andean Textile Economy." In
         Coca, Cocaine, and the Bolivian Reality. M. B. Leons and H. Sanabria,
         eds. Pp. 71–98. Albany: State University of New York Press.

1999   [1998] "(Re)Fashioning the Self: Dress, Economy, and Identity
         among the Sakaka of Northern Potosí, Bolivia." *Revista Chungará*
         (Arica, Chile) 30(2): 161–96.

[1999]   "Time and History in Taquile, Peru." Paper presented at the
         American Society for Ethnohistory Meeting, Mashankucket, CT,
         1999.

2000   "When Incas Travel Abroad: Tourism to and from Peru." In
         Transforming Cultures in the Americas. Vol. 4. D. Castillo and M. J.
         Dudley, eds. Pp. 21–30. Ithaca, NY: Latin American Studies
         Program/Cornell University.

[2001]   "Tourism and the Gendering of Indigenous Identity and Power in
         Highland Peru." Paper presented at the 100th Annual Meeting of
         the American Anthropological Association, Washington, D.C.,
         2001.

2002   "Dangerous Encounters: Ritual Battles in Andean Bolivia." In
         Combat, Ritual, and Performance: Anthropology of the Martial Arts.
         D. E. Jones, ed. Pp. 119–52. Westport, CT: Praeger.

Zorn, Elayne, and Rita Prochaska

[1986]   "Local Control Over the Production of Tourist Services." Paper
         presented at the 85th Annual Meeting of the American
         Anthropological Association, Washington, D.C.

Zuñiga, Edgar Edwardo

1980   Estudio de factibilidad económico financiero de la "Empresa de
         Transporte Turístico Lacustre Taguile S. R. Ltda." Report typed
         1980.

FILMS AND CDS

Bellenger, Xavier, recorder

1992   *Perou. Taquile, île du ciel: Musique quechua de lac Titicaca.* OCORA
         (CD 558 651).

Conjunto Las Nuevas Ondas

2001   *Las Nuevas Ondas.* Vol. 2. (CD). Taquile, Puno, Perú.

Freeman, Mark

    1997   *Weaving the Future* (film.) Distributed by Documentary
        Educational Resources, Watertown, MA.

Gelles, Paul H., and Wilton Martínez

    1992   *Transnational Fiesta: 1992* (film.) Distributed by the University of
        California Center for Media and Independent Learning, Berkeley.

WEBSITES

AAA (American Anthropological Association).
    http://www.aaanet.org

CTTC (Center for Traditional Textiles of Cusco).
    http://www.incas.org/SPChinchero.htm

INDEX

adolescence and textiles, 78, 154
Adventists, 119
aesthetics, 73, 82–84, 155
agriculture, 1, 8, 40, 99, 135, 160; crops, 30, 33, 40, 99; fertility, 65; sectoral fallowing, 33, 34, 78, 99; subsistence, 8, 41–42; and textiles, 54, 58, 167n2
agro-pastoral economy, 10, 42, 76, 79–80, 153–56. *See also* agriculture; animal husbandry/herding
Albó, Xavier, 160–61, 163
Allen, Catherine J., 38, 168n7
alpacas. *See* camelids
altiplano, 4, 6, 28, 30, 44–46, 112
Amantani Island, 7, 26, 30–31, 33, 34, 47, 90, 122, 143, 175n4
amautas. See National Grand Prize Amautas of Peruvian Crafts
American Museum of Natural History, 3, 52, 124, 167–68n3
Andeanness, xv. *See also* Murra, John
Andes, 79
animal husbandry/herding, 8, 10, 40, 58, 75, 154
anthropology: and theorizing change, 19; and transnationalism, 17
Antigua, Guatemala, x
antique textile market. *See* ethnic textile market
Antropólogos del Surandino (ASUR), 154, 160, 176n4

apprenticeship, 63, 120; of author, xiii, 3, 22–23
aqsu. See women, clothing
Arequipa, Peru, 88, 173n15
Arnold, Denise, 57, 173n12
art, 155, 159–60; commercialization of, 11, 79, 155; commoditization of, 169n9, 173–74n2; creation of new objects, 12, 85, 160; textiles as, 19, 52–53, 155, 159–60, 176n4. *See also* crafts
Asociación Artesanal "Manco Capac" Taquile, 88–89
authenticity, 5, 122, 142, 151–53, 169n9
Avalos de Matos, Rosalía, 12
awana. See looms, Andean-type
ayllu, 8, 33, 36, 53, 80, 168n5; *ladus*, 32, 36, 41, 115; legal recognition as community, 152; in Peru and Bolivia, 32, 176n4; *suyo* system, 33; and tourism, 14, 141; and weaving, 83, 173n12
Aymara language, 8, 30, 43, 77, 86
ayni, xix, 36, 87, 124; owed by author, 24

Bastidas, Micaela, 158
Bay of Puno, 7, 28, 34. *See also* Urus Islands
belts, 1, 74, 77, 82, 83, 88; changes in, 74, 82, 83, 88, 98; looms for, 62; *mama chumpi*, 77, 173n14; in museums, 174n6; types of, 74, 77;

belts (*continued*)
underbelt, xiv, 77. *See also* calendar belts
Berlo, Janet, 157
Berra, Yogi, 111
boats, xi, 5, 8, 44, 118–21, 137, 141; associations for, 13, 37; building of, 3, 32, 47, 119, 138; cooperatives for, 13–14, 37, 49, 117, 119–20, 142; *Corsario*, 120; crews, 118, 138; dangers of, 27; Motorboat Committee, 120; ownership of, 120–21, 134; reed, 8, 44; *San Miguel*, 44; wooden sailboats, 8, 31, 118–19, 120
Bolivia, 44
Bourdieu, Pierre, xii, 14
braids and braiding, 58, 63, 67
Brooklyn Museum, xv, 1–2, 5, 35, 61, 155, 174n6, 174n7
Bubba, Cristina, 172n3

calendar belts, 12, 35, 73, 97–105, 173n1, 174n8; gender and, 12, 160; meta-discourse about, 97
calendars, 97–105; annual, 12, 41–42; created on Taquile, 12
Callañaupa, Nilda, 176n3
Callañaupa, Wilton, 2
camelids, 58, 75; alpaca, 58, 155, 173n13; colors of, 59; fleece of, 42, 43, 55, 58, 86; llama, 43, 58, 172n7, 173n13; vicuña, 58, 172n5; wool production, 42, 58. *See also* animal husbandry/herding
campesino. See peasants
campo runa. See peasants
Candelaria, Feast of, xiii, 28, 51
Candlemas, Feast of Virgin, xiii, 28, 51

Capachica Peninsula, Peru, 28–29, 46–48, 114, 122
Capitanía del Puerto, 147–50
cargo system, 34, 36
Catholicism, 49, 119, 133
Center for Renewable Energies, National Engineering University (CER-UNI), 49, 122
Center for Traditional Textiles of Cusco (CTTC), 154, 160, 176n3
Cereceda, Verónica, 56–57
chaleco músico, 68, 90
ch'aska. See images
Chibnik, Michael, 155, 167n2
chola/o, 68, 69–70, 143, 150–51, 158, 168n6
Chucuito Peninsula, Peru, 28
chuku. See clothing, women's
ch'ullo. See clothing, men's
chumpi. See belts
chumpi calendario. See calendar belts
ch'uspa, 1. *See also* clothing, men's
Clifford, James, 170n2
clothing, 54, 65–67, 173n15; Andeantype, 58, 61; changes in, 68–69, 71, 153–56; colonial prohibitions on, 53; effects of tourism on, 70, 136, 138, 142, 159–60, 165; ethnic, 10, 12, 53–54, 66–68, 71, 79–80, 138, 151, 165, 173n15; handmade, 6, 65–66; and identity, 69–71, 80; men's, 1, 15, 64, 66–67; politics of, 15; and race, 51, 139–40, 151–53; and racism, 14, 65; *runa p'acha*, 27, 53–54, 65, 75, 153–56; and semiotic analysis of, 55–56, 72–73; Spanish-type, 58, 61; strategic use of, 80, 138, 165; styles of, 65–66; as visual language, 57–58, 72; worn on Ta-

quile, 54, 58, 66–67, 69, 111, 130,
165; Western–type, 10, 64, 68–70,
138; women's, 66, 76–77. *See also*
belts; shawls; textiles
coca leaf, 1, 42, 44
Cohen, Jeffrey, 127, 137, 161, 167n2
Cohen, John, 48
Colla Aymara kingdom, 30
Colloredo-Mansfeld, Rudi, 141
colonial period, 53, 61
color, 82, 83, 153–54
commercialization, 56–57, 71, 90,
145, 157, 159–60
commoditization, 10, 85–110, 142,
155, 169n9, 173–74n2; of culture,
12; definition of, 11, 168n8; and
gender, 16, 56; as process, 86,
173–74n2; of textiles, 12, 82–110,
155–56; and tourism, 11, 16, 85,
159–60; of traditional arts, 85–95,
153–56, 160, 173–74n2
communalism, 114–16, 143, 145, 161.
See also community; labor
community, 14, 114, 116, 119, 140–41,
148, 165. *See also ayllu*
conflicts, 6, 115, 119, 175n1
Conklin, William, 55
Consejo Indio de Sud America
(CISA), 49
"contact zones," 11, 85
cooperatives, 83–89; boat, 13, 14,
117–19, 137; fishing, 122; membership in, 89, 119–20, 137; for
selling textiles, 13, 51, 87–89, 125,
126, 137, 174n9; tourism-related,
117, 126; transportation, 4, 118;
weaving, 125, 126, 174n9
Cornejo, Mariano, 117, 123
Coroma, Bolivia, 57, 162, 172n3
crafts, xii, 155–56, 159–60; coopera-

tives, 51, 88–89, 117, 125, 131;
cottage industry, 66; demon-
strations of, 4; fairs, 88, 123–27;
Grand Master of Peruvian
Crafts, xiv, 94; Handicraft Committee, 125; prizes, 94; producers, 6, 84, 94, 173n15; reorganization of production of, 12, 90; as
source of income, 10, 155–56,
159–60; textiles as, 19
crochet, 58
cross-dressing, 68
Cruz Machaca, Fortunato, 128
cultural preservation, 13, 136–37, 146
culture, 5; choices about, 11; commercialization of, 12, 159–60; expressive, 5–6; and gender, 11, 56;
impact of globalization on, 11,
162; impact of tourism on, 14,
69, 138–45; popular, 18; and race,
69, 139
cumbi. See textiles, *cumbi*
Cusco, Peru, 87–88, 132, 149, 154
Cutipa, Juan, 148, 169n14

Davis, Fred, 55
de Amat Quiroz, Gamaliel, 111
de la Cadena, Marisol, 150, 168n6,
171n9, 171n10
de Solari, Gertrudis, xi–xii, 88, 123,
175n6
death, 65
designs. *See* images
development, 57–59, 63, 123–27, 157,
163; grassroots, 124
diet, 8, 9, 30, 42, 47, 117, 122, 170n3,
175n5. *See also* tourism, food and
restaurants
discrimination, 11, 48, 65, 79, 139–40
dyes, 58–59, 153–54

economy: agro-pastoral, 79–80, 153–56; barter and exchange, 6, 42, 75–76, 86, 150; capitalism, 116; cash, 10, 16, 42–44, 86–88, 112, 136, 140, 160; changes in textile, 73, 79, 142, 153–56; ethnic, 75, 86, 169n11; formal, 42; inter-zonal exchange, 75; money, 4, 10, 42, 86–87, 140, 142, 145, 149–50, 161, 174n3; in Puno region, 9, 58, 144–45; and tourism, 136, 142, 145, 159–60; wool, 9, 42, 43, 58, 79; women and, 73, 144–45, 154, 174n3. *See also* exchange

education, 8, 9, 45–46, 49, 60, 72, 136, 144, 154, 157–59; effects on community, 6, 49; formal, 45, 136, 154; incompatibility with cloth production, 72, 77, 79–80, 154; informal, 45, 60, 77; teach-ers, 12; of women, 9, 154

elders, 63, 93

electricity, 1, 5, 122

Elvehjem Museum of Art, 174n6

Empresa de Transporte, 120

Energy Saving Project of the Min-istry of Energy and Mines (PAE-MEM), 49, 122

envidia, 140

Espejo, Elvira, 176n4

Esteves Island, Peru, 147–50

ethnicity. *See* race and racism

ethnography, xiii, 20, 39, 113, 152, 169n12, 169–70n15; ethical issues, 20, 168n4; and gender, 21; methodology, 20–22; multi-sited, xiii, 17; obligations to com-munity, 21, 24, 169–70n15, 175n3; as rite of passage, 28; and

transnational subjects, 17, 175n3; and writing, 152

exhibitions, 123–27. *See also* museums

faena. See labor

faja calendario. See calendar belts

family life: childlessness, 37, 171n11; children, 37, 70; family size, 29; inheritance patterns, 40

fashion, 19, 52

Femenías, Blenda, 71

Festival of American Folklife, xv, 47, 103, 122, 124, 125, 159

festivals, xiii, 13, 47, 125, 136, 173n13

fiber, 43, 58, 59, 75–76, 86, 173n13

fiesta-cargo system. *See cargo* system

fishing, 1, 42, 44, 46, 122; coopera-tives, 122; in Lake Titicaca, 8, 44

fleece, 42, 43, 55, 58, 63, 76, 86, 153–56, 173n13. *See also* fiber

Flores Huatta, Alejandro, 43–44, 82, 103, 127, 173n1, 174n7

Flores Quispe, Cayetano, 63

folklore, 51, 123–24; associations, 3, 14, 98, 117, 123–24; presentations of, 4–5, 117. *See also* Festival of American Folklife

Frame, Mary, 73

Franquemont, Edward, 53, 55

Fujimori, Alberto, 14–15, 49–50, 133–34, 152, 175n4

García Canclini, Nestor, 18

gender, 37–41, 144, 156–59; and ac-cess to resources, 75; activities proper to, 59–61, 116, 148; and cloth, 10, 19–20, 72–80; comple-mentarity of roles, 34, 41, 59–60, 76; cross-dressing, 68; and devel-

opment, 20, 75, 144, 157–59; and
exhibitions, 123; imagery, 78,
171n10; inequality, 40, 94; and
interpreting textiles, 56, 78; and
modernization, 20, 40, 143–45,
154, 159, 170n17; and performance, 123; and race, 171n10;
reciprocity, 115; status, 119, 144;
stereotypes, 79; and textiles,
76–77
globalization, 157, 162; coping with,
15; definition of, 17; and gender,
11
González de Taquila, Pedro, 26, 30–
31
Gramsci, Antonio, 55
Grand Master of Peruvian Crafts.
See Huatta, Francisco
Greimas, Algirdas Julien, 57
guaca. See waka
Guatemala, 56. See also Maya

Hall of the Americas. See Brooklyn
Museum
Harris, Olivia, 78
Healy, Kevin, 11, 48, 87, 114, 146,
175n3
Hendrickson, Carol, 70
herding. See animal
husbandry/herding
Hobsbawm, Eric, 19, 82
hotels. See tourism, lodging
houses and housing, 29, 38, 46, 117,
121–23, 141, 147–50. See also tour-
ism, lodging
Huatta, Agustina, 174n8
Huatta, Alejandro, x, 3, 86
Huatta, Alicia, 89
Huatta, Calixto, 23, 61
Huatta, Elias, 39, 65

Huatta, Feliciana, 73
Huatta, José, 31, 88
Huatta, Lino, 63
Huatta, Lucía, 22
Huatta, Manuel, 88
Huatta, María, x, 1, 82–85
Huatta, Marta de, 60
Huatta, Petrona, 62, 156
Huatta, Prudencio, 32
Huatta, Regoria de, 63
Huatta, Santiago, 119
Huatta, Toribio, 119, 120
Huatta Cruz, Francisca, 1, 135
Huatta Cruz, Sabina, 128
Huatta Flores, Fortunato, 95
Huatta Huatta, Dario, 89
Huatta Huatta, Francisco "Pancho,"
xii, xiv, 1, 15, 21, 28, 54, 60–61, 64,
73, 77, 87–88, 94, 114, 119, 123, 156,
174n6
Huatta Machaca, Alejandrina, x, 3,
16, 22, 61–62, 82, 85, 144
Huatta Machaca, Gerardo, 73, 156

Ichu, Peru, 75–76, 173n13
iconography: changes in, 73, 78, 153–
56
identity, 5, 84, 138–39, 147–53; and
art, 19; and cloth, 52–53, 63–65,
80; as commodity, 14; and dress,
69–71, 80, 138; effects of tourism
on local, 11, 14, 70, 138–45; ethnic, 70–71, 80, 149–52; new forms
of, 80
Ilave, Peru, 7, 42, 43
images on textiles, 74, 82, 83, 98,
103, 154; birds, 74, 83, 98, 99; in
calendar belts, 35, 98; changes
in, 73, 74, 78, 83, 98, 154; fish,
98, 99; flowers, 35, 74, 78, 83, 99;

images on textiles (*continued*)
gendered, 78; geometric, 5–6, 74,
83; naturalistic, 5, 73, 74, 78, 83,
154; representational, 4–6, 74, 78,
83, 154; shared, 78; sources of,
73, 78, 83; of Taquile, 74, 78, 83;
weaving of, 62, 83
Incas, 30, 89, 142, 151; *awasqa*, 54;
categories of cloth, 54; *cumbi*, 54;
and ethnic identity, 68; *moieties*,
41; social organization, 32
indians, 6, 142–44, 150–53, 160–63,
167n1. *See also mestizos*; race and
racism
Inter-American Foundation, 22,
49, 103, 119, 125, 126, 139, 151,
175n3
intersubjectivity, 26
Isbell, Billie Jean, 175n6

Janaq Ladu, 32, 115
Jilaqata. *See* political organization
and participation
Jones, Tristan, 113–14
Juli, Peru, 31
Julien, Catherine, 170n1

khipu, 127
Kincaid, Jamaica, x
kinship, xiii, xiv, 3, 22, 39, 47, 116,
168n5; and access to resources,
76; *comadre*, xiv, 22, 39, 131; *compadrazgo*, 39, 130, 156; *compadre*,
2, 156; ethnic group, 185n5; and
textiles, 61; and tourism, 116;
transnational, 14, 130, 156
knitting, 58–59, 60, 90; and commercialization of textiles, 89–90,
145
Kottak, Conrad Phillip, 113

La Paz, Bolivia, 132, 173n15
labor: communal, 36–37; effects of
tourism on, 115, 141; exchange,
36–37, 86–87, 114–15, 141; *faena*,
37, 38, 114, 115, 117; forced, 37;
mit'a, 37, 170n6; and textiles, 58–
59, 87; sexual division of, 37, 40,
61, 76, 170n17
Lake Titicaca, vi, xi, 7, 8, 43, 44, 147,
151; maps, 7, 34; as national
boundary, 28; traveling on, 8, 27,
47, 165
land tenure, 29, 31–33, 116, 145
Lima, Peru, 46, 84, 86–89, 117, 122–
23, 144, 176n2
literacy, 6, 29, 45–46, 82, 83, 117, 137,
148, 154
llamas. *See* camelids
lliqlla. See shawls
Loits, Padre "Pepe," 48, 114
looms: Andean-type, x, 3, 59–63,
167–68n3; body-tension, 61;
European-type, 59–61; hole-and-
slot heddle, 63; ground, 3, 59–63,
167–68n3; materials for, 42, 60–
61; new types, 167–68n3; production of yardage, 60–61; rigid
frame, 3, 61–63; set-up, 61; treadle, 59–61; yarns suitable for, 63.
See also weaving
Lupaca "kingdom," 30, 170n4

Macha ethnic group, 56
Machaca Huatta, Agustín, 58,
169n14
Machaca Quispe, Natividad, xiii–
xiv, 22, 28, 39, 54, 66, 75, 77, 130
Macusani, Peru, 23
Mamani, Casimiro, 60
mañarikuy, 36

Manco Capac Taquilean Crafts Association, 88–89
maps, 7, 34
Marca, Sebastián, 128
Marca, Victorio, 38
Marca Flores, Casimiro, 44
Marca Huatta, Juana, 68, 135–36
Marca Willi, Teodosia, 35, 174n7
Marca Willi, Terencia, 98, 125
marriage, 29, 37, 170n3; competing with weaving, 77; domestic violence, 38; endogamy, 29; and textile skills, 59, 77–78
Martin, Richard, 56
Matos Mar, José, 12, 30–32
Maya ethnic group, 70, 157
Mayer, Enrique, 86
Medlin, Mary Ann, 71
Meisch, Lynn, 70–71, 130
Menchú Tum, Rigoberta, 51
mestizaje, 168n6
mestizos, 6, 8, 147–53, 168n6, 171n14; Taquileans as, 176n2. *See also q'ara*; race and racism; *runa*
meta-discourse, 55–56; of calendar belt, 97
migration, 9, 42–43, 72, 79–80, 86, 89, 137, 143, 158, 176n2; effects of tourism on, 13, 137, 143; reverse (return), 89, 122, 137, 143, 158; seasonal, 43, 86; urban, 43, 158
Ministry of Tourism and Industry (MITINCI), 118, 131–32, 147–50
mink'a, 36
mismiy. *See* spinning
Mitchell, Ross E., 118, 136–37, 141–42
modernity, 18, 157, 160, 169n10
modernization, 11, 20, 140, 150–54
moieties, 170n5
money, 140, 145, 149–50, 161; earned from crafts, 10, 86–88, 145. *See also* economy
Mosoq Wayra youth group, 130
motifs. *See* images
Murra, John, xv, 53
Murúa, Father Martín de, 26, 170n1
museums, 2, 3, 5, 13, 52, 84, 123–27, 155–56. *See also* American Museum of Natural History; Brooklyn Museum; Smithsonian Institution
music, 67, 124; panpipe, 130; for tourists, 24

Nash, June, ix, 137
National Grand Prize Amautas of Peruvian Crafts, 123
"Natives of Taquile" Folklore Association, 3, 97, 98, 99, 102, 103, 104, 124, 173n1
ñawsa, 154
New York City, 17, 52, 124
non-governmental organizations (NGOs), 49, 84, 130–31, 133

Orlando, Florida, x, 149
Orlove, Ben, 44, 167n1, 175n4
Otavalo ethnic group, 70, 86, 130–31, 141, 155
Oviedo, Florida, 149

pastoral economy. *See* agro-pastoral economy
Peace Corps, 11, 86–87
peñas, 124
performance, 123–27
Peru, 142, 151–52; civil war, xv, 8, 71, 79; recent history, 8–9, 79; Shining Path guerilla group, xv, 8, 71, 79; symbols of, 83; travel be-

Peru (*continued*)
tween Bolivia and, 44; Taquilean interactions with, 119, 131–32, 147–53, 162
Peruvian Social Investment Fund (FONCODES), 175n4
plying. *See* spinning
political organization and participation, 15, 49–50, 116, 144; authorities, 34, 37, 58, 65, 116, 127, 128, 134, 144, 148, 158, 160–63, 175n1; female role in, 38, 148, 170–71n7; male role in, 34, 116, 148; nation and nation-state, 83, 134, 158, 160–63; political parties, 140, 153, 163; protest, 133; *teniente governador*, 88; traditional, 34
polleras, 27–28, 66–67
Potosí, Bolivia, xv, 153
postcolonialism, 26
poverty, 11, 137, 158–59
Pratt, Mary Louise, 11, 85
Protestantism, 49
Pulido, Guillermo, 65, 169n14
Puno, Peru, 5, 34, 44, 46, 75, 84, 86, 118, 120–21, 123, 132, 134, 139–40, 144, 147, 165; attitudes about, 8, 139–40, 148; city, 8, 44, 139–40, 165; department, 8, 33; dock, xii, 27, 44, 120, 165; lodging, 121; map, 7, 34; market, 51; November 4th anniversary, 51; province, 33; region, 8, 33; as source of textile materials, 58; Taquile as tourist attraction in, 132, 139–40, 147–50; Taquilean tour agency in, 34, 121, 134–35, 165; travel between Taquile and, xi, 8, 44, 47, 118–19, 165; tour agencies,

xvi, 34, 132, 134–35, 147–50, 165; working in, 42
pushkay. *See* spinning

q'ara, 65
qhariwarmi, 41
Quechua language, xii, 8, 29, 45, 66, 77, 99, 158, 174n8; author's orthography of, 177; mix of Spanish and, 99, 171n8, 173n1, 174n8; origin in Taquile, 30; term for Taquileans in, 167n1
quipu (knotted cord). *See khipu*
Quispe, Antonio, 38
Quispe, Sebastián, 89
Quispe Cruz, Paula, 43–44, 125, 159
Quispe Huatta, Juan, 1–2, 33, 34, 127, 130, 134, 150, 153
Quispe Huatta, Julio, 2, 88, 135
Quispe Quispe, Félix, 127

race and racism, 5, 48, 65, 73, 80, 131–32, 139–40, 143–44, 147–53; antiracist strategies, 6, 14, 131; and cloth production, 22, 79; and culture, 69, 150–53; and dress, 14, 65, 139–40; food as symbol of, 42, 171n13; and identity, 63–65, 138–40, 147–53; and tourism, 139–40, 143–44, 147–53; and transnationalism, 14, 131
Ranger, Terence, 19
reciprocity and redistribution, 115–16
Reid, Donald G., 118, 136–37, 141–42
representation, 5, 51, 151–53
rites of passage: of anthropologists, 26–28, 39; first haircutting, 39, 65
Rosoff, Nancy, 1, 155, 174n7
runa, 10, 47, 151, 153; community-

level identification, 33; definition of, 167n1; and ethnicity, 65, 150–53; and identity, 72, 150–53, 167n1; as perceived by *mestizos*, 147–53; and *runa p'acha*, 47, 65, 75, 153–56

runa p'acha, 58, 61, 65–67, 75, 153–56

Sacaca, Bolivia, 23
Sakaka ethnic group, 65
San Isidro, Feast of, 68
San Juan, Feast of, 75
Sánchez Cerro, Luis (Peruvian president), 31
Santa Ana del Valle, Mexico, 116, 161
Santa Cruz (Holy Cross), Feast of (3 May), 67
Santiago (Saint James), Feast of (25 July), 97
schools and schooling. *See* education
semiotics of cloth, 55–57, 60, 72–73, 80
September 11, 130, 155, 175n7
shawls, 1, 3, 76–77
sheep, 8, 42, 43, 58–59
sikuris, 67
Sikuris de Santa Cruz, 67
Smithsonian Institution, xv, 47, 103, 122, 124, 125, 159
Socca, Peru, 42, 86
social divisions, 33, 35–36, 46–50, 65, 116, 131–32, 140–41, 150–53; Inca, 41; *moieties*, 8, 32, 41; peasant class, 112, 119, 127, 152, 176n1
solar power, 1, 49, 122
South American Handbook, 113–14
Spanish language, xii, 8, 29, 82, 99, 137, 144, 167n1, 174n8, 175n7; and status, 35–36, 168n6

spinning: Andean drop spindle, 22, 63, 64; author learning, xiii, 23, 63; changes for marketing, 6, 90, 153–56; decline of handspinning, 63–64, 153–56; handspinning, 4, 58, 154–55; importance of, 59, 63; learning, 60, 77; machine-spinning, 4, 6, 63, 90, 153–55; *mismiy*, 63, 172n8; plying (doubling), xiii, 58–59, 63–64; *pushkay*, 172n8; reasons for decline of, 63, 79, 153–56, 174n4; on wheel, 64; yarns, 55, 63, 153–55
Stein, William, 171n14
suyo system, 34; map, 34; woven image of, 34–35, 83, 99
symbolism: changes in meanings, 73, 153–56; and gender, 170n17; meaning of, 6; of Taquile, 78

Taquila, 31
Taquile island, 26, 29, 31; altitude, 6, 111, 123; anthropologists' writings about, 12, 151–52; arable land, 28; author's first trip to, 27, 169n14; compared to other communities, 17, 149, 151–56, 162–63; effects of isolation, 13–14; gross national product, 137; halves, 32–33; history, 30–32, 104, 109–10; and Incas, 30, 53, 151; interzonal exchange, 75; languages spoken on, 29; maps, 7, 34; mayor, 127; museums on, 13, 123–27, 152; patronal saint, 97; plaza, 89, 125, 126, 128, 130, 148; political prison on, 31; population, 6, 9, 28–29, 43; ports, xi, 22, 34, 147–50; size, 28; stores, 121–27, 159; symbol of, 34–35, 83; travel between

Taquile island (*continued*)
  Puno and, 8, 44, 111–12, 120, 165;
  urbanization, 11
Taquileans: author's terms for,
  167n1; author dressed as, 47; cultural identity, 1, 13, 72, 80, 136–37,
  142, 147–53, 161; female entrepreneurs, 144; generational changes
  and conflicts, 84, 143, 154, 174n5;
  health, 13, 44–45, 127, 137, 170n3;
  leveraging relations with outsiders, 31; lifespan, 13; male entrepreneurs, 11, 87–88; mortality,
  9, 170n3; regaining title to land,
  31; interactions with outsiders,
  29, 46–50, 124, 127–31, 147–53;
  standard of living, 13; stories,
  26; surnames of, 32; terms for
  themselves, 167n1; traveling outside Peru, 5, 49, 116, 123–24, 153,
  173n1; value of dress, 69, 136, 165;
  youth, 130, 174n4
Tarabuco ethnic group, 56
technology, 58–63, 73, 172n4; research on, 17
terms, 48, 167n1
Textile Museum, xiii
textiles, 51–81; Andean, 53–58, 77,
  101, 103; anthropomorphic aspects of, 55; *awasqa*, 54; and
  ayni, 124; and birth, 65; as capital, 16, 122, 145; changes in, 4–6,
  10–11, 18, 73, 79, 82, 90, 142, 153–
  56, 176n4; codes, 55–56, 60, 67–
  68, 72–73, 80; commercialization
  of, 12, 42, 47, 51, 56–57, 84–88, 90,
  143, 145, 153–57, 159–60; commoditization of, 85–95, 155–56;
  cooperatives, 4, 51, 87–89, 117,
  125, 126; *cumbi*, 54, 171n1; and
  death, 65; declining sales of, 9–

10, 53, 84–85, 133, 153–56; effects
of changes in, 79, 142, 153–56;
evaluating quality of, 4, 155; first
sales of on Taquile, 86–89; functions in Andes, 5, 9, 10, 52, 80;
and gender, 19–20, 56, 59, 61, 65,
72, 76–78, 80, 94, 158; and identity, 52–53, 63–65, 69–71, 80, 84;
importance to tourists, 17; income derived from, 10, 136, 155–
56; incompatibility with education, 72, 154; as language, 57–58,
72, 97–105, 160; and magic, 58;
marketing of, 86–90, 97–105,
125, 155–56; military use of, 54;
modifications for sale of, 11, 84–
85, 88, 90; new traditional textiles, 82, 153–56; as organizing
principle, 54; political use of, 58;
prices, 4, 87–89; production of,
55, 58–63, 77, 90; and racism, 22,
65, 68–69; raw materials needed
for, 10, 42, 58, 76, 86, 173n13,
174n4; and religion, 55; ritual
use of, 54; selling of, 4, 51, 87–89,
125, 155–56; selvedged, 59–60;
semiotics, 55–57, 60, 72–73, 80;
as site of social identity, 19, 52–
53, 65, 69, 80, 151–53; as source
of income, 6, 16, 89, 155–56;
study of, xi–xii; technology, 53,
58–63, 65–66, 73; traditional, 82,
153–56; transformations in, 5;
vocabulary, 77; as wealth, 10, 54;
women's special relationships
to, 73–75, 79, 160; as writing,
57–58, 82; zoomorphic aspects
of, 55
time, 6, 54; travel between Puno
and Taquile, 8, 44, 119, 165. *See
also* calendar belts